IMAGES
Building English Vocabulary
Through Etymology from Greek
Book IV

Peter R. Beaven with Eugenia Georges

Images for Building English Vocabulary through Etymology
from Greek Book IV

Peter R. Beaven with Eugenia Georges

Editor: Christian Waters

Version 1.0 Revised: 25 August 2018

Published by
The Cheshire Press
an imprint of The Cheshire Group
Andover, MA 01810
www.cheshirepress.com

All rights reserved. No part of this book may be
reproduced or transmitted in any form or by any means
without the express written consent of the author, except for
the inclusion of quotations in reviews.

Copyright ©2017 by Beaven & Assocites

ISBN: 978-0-9995092-9-6

Library of Congress: 2018955373

Printed in the United States of America

Beaven & Associates
3 Dundee Park, #202 A
Andover, MA 01810
978 475-5487
www.beavenandassociates.com

Beaven, Peter R.; Georges, Eugenia
Images for Building English Vocabulary through Etymology
from Greek Book IV

Etymology in Building English Vocabulary

The word "etymology" refers to tracing the origin and historical development of words in a language. How is a given word derived from an earlier word or words in a native or foreign language?

Just as we can "parse" or break up a sentence into parts of speech - noun, verb, adjective, adverb, etc. - so we can deconstruct a given word into its constituent meaning elements and trace their origins. For example, the word "etymology" consists of an original Greek root "etymon" - meaning "an earlier form of the same word" - and the Greek "logos" - meaning "word" or "speech", which took on the later form "-ology" - meaning "study of." So, there we have the etymology of the word "etymology."

Studying the etymology of vocabulary words reveals repeated word-formation patterns, so that we can dissect or guess the meanings of unfamiliar words based on their constituent prefixes and roots that we have encountered earlier. For example, by knowing that the prefix "pre-" means "before" or "ahead" and that "dict" is rooted in "speaking" or "saying," we can surmise that "predict" means to foretell or talk about something before it happens.

The English language is built primarily from the Anglo-Saxon (Germanic), Latin, and Greek languages. Historically, the Angles and Saxons drove out the original Celtic inhabitants and occupied Britain, and after a few brief occupations by the Roman legions, in 1066 the tribes were defeated by the Norman leader William the Conqueror, who spoke French - a language derived almost entirely from Latin. Over time, the Germanic and Latinate languages blended to become what we know as English.

Because Latin is such a fundamental basis of English and because Latin is built from a regular system of "reusable" prefixes and roots, studying these elements makes learning vocabulary more efficient. Instead of learning word meanings in isolation, by learning a standard set of Latin prefixes and common roots we can "mix and match" to learn several new words or variations. The study of etymology thus can accelerate the expansion of our vocabulary while helping us appreciate how meanings and usages have evolved.

For example, knowing that the root "gress" means "step" or "advance", and knowing a series of prefixes, we can deduce word meanings:

Prefix	Meaning	Example
"ad"	= to, toward	address ("g" in "gress" becomes a "d")
"co, con"	= together	congress (movement together)
"di"	= split	digress (move away from)
"e, ex"	= out of, from	egress (way out, exit)
"in"	= in, into	ingress (way in, entrance)
"pro"	= forward, for	progress (move forward)
"re"	= back	regress (move backward)
"trans"	= across, over	transgress (move across)

ETYMOLOGY IN BUILDING ENGLISH VOCABULARY

So many of the words in English that relate to the intellect, words that make us pause to think and study, come from the Greek. The Roman conquest of Greece and admiration for its culture led to the incorporation of many Greek terms into Latin. So we make a point of studying Greek roots and prefixes as well. For example, the Greek root "pathos" means "feeling" or "suffering", from which come such words as:

"a"	= not	apathy (not caring)
"anti"	= against	antipathy (dislike or hostility)
"em, en"	= into, in	empathy (sharing in another's feeling)
"sym"	= together, with	sympathy (feeling sorrow for another)

In addition, there are other English words based on the same root, such as "pathetic", "pathology", "pathos", and so on.

Consider the common prefixes and cross-connections of the words below:

telecommute	micron	automaton	extrasensory	intercede
telegraph	micrograph	autobiography	extravehicular	intercept
telephone	microphone	automobile	extraterrestrial	interrupt
telescope	microscope	autograph	extraordinary	interdict
television	micromanage	autonomy	extralegal	intervene

or the roots "duc" ("lead"), "fer" ("bear, bring"), "port" ("carry") and "vers" ("turn") as below:

aqueduct	confer	report	converse
conduct	defer	deport	diverse
deduce	refer	transport	reverse
duct	transfer	teleport	adverse
ductile	prefer	airport	perverse
educate	offer	purport	obverse
induce		export	averse
produce		import	inverse
seduce		comport	transverse
viaduct		support	controversy

In the series Building English Vocabulary, a student discovers that from just one Latin or Greek root springs an exponential growth in his vocabulary, sharpened tools to articulate the written or spoken word. A broader knowledge of English leads him to greater ties to the shared cognates of French, Spanish, Italian, and Greek. A stronger grasp of English brings a deeper understanding of the plays of Shakespeare, the novels of Dickens, the essays of Emerson, the poetry of Emily Dickinson, or the oratory of Lincoln and Churchill., who as national leaders, marshaled the English language — the former to invoke peace — the latter to evoke resolve for impending battles, the victories of which in the post bellum of the twentieth century helped thrust English into its role as the lingua franca of the modern world.

Contents

Lesson I	7
Lesson II	18
Lesson III	29
Lesson IV	39
Lesson V	50
Lesson VI	58
Lesson VII	72
Lesson VIII	79
Lesson IX	88
Lesson X	96
Lesson XI	106
Lesson XII	117
Lesson XIII	127
Lesson XIV	143
Lesson XV	152
Lesson XVI	161
Lesson XVII	168
Lesson XVIII	177
Lesson XIX	190
Lesson XX	200
Lesson XXI	208
Lesson XXII	217
Lesson XXIII	226
Answer Key	239

Lesson I

Amoral

A-, AN-
without, lacking, not

MORES-
custom

Definition: **adj.** lacking any morals, principles; having no sense of right and wrong

Sentence: The philosopher Nietzsche believed that society should be <u>amoral</u> as a whole and that it was each individual's own responsibility to define his or her own morals for himself or herself..

Amorphous

A-, AN-
without, lacking, not

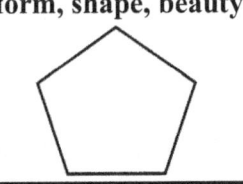
MORPHE-
form, shape, beauty

Definition: **adj.** shapeless; having no definite form

Sentence: The blob of clay, though it can hold its shape well when molded, is <u>amorphous</u> because it has no rigid or defined shape.

Anarchy

A-, AN-
without, lacking, not

ARKHE-
ruler, rules

Definition: **n.** the state of being without a political authority; lacking any common purpose or goal; chaos; rebellion; absence of order.

Sentence: Communists believed that government would eventually wither away and leave a state of <u>anarchy</u>.

Anecdote

A-, AN-	*EKDOTOS-*
without, lacking, not	published, given out

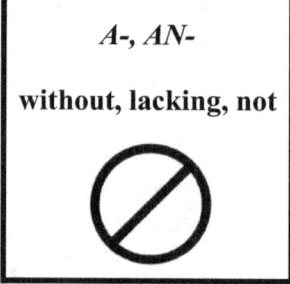 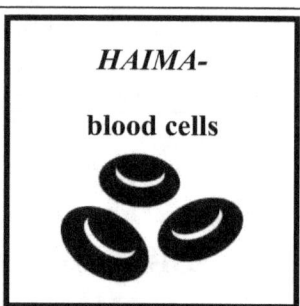

Definition: **n.** a short, humorous or intriguing tale; a previously untold part of history or biography

Sentence: My grandfather always relates amusing <u>anecdotes</u> about his life at family gatherings.

Anemia

A-, AN-	*HAIMA-*
without, lacking, not	blood cells

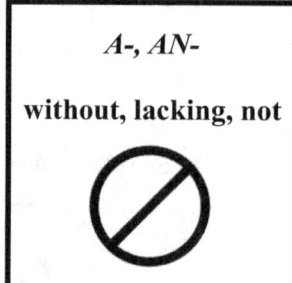 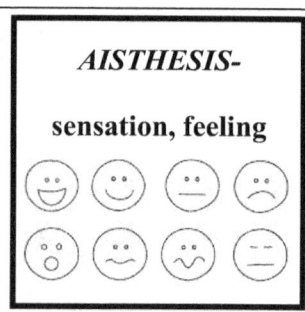

Definition: **n.** a deficiency in the oxygen-carrying component of blood; a disease of iron deficiency

Sentence: People who have <u>anemia</u> are not able to give blood because they are not able to reproduce their red blood cells at a fast enough rate.

Anesthesia

A-, AN-	*AISTHESIS-*
without, lacking, not	sensation, feeling

Definition: **n.** the loss or lack of sensation, especially feeling, due to disease, injury, acupuncture or drug-induced insensibility or numbness

Sentence: In the middle of the 19th century doctors were reluctant to give pregnant mothers chemicals that would induce a state of <u>anesthesia</u>, fearing that the absence of pain would impair the bond between mother and child.

Anodyne

A-, AN-	ODYNE-
without, lacking, not	pain

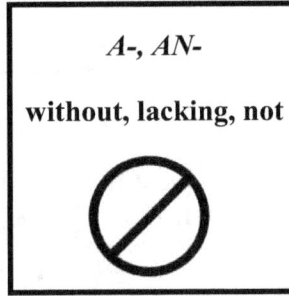

Definition: **n.** a medicine or anything that has the ability to ease pain or distress

Sentence: On the battlefield, army medics are often called upon to administer morphine, an <u>anodyne</u>, in order to ease the pain of wounded soldiers.

Anomaly

A-, AN-	OMALOS-
without, lacking, not	even, normal

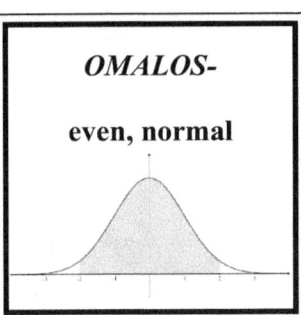

Definition: **n.** something that is abnormal or sits outside the bounds; an erring or deviation from what is common or expected, an incongruity or inconsistency, irregularity.

Sentence: The 'F' received by a straight-A student was clearly an <u>anomaly</u> on the otherwise perfect transcript.

Anonymous

A-, AN-	ONYMA-
without, lacking, not	name

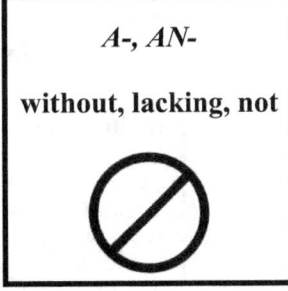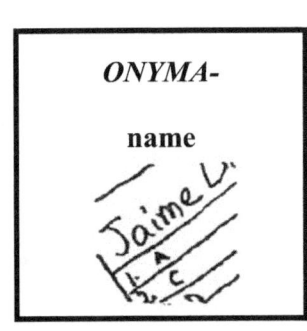

Definition: **adj.** lacking the name of an author or of unknown authorship

Sentence: On Valentine's Day, unsigned cards allow the sender to remain <u>anonymous</u>.

Apolitical

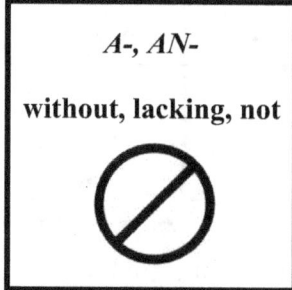

Definition:	**adj.** Not concerned with politics
Sentence:	The <u>apolitical</u> student was more interested in becoming a veterinarian than in analyzing current events and political theories.

Apnea

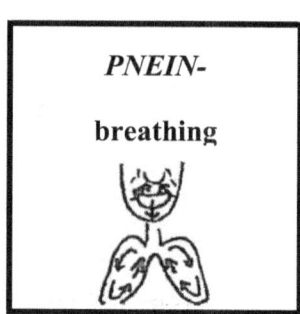

Definition:	**n.** a caesura or interruption of breathing, usually during sleep
Sentence:	The heart attack victim suffered from temporary <u>apnea</u> while he struggled desperately to breathe.

Aseptic

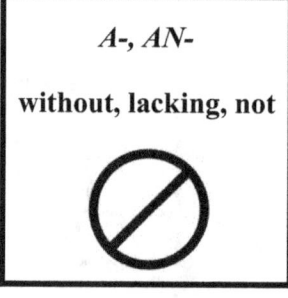
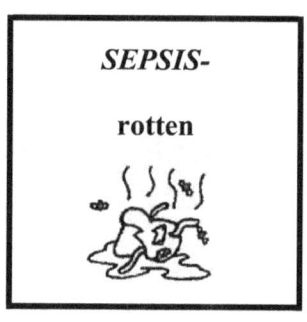

Definition:	**adj.** clean of any microorganism; sterilized; germ-free
Sentence:	It is critical to use <u>aseptic</u> surgical instruments when operating to minimize the risk of infection.

Asylum

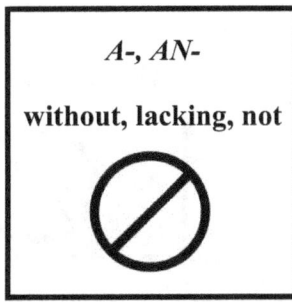

	A-, AN-	SYLON-
	without, lacking, not	right of seizure

Definition: **n.** a place for the care of people who are unable to care for themselves; a place of refuge or safety; protection from extradition

Sentence: In medieval times, the church was an <u>asylum</u> where a fugitive was safe from arrest.

Asymptomatic

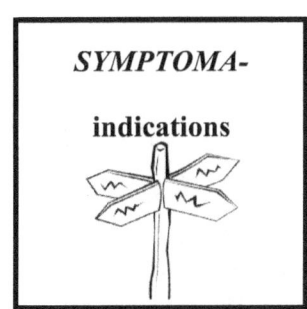

	A-, AN-	SYMPTOMA-
	without, lacking, not	indications

Definition: **adj.** showing no signs of ailment or symptoms realize they are infected.

Sentence: Many people who are HIV positive remain <u>asymptomatic</u> for upward of ten years and do not even realize they are infected.

Atheism

	A-, AN-	THEOS-
	without, lacking, not	god

Definition: **n.** having no belief in the existence of god(s)

Sentence: Writing that 'religion is the opiate of the people', Marx called for communists to embrace <u>atheism</u>.

Atom

A-, AN- without, lacking, not 	*TOM-* cut 

Definition: **n.** an irreducable part of a system; the smallest unit of an element

Sentence: Democratis first proposed that the smallest unit of matter was the <u>atom</u> – *not* able to be *cut* any further.

Atrophy

A-, AN- without, lacking, not 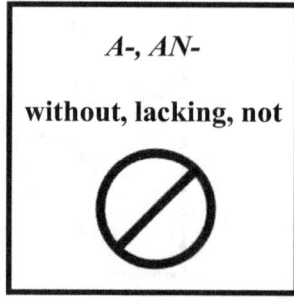	*TROPHIE-* food, nourishment 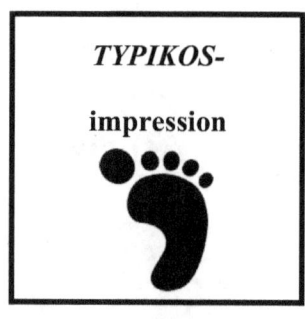

Definition: **n.** a deterioration of muscle mass or tissue, caused by disease, injury, or lack of use
v. to deteriorate, used of muscle mass or tissue

Sentence: A paralysis victim suffers from weakened or shriveled limbs - <u>atrophy</u> caused by lack of muscle movements.

Atypical

A-, AN- without, lacking, not	*TYPIKOS-* impression

Definition: **adj.** irregular or not fitting in the usual mold; not conforming to type

Sentence: This lizard exhibits an <u>atypical</u> coloring pattern as it is polka-dotted while all others of its kind are striped.

Exercise A: *Fill in the blanks below with the correct form of a word from the lesson*

1. During World War II, many German civilians sought an _____ to escape from the war

2. Arriving home in the snow, Johnny saw that the front door was wide open. Because of this _____, he was frightened to go inside.

3. After the U.S. captured Saddam Hussein, Iraq fell into a brief period of chaos and _____.

4. Before performing invasive surgery, the doctor administrated _____ to the patient.

5. Science is often regarded as _____, as it is concerned only with progress, not with right and wrong.

6. Many overweight people suffer from sleep _____. It is a condition that occurs when a one's airway is obstructed, causing airflow to be restricted.

7. After her car crash, Sara found her legs beginning to _____, as she lay in the hospital for many months.

8. Due to the recent scandal in the Roman Catholic church, many of the laity have renounced their faith, turning to _____ in disbelief that if a God existed he would allow such behavior.

9. The students were stuck waiting for hours for Laurel. They regarded her behavior as _____, as she was always punctual.

10. The entire town was up in arms over the _____ letter in the town paper. Everyone was trying to find out who wrote it.

11. The theory of evolution states that we all began as _____ blobs which eventually, through survival of the fittest, took form and evolved into modern man.

12. Jane was suffering from _____. Because of her poor blood circulation, she often felt cold.

13. My father told me a humorous _____ about the time he went into the women's room by accident.

14. The doctor made sure that the needle was _____ before injecting the patient so that the patient did not get an infection.

15. For a long time, scientists believed that _____ could not be reduced any further. But with new technology and expensive machines, scientists have managed to split them.

16. Although he was diagnosed with cancer, Joseph appeared _____, without any noticeable changes in his appearance or daily activity.

Exercise B

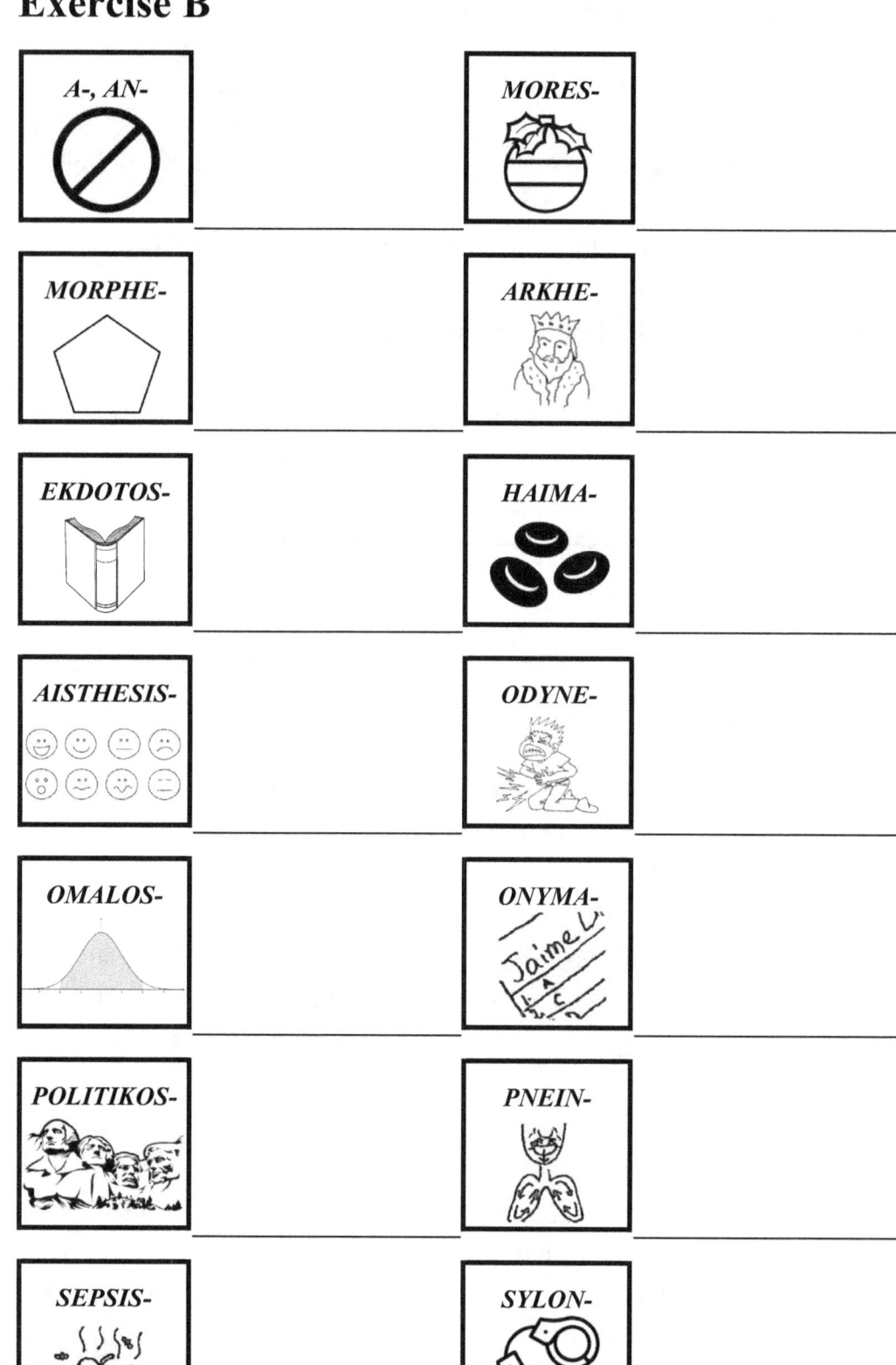

SYMPTOMA-	THEOS-
TOM-	TROPHIE-
TYPIKOS-	

EXERCISE C

Complete the following crossword puzzle on Lesson 1:

Across:
1. Irreducible part of a system
2. Caesura from breathing
5. Deviation from the norm
8. Drug that induces lack of feeling
9. Deficiency in the oxygen carrying part of blood
10. Being without a political authority
12. Lack of the sense of smell
13. Short humorous tale
14. Lacking any morals

Down:
1. Devoid of any water
2. Lacking the name of an author
3. Showing no signs of ailment
4. Deterioration of muscle mass
5. Severe asphyxia
6. Clean of any microorganism; sterile
7. Place for care of those who cannot take care of themselves
8. Having no belief in the existence of god(s)
11. Shapeless
12. Lack of conjunction
15. Irregular or not fitting in the usual mold

Exercise D

Match the word with the letter of its definition.

1. ___ amoral
2. ___ amorphous
3. ___ anarchy
4. ___ apolitical
5. ___ anemia
6. ___ anesthesia
7. ___ anhydrous
8. ___ anomaly
9. ___ anonymous
10. ___ anosmia
11. ___ anoxia
12. ___ apnea
13. ___ aseptic
14. ___ asylum
15. ___ asymptomatic
16. ___ asyndeton
17. ___ atheism
18. ___ atom
19. ___ atrophy
20. ___ atypical

a) having no belief in the existence of god(s)
b) irregular or not fitting in the usual mold
c) clean of any microorganism; sterile
d) showing no signs of ailment
e) lacking any morals
f) place for care of those who cannot take care of themselves
g) irreducible part of a system
h) shapeless
i) caesura from breathing
j) lack of conjunction
k) deterioration of muscle mass
l) severe asphyxia
m) lacking the name of an author
n) uninterested in government or election issues
o) deficiency in the oxygen carrying part of blood
p) lack of the sense of smell
q) devoid of any water
r) being without a political authority
s) drug that induces lack of feeling
t) deviation from the norm

Lesson II

Amphibious

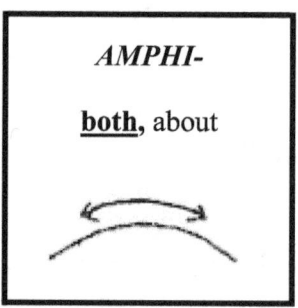
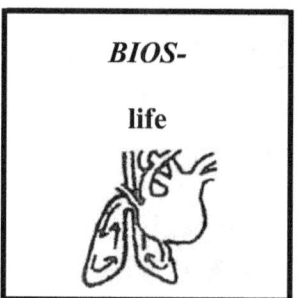

Definition: **adj.** capable of living or operating in or out of water

Sentence: Able to live in the water and on dry land, the frog is an example of an <u>amphibious</u> creature.

Amphitheater

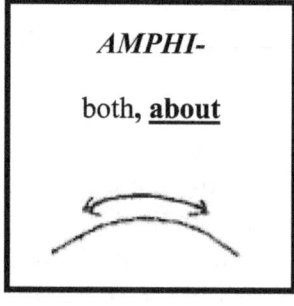

Definition: **n.** a rounded structure with tiered seating for viewing a show or lecture

Sentence: The Colosseum of Rome, though half of it has crumbled or been carted off, has stood for over 2,000 years. It was originally an <u>amphitheater</u> in which gladiatorial and perhaps naval battles took place.

Anabasis

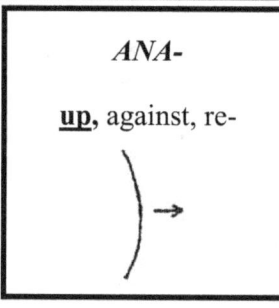
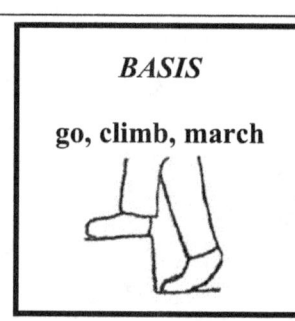

Definition: **n.** an advance; expedition; stepping up

Sentence: Xenephon's book <u>Anabasis</u> or *March Up Country* describes the ten thousand Greek mercenaries fighting under Cyrus in Babylon and their homeward journey from Persia to Greece.

Anachronism

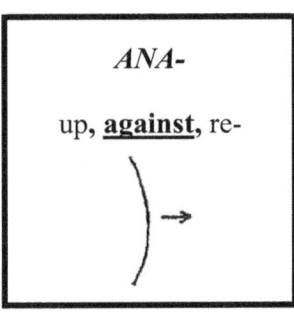

Definition: **n.** someone or something that is out of its proper order in time

Sentence: A clock striking the hour in Shakespeare's 'Julius Caesar' is an <u>anachronism</u>, since mechanical clocks did not exist at the time.

Anagram

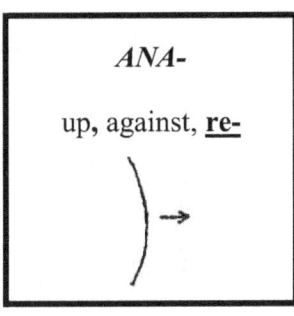
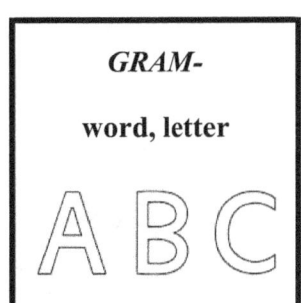

Definition: **n.** a word formed by rearranging the letters in another word

Sentence: In J.K. Rowling's Harry Potter series, 'I am Lord Voldemort' is an <u>anagram</u> of the villain's real name, 'Tom Marvolo Riddle'.

Analgesic

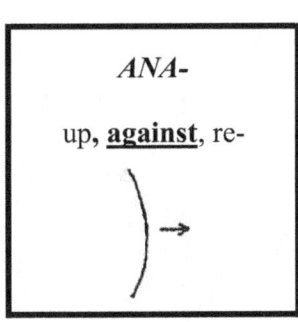
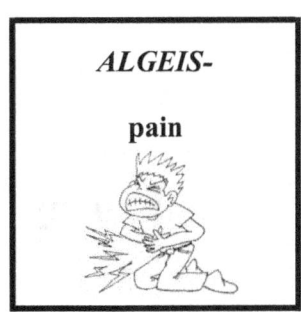

Definition: **n.** a medicine that eases pain
adj. easing pain

Sentence: The drug in Tylenol, which is used to relieve headaches, is an <u>analgesic</u> whose proper name is acetaminophen.

Analysis

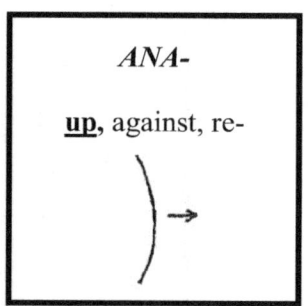

Definition: **n.** the separation of something into its constituent pieces to determine its nature

Sentence: One aspect of psycho<u>analysis</u> involves interpretation of dreams as a window into the patient's subconscious mind.

Anaphora

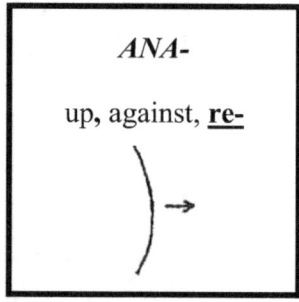

Definition: **n.** the purposeful repetition of a word or phrase for rhetorical effect.

Sentence: Winston Churchill employed <u>anaphora</u> in his 'We shall fight them on the beaches' speech, repeating 'we shall' before every clause.

Anatomy

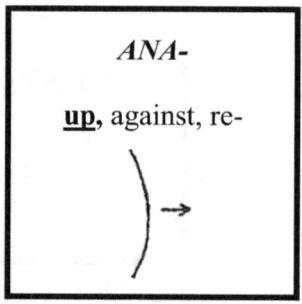
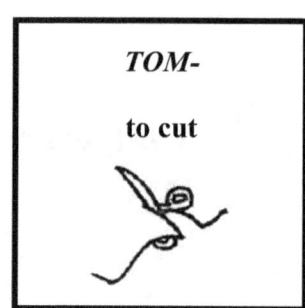

Definition: **n.** the science concerned with the structure of organisms

Sentence: Gray's '<u>Anatomy</u>' is the standard medical student text describing and illustrating the various structures and systems of the human body.

Authentic

Definition: **adj.** trustworthy, reliable, or believable, genuine; one who does things himself

Sentence: Some people believe that the Shroud of Turin, bearing the image of a man who was crucified, is the actual cloth which covered Jesus in burial, but others contend that it is not authentic and merely a medieval hoax.

Autobiography

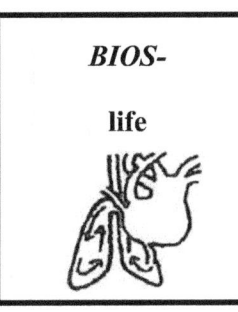

Definition: **n.** an account of one's life written by oneself

Sentence: St. Augustine's self-composed life story entitled 'Confessions' is considered to be the first Western autobiography.

Autocrat

Definition: **n.** a person with ultimate or complete power or authority.

Sentence: Today, the words 'tyrant,' 'despot,' and 'autocrat' can be used interchangeably, although they originally had subtle differences.

Autograph

Definition:	**n.** a person's own signature **v.** to sign one's name
Sentence:	A rare book is enormously more valuable if it contains the author's signature or <u>autograph</u>.

Automatic

 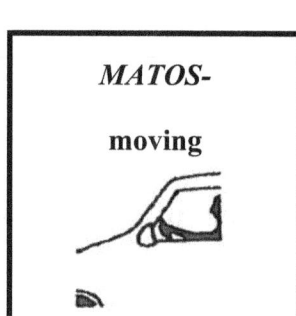

Definition:	**adj.** capable of operating independent of any external influence
Sentence:	Reflexes such as blinking are typically <u>automatic</u> or involuntary nervous system phenomena.

Automaton

 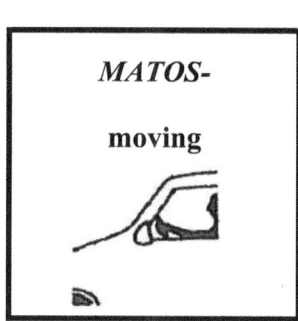

Definition:	**n.** a device that is automatic
Sentence:	The Museum of Science in Boston has an <u>automaton</u> made entirely out of Tinker-Toys and string that is able to play tic-tac-toe.

Automobile

Definition: **n.** a self-propelled vehicle for land travel, having four wheels and an internal combustion engine; car

Sentence: The first <u>automobile</u> patent in the United States was issued to Oliver Evans in 1789.

Autonomous

Definition: **adj.** independent; self-governing; subject to its own laws only.

Sentence: Even though it does not have independence from China, Hong Kong is <u>autonomous</u> because it is self-governing.

Autopsy

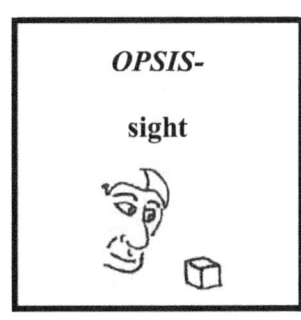

Definition: **n.** an examination of a dead body to determine cause of death; post mortem

Sentence: The <u>autopsy</u> performed on the corpse of Terry Schiavo revealed that her brain had diminished significantly and that she was incapable of complex thought at the time of death.

Exercise A

1. In college, Pedro wishes to study _____ as he has always been fascinated by the human body.
2. The sword is an _____ Civil War saber, handed down from generation to generation within my family.
3. In the replica of the old Lowell textile mills, the computer monitors within the displays are _____ because they did not exist at that time.
4. I was relieved when my mother bought an _____ vacuum. Because of this feature, I no longer had to sweep the house by hand.
5. Whenever I get a sunburn I rub aloe, an _____, on it so that it is not as painful.
6. For the D-Day beach landings, British engineers developed _____ tanks that could move through water and land alike.
7. Many people think that it is not just a coincidence that the word "lives" is an _____ of "Elvis".
8. The girl drove in her convertible _____ to the store.
9. Martin Luther King's famous speech is known for its _____ using the repeated phrase "I have a dream!"
10. After Terry Schiavo died, doctors performed an _____ on her to determine her cause of death.
11. Augustus Caesar led a famous military _____ against Marc Antony in Egypt.
12. Bill Clinton's _____ is titled "My Life"
13. The baseball player signed his _____ for any fan that asked for it.
14. The complex system requires much _____ in order to determine how it functions.
15. The Native Americans are an _____ people, who are not subject to the rule of the U.S. government.
16. Many monarchs are _____, who have the ability to make any law that they wish to.
17. Because they are self-propelled, the cuckoos on a clock are _____.
18. Many college classrooms are in the shape of an _____ because the tiered seating with one focal point is suitable for that environment.

Exercise B

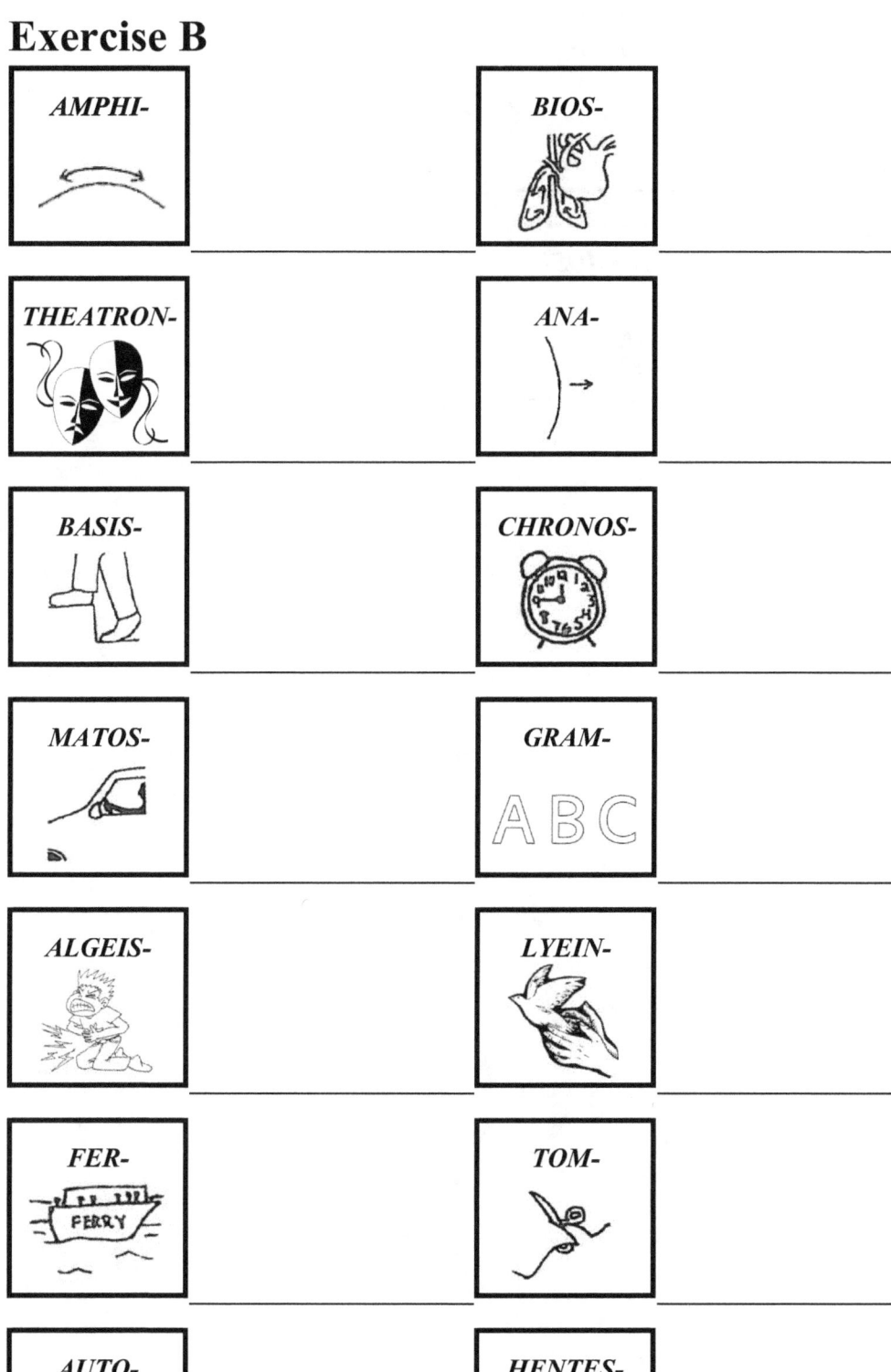

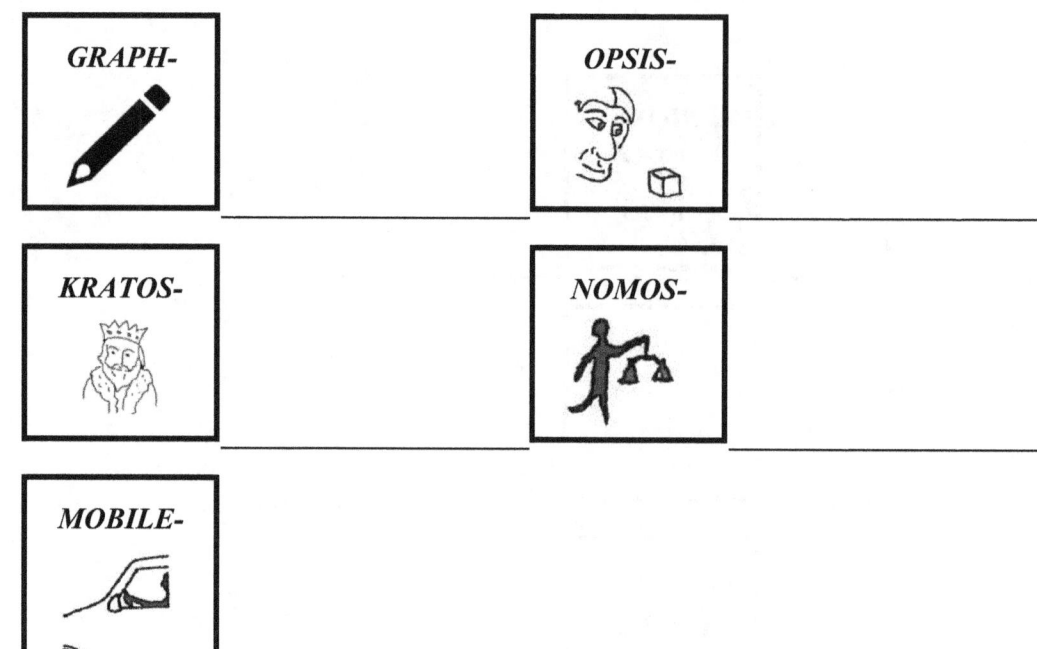

EXERCISE C
Complete the following crossword puzzle on Lesson 2:

Across:
2. Separation to study the parts
4. One with complete power
6. Capable of living both on land and in water
8. Word formed by rearranging another word
9. The study of an organism's structure
10. Examination of a dead body
11. Rounded tiered area for viewing a show
13. Easing pain
14. Something out of its proper time
15. Reliable, trustworthy

Down:
1. Signature
2. Car
3. Self-operating
5. Self-governing
6. Repetition of a word or phrase
7. Book about someone's life, written by himself or herself
8. Expedition; advance
12. Grammatically able to be interpreted multiple ways
13. Automatic device

EXERCISE D

Match the word with the letter of its definition:

1. ___ **amphibious**
2. ___ **amphibolous**
3. ___ **amphitheater**
4. ___ **anabasis**
5. ___ **anachronism**
6. ___ **anagram**
7. ___ **analgesic**
8. ___ **analysis**
9. ___ **anaphora**
10. ___ **anatomy**
11. ___ **authentic**
12. ___ **autobiography**
13. ___ **autocrat**
14. ___ **autograph**
15. ___ **automatic**
16. ___ **automaton**
17. ___ **automobile**
18. ___ **autonomous**
19. ___ **autopsy**

a) separation to study the parts
b) self-operating
c) expedition; advance
d) easing pain
e) one with complete power
f) capable of living both on land and in water
g) examination of a dead body
h) word formed by rearranging another word
i) something out of its proper time
j) signature
k) rounded tiered area for viewing a show
l) automatic device
m) repetition of a word or phrase
n) conforming to fact, real
o) grammatically able to be interpreted multiple ways
p) book about someone's life, written by himself or herself
q) self-governing
r) car
s) the study of an organism's structure

Lesson III

Antagonist

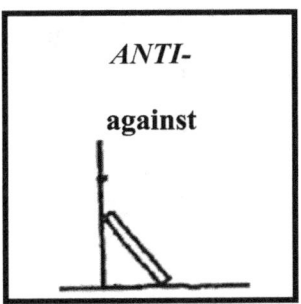

Definition: **n.** an adversary; the character opposite the protagonist in a novel, i.e. the main villain

Sentence: In *Les Miserables*, the hero Jean Valjean is continually hounded and pursued by his police inspector antagonist, Javert.

Antibiotic

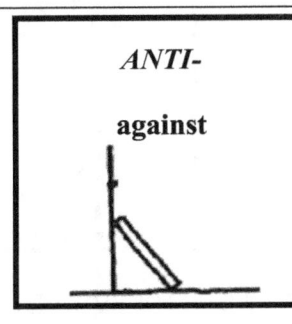
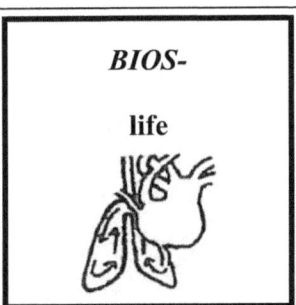

Definition: **n.** a fungus-, bacterium-, or other organism-derived substance that destroys or inhibits microorganism growth. Antibiotics are used in disease treatment.

Sentence: The first effective antibiotic discovered was penicillin."

Antibody

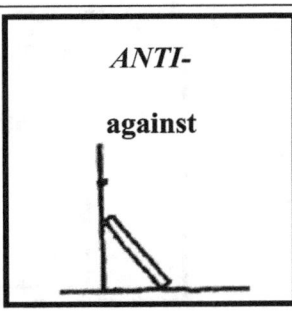
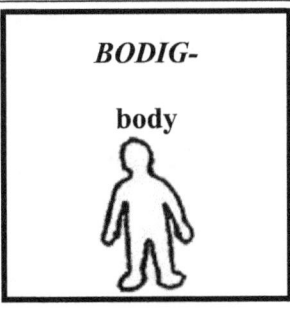

Definition: **n.** a protein that responds to an infection or a virus within the body; antagonistic

Sentence: Without antibodies, our bodies would be vulnerable to every infection and virus.

Antidote

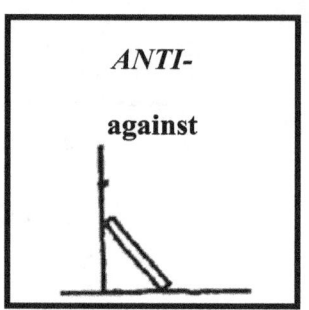

Definition: **n.** a remedy for a poison

Sentence: Poisonous bites, such as those from certain snakes, require an immediate <u>antidote</u> in order to counteract the venom.

Antipathy

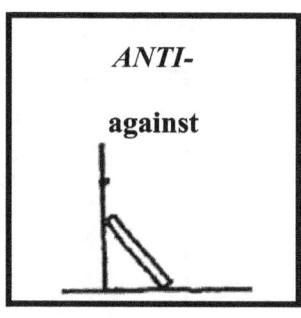 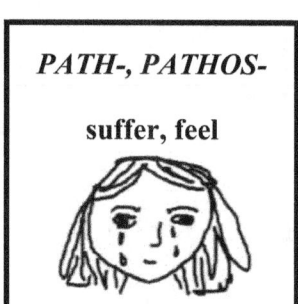

Definition: **n.** a feeling of repugnance or hostility

Sentence: Hamlet felt great <u>antipathy</u> toward his usurping Uncle Claudius, who had murdered Hamlet's father then married Hamlet's widowed mother.

Antiseptic

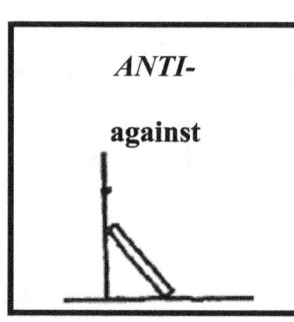 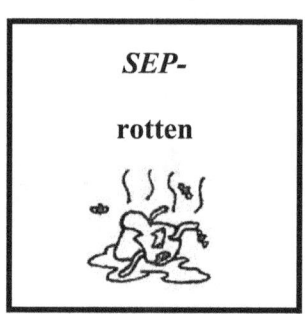

Definition: **adj.** preventing of infection

Sentence: Rubbing alcohol, a common household <u>antiseptic</u>, is placed on wounds in order to prevent infection.

Antithetical

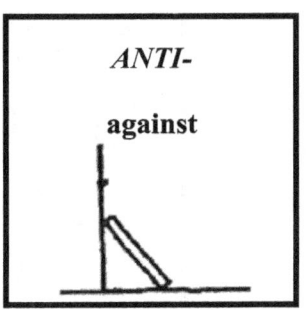 

ANTI- against

THETIKOS- to contend

Definition: **adj.** in opposition to

Sentence: Suburban sprawl was seen as <u>antithetical</u> to the efficient use of land in the United Kingdom after World War II.

Antonym

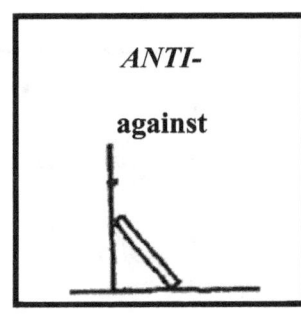 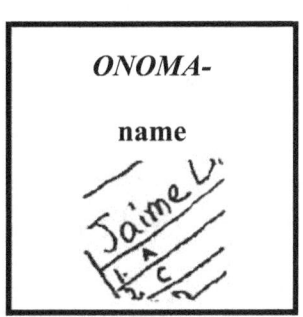

ANTI- against

ONOMA- name

Definition: **n.** a word that means the opposite or nearly opposite of another word

Sentence: The words 'punctual' (on time) and 'dilatory' (tardy) are <u>antonyms</u>.

Aphorism

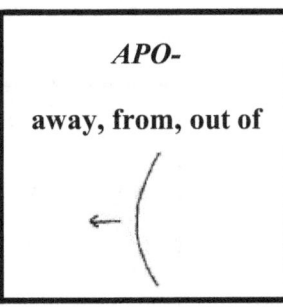 

APO- away, from, out of

HORIZ- define, limit

Definition: **n.** an adage or folk saying

Sentence: A famous <u>aphorism</u> of Benjamin Franklin is: 'A stitch in time saves nine.'

Apocalyptic

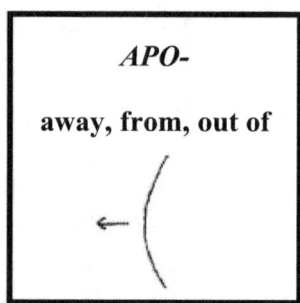
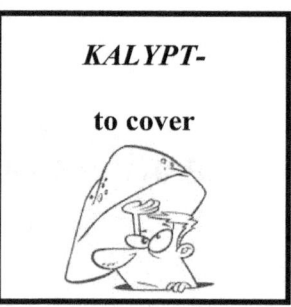

Definition: **adj.** having to do with a natural disaster or cataclysm; bringing on the end of the world

Sentence: Many feared that the Cold War would turn <u>apocalyptic</u> with the potential launch of thousands of U.S. and Russian nuclear warheads.

Apogee

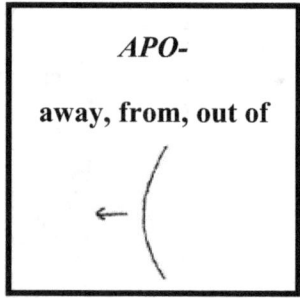

Definition: **n.** the point at which an orbiting body is farthest from the Earth's center; pinnacle or zenith

Sentence: The moon reaches <u>apogee</u> approximately once per month.

Apocryphal

Definition: **adj.** fictitious; erroneous; inauthentic; of doubtful sanction; uncanonical

Sentence: The anti-Semitic tract 'The Protocols of the Elders of Zion' has been shown to be a fake and therefore untrue and <u>apocryphal</u>.

Apology

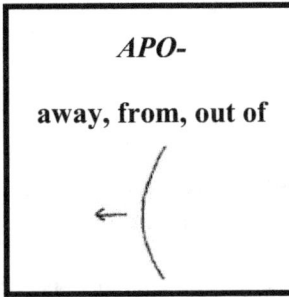

Definition:	**n.** an expression of regret for a transgression; an explanation or rationale; a defense, excuse, or justification in speech or writing
Sentence:	Plato's '<u>Apology</u>' is an account of Socrates' self-defense in his trial for corrupting Athenian youth and his subsequent condemnation.

Apostate

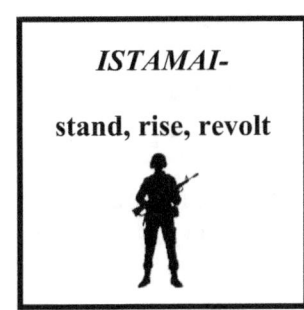

Definition:	**n.** one who has renounced his faith, political party, cause, or principles
Sentence:	When King Henry VIII argued with the Pope and formed the Anglican Church, he was excommunicated from the Catholic church as an <u>apostate</u>.

Apostle

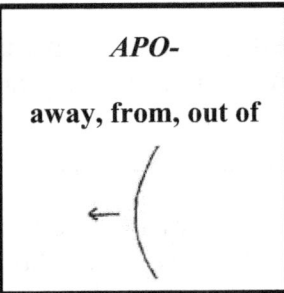

Definition:	**n.** a passionate supporter or follower
Sentence:	Jesus' closest disciples became known as the Twelve <u>Apostles</u>.

Exercise A

1. After Zorro realized he had been poisoned, he quaffed a vial of the _____ to cure himself.

2. When Nathan fell and skinned his knee, his mother applied an _____ to clean the wound and ward off infection.

3. Since Jerome had already endured the chicken pox, his body had developed _____ to fight off the disease, and he was unlikely to contract it again.

4. Dr. Atkins had reached the _____ of fame and fortune when he fell on the ice and died of a heart attack.

5. The old _____, "an apple a day keeps the doctor away," has received support from the health community but serves better as a proverb than actual nutritional advice.

6. After breaking the rules at school, Eric was asked to write an _____ atoning for his actions.

7. Medical experts worry that doctors are prescribing too many _____ and that bacteria will soon be immune to their effects.

8. Peter & Paul are not only the names of two thirds of the folk trio that perform the song "Puff the Magic Dragon" but also the names of two of the _____ of Jesus Christ.

9. The Cuban Missile crisis nearly led to an _____ war between the United States and the Soviet Union. A nuclear holocaust was narrowly averted.

10. Many novels tell a tale of a protagonist facing off against his or her adversary, the _____.

11. The famous tale of William Tell splitting an apple on the head of his son with an arrow is _____; it almost certainly never happened.

12. Do you think that Hilary's _____ for Lindsay stems from jealousy?

13. Mitch seemed puzzled when the crossword clue asked him for the _____ of "bouncy," and he was only able to think of "not bouncy."

14. The Pope declared King Henry VIII an _____ after he divorced Queen Katherine thereby defying a papal order.

15. Cindy's purchase of a fur coat was _____ to her actions as an animal rights activist.

Exercise B

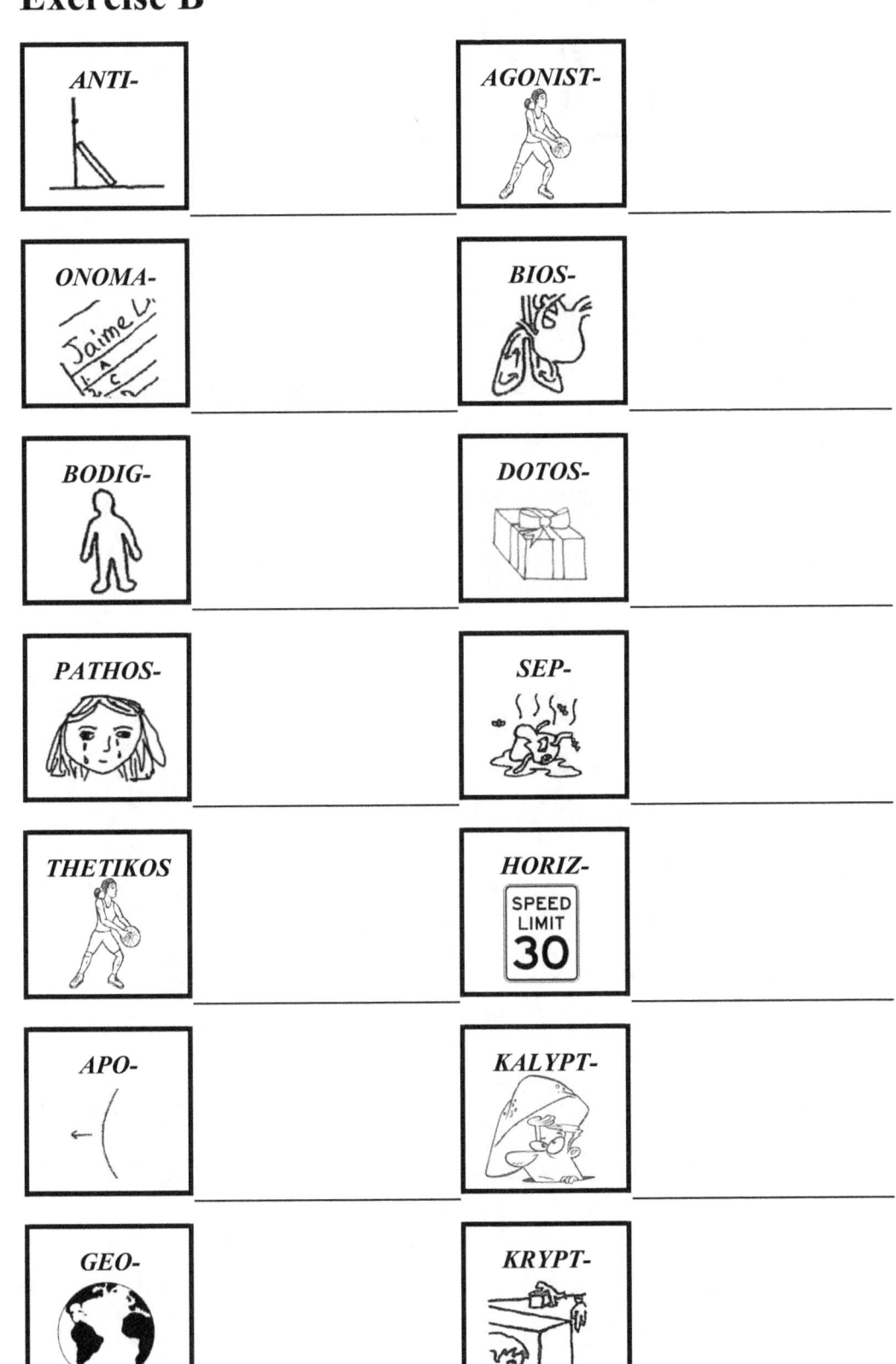

LOGOS-  _____ **ISTAMAI-**  _____

STELL- _____

EXERCISE C

Complete the following crossword puzzle on Lesson 3:

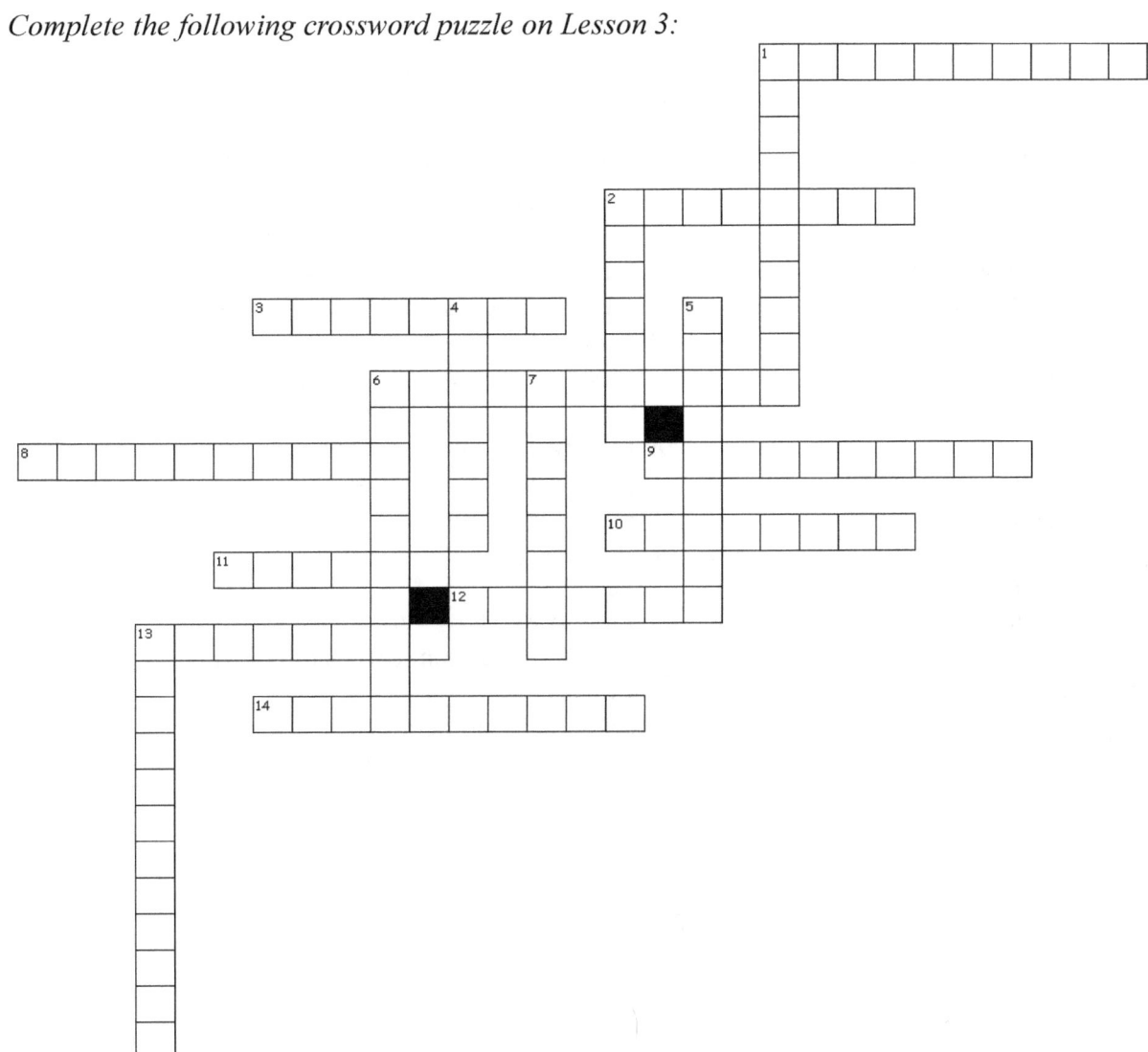

Across:
1. Substance derived from a fungus or bacterium that weakens or destroys bacteria
2. Proverb
3. One who forsakes his or her religion or beliefs
6. Having to do with a natural disaster
8. Person who contends against another
9. Consumed by rage that leaves one unable to act or think clearly
10. Protein that prevents infection
11. Pinnacle
12. Expression of regret
13. Medicine that counteracts a poison
14. Of questionable origin

Down:
1. Intended to ward off evil
2. Word meaning the opposite of another word
4. Devout follower
5. Feeling of disgust or dislike
6. Preventing of infections
7. Farthest point from the sun
13. Completely opposite in nature

EXERCISE D

Match the word with the letter of its definition:

1. ___ antagonist
2. ___ antibiotic
3. ___ antibody
4. ___ antidote
5. ___ antipathy
6. ___ antiseptic
7. ___ antithetical
8. ___ antonym
9. ___ aphelion
10. ___ aphorism
11. ___ apocalyptic
12. ___ apogee
13. ___ apocryphal
14. ___ apology
15. ___ apoplectic
16. ___ apostate
17. ___ apostle
18. ___ apotropaic

a) feeling of disgust or dislike
b) expression of regret
c) word that means the opposite of another word
d) person who contends against another; an opponent
e) medicine that counteracts a poison
f) devout follower
g) one who forsakes his or her religion or beliefs
h) protein that prevents infection
i) substance derived from a fungus or bacterium that weakens or destroys bacteria
j) completely opposite in nature
k) furthest point from the sun
l) preventing infections
m) proverb
n) pinnacle
o) intended to ward off evil
p) consumed by rage that leaves one unable to act or think clearly
q) of questionable authenticity
r) having to do with a natural disaster or cataclysm

Lesson IV

Cataract

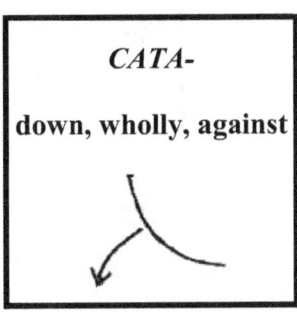

Definition:	**n.** a waterfall; a large downpour; an eye condition in which the lens is opaque; to dash down
Sentence:	The Upper Nile is unnavigable owing to its plunging and precipitous <u>cataracts</u>.

Cataclysm

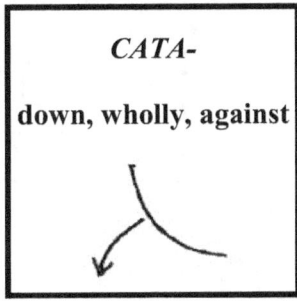 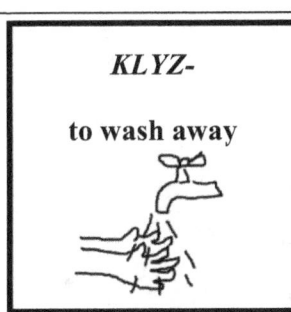

Definition:	**n.** a violent and sudden upheaval that bears great destruction or change; a great flood
Sentence:	The great Biblical Flood was a <u>cataclysm</u> of forty days and forty nights of rain that washed away everything on earth save Noah's Ark.

Catacomb

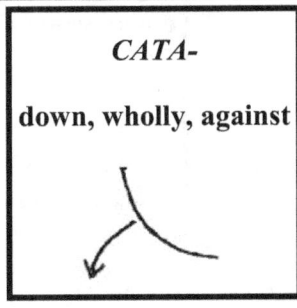 

Definition:	**n.** an underground labyrinthine passageway, often containing sections for graves
Sentence:	In *Indiana Jones - The Last Crusade,* Jones and his sidekick Marcus explore the <u>catacomb</u> under an Italian church leading to Sir Richard's tomb.

Catalog

CATA-	LOGOS-
down, wholly, against	word, speech, study

Definition: **v.** to order into a list; to make a catalog
n. a list of things for exhibition or sale; a publication containing such a list

Sentence: The inscribed clay cuneiform tablets unearthed in ancient Iraq are largely catalogs of business transactions.

Catharsis

KATHAIR- to cleanse

Definition: **n.** A cleansing of emotional tension in the wake of an overwhelming experience; a purgative

Sentence: Aristotle claimed that many tragedies offered catharsis to their audiences; that upon leaving the play and returning to the real world they would feel emotionally purged.

Cathedral

CATA-	HEDRA-
down, wholly, against	seat

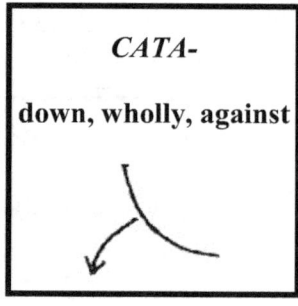 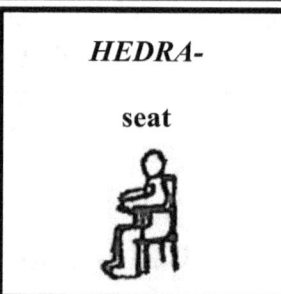

Definition: **n.** a large church
adj. anything which is of, relating to, or reminiscent of a large church

Sentence: Germany's Romantic Road winds through many medieval cities boasting cavernous houses of worship called cathedrals.

Cathode

	CATA-	HODOS-
	down, wholly, against	way, path

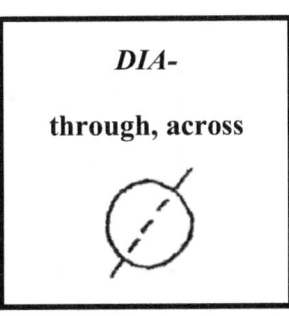

Definition: **n.** a negatively charged electrode; the positively charged lead of a battery supplying current

Sentence: The <u>cathode</u> of a standard flashlight battery is the flat end, carrying a negative charge.

Diadem

	DIA-	DEIN-
	through, across	to bind

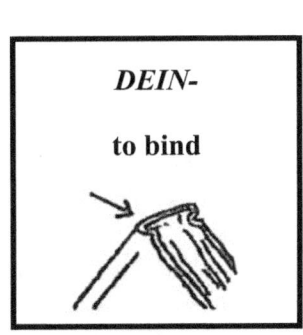

Definition: **n.** a crown worn as a symbol of power; power or dignity
v. to adorn with a diadem

Sentence: At her coronation, Queen Elizabeth donned the crown - a <u>diadem</u> symbolizing the British monarchy.

Diagnose

	DIA-	GIGNOSK-
	through, across	to know

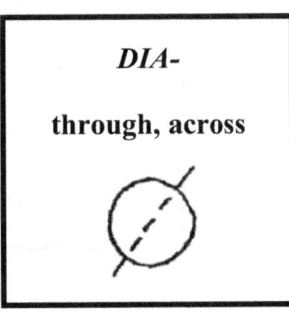

Definition: **v.** to determine the cause of; to determine what is ailing a person

Sentence: Based on descriptions from the time, historians were able to <u>diagnose</u> Caesar's condition as epilectic seizures.

Diagram

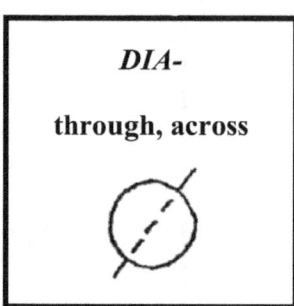

DIA- through, across

GRAPH- to write, to sign

Definition: **n.** a chart or graph showing how parts work in relation to each other

Sentence: Arithmetic and geometric relationships may be represented in figures or in the pictoral form of a <u>diagram</u>.

Diameter

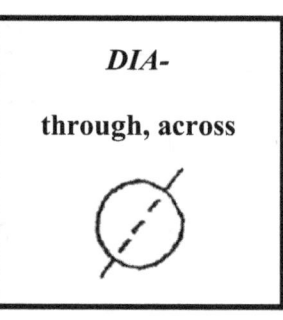 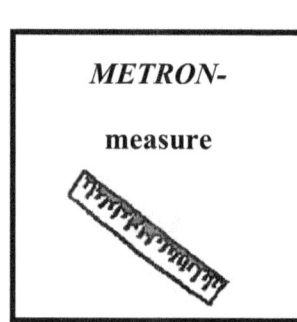

DIA- through, across

METRON- measure

Definition: **n.** the width of something; a line segment through the center of a circle and ending at the intersections with the circle

Sentence: Doubling the cross-section or <u>diameter</u> of a circle quadruples the area.

Diagonal

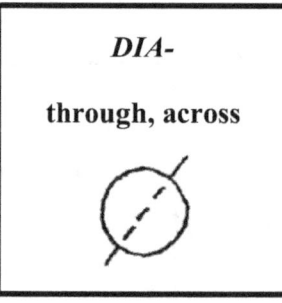 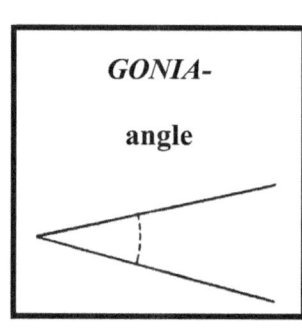

DIA- through, across

GONIA- angle

Definition: **adj.** slanted
n. a slanted line

Sentence: The back-slash (/) and forward-slash (\) characters are neither vertical not horizontal, but <u>diagonal</u>.

Dialect

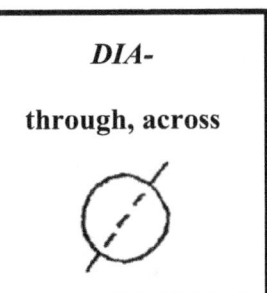

DIA-
through, across

LEG-
to speak

Definition: **n.** a regional variant of a common language

Sentence: Although people in Mexico and Spain both speak Spanish, they speak different <u>dialects</u> and therefore often have trouble communicating.

Dialogue

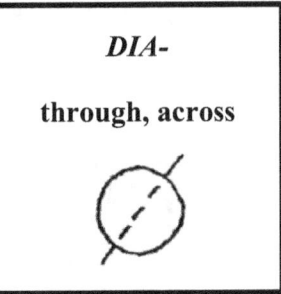

DIA-
through, across

LOGOS-
word, speech, study

Definition: **n.** a conversation between two or more people
v. to hold a conversation

Sentence: Galileo's 'Dialogue Concerning the Two Chief World Systems' consists of an argument among three Italians over a Ptolemaic (earth-centered) versus Copernican (sun-centered) universe.

Dysfunction

DYS-
difficult, faulty

FUNGIO-
to perform

Definition: **n.** improper operation; abnormal or poor function

Sentence: Diabetes is a sugar disease brought on by a <u>dysfunction</u> of the pancreas when it fails to produce sufficient glucose-bearing insulin.

Dyslexia

DYS- difficult, faulty

LEG- to speak

Definition: **n.** a learning disorder that impairs the ability to read and comprehend words

Sentence: Those who suffer from severe <u>dyslexia</u> need to be put in special, slower reading classes as they are unable to process words as quickly as people who don't have the condition.

Dysphoria

DYS- difficult, faulty

PHER- to bear

Definition: **n.** unhappiness; depression; anxiousness

Sentence: 'The Sorrows of Young Werther' is a Goethe novella describing a young man's unrequited love for already engaged Lotte, his consequent <u>dysphoria</u>, and subsequent suicide.

Dystopia

DYS- difficult, faulty

TOPOS- place

Definition: **n.** an imaginary place in which life is the worst possible

Sentence: Orwell's '1984' and Huxley's 'Brave New World' describe futuristic <u>dystopias</u> in which life has become hellish, commodified, and under oppressive government control.

Exercise A

1. Even though I have been studying the _____ of the air conditioning unit for the entire day, I still am unable to understand how it works.
2. The novel *A Clockwork Orange* is about a totalitarian _____, and it discusses just how terrible life in such a society can be.
3. After the enormous _____ that soaked everything in sight, there was no more rain for a week.
4. When I was attempting to fit the screw into the hole, I realized that the screw's _____ was too wide to fit in the hole.
5. Jim went to the doctor, and the doctor _____ Jim with pneumonia.
6. The king wore a _____, which showed how powerful he was.
7. When jump-starting a car, you must first connect the wire to the _____ of the working car so that you do not risk a shock when you complete the circuit.
8. The large deluge left an even larger _____, forcing people to wade down the road rather than simply walking.
9. The _____ at the Vatican is known as St Peter's Basilica.
10. An underground graveyard like the ones constructed by the Romans is known as a _____.
11. The building seemed to be askew because it was formed by a modern artist known for his use of _____ lines rather than traditional rectangular ones.
12. Bob's _____ impaired his ability to read and caused him to stay back a grade.
13. The _____ for my favorite company came today, and I look forward to perusing it for any new items I may wish to purchase.
14. While visiting Alabama, the _____ of English was so varied from my own that I had trouble understanding people.
15. Every year that the Red Sox did not win the World Series plunged me deeper into _____.
16. Because we were unsure what we would do that evening, the five of us engaged in _____, discussing possible plans.
17. After imbibing too much alcohol, the man's liver suffered from _____ and no longer functioned correctly.

Exercise B

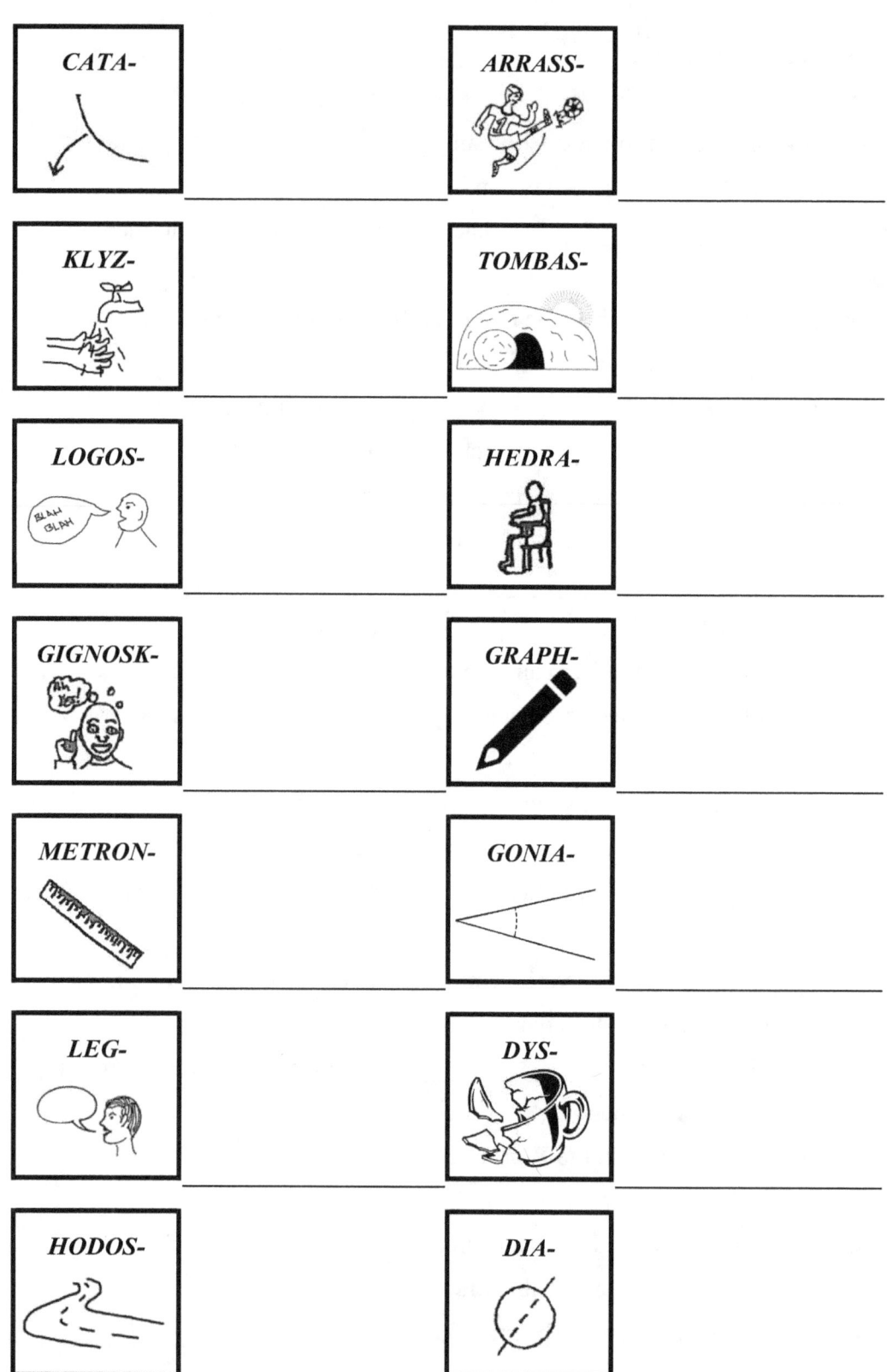

 DEIN-	 KATHAIR-
 PHER-	 TOPOS-
 FUNGIO-	

EXERCISE C

Complete the following crossword puzzle on Lesson 4:

Across:
3. Condition of muscle deterioration
5. Improper operation
6. Positive lead on a source of current
8. Distinguishing
10. Unhappiness
11. Regional variant of a language
12. Giant flood
13. Crown worn symbolizing power
15. Large church

Down:
1. Large downpour
2. Slanted
3. Learning disorder impairing reading
4. Assess ailments
7. Conversation between multiple people
8. Chart or graph
9. Inflammation of mucous in the nose
10. Imaginary, terrible place
13. Angry tirade
14. Underground passageways for tombs
15. List of items for exhibition
16. Width

EXERCISE D

Match the word with the letter of its definition:

1. ___ cataract
2. ___ cataclysm
3. ___ catacomb
4. ___ catalog
5. ___ catarrh
6. ___ cathedral
7. ___ cathode
8. ___ diadem
9. ___ diacritical
10. ___ diagnose
11. ___ diagram
12. ___ diameter
13. ___ diagonal
14. ___ dialect
15. ___ dialogue
16. ___ diatribe
17. ___ dysfunction
18. ___ dyslexia
19. ___ dysphoria
20. ___ dystopia
21. ___ dystrophy

a) inflammation of mucous in the nose
b) conversation between multiple people
c) chart or graph
d) underground passageways for tombs
e) learning disorder impairing reading
f) distinguishing
g) large church
h) regional variant of a language
i) large downpour
j) improper operation
k) positive lead on a source of current
l) imaginary, terrible place
m) giant flood
n) angry tirade
o) assess ailments
p) list of items for exhibition
q) condition of muscle deterioration
r) width
s) crown worn symbolizing power
t) unhappiness
u) slanted

Lesson V

Endocrine

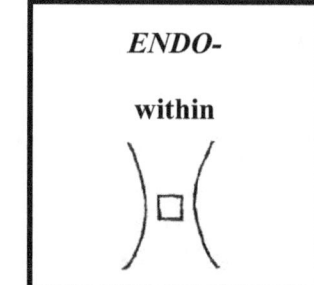

Definition: **adj.** secreting internally

Sentence: One whose <u>endocrine</u> glands secrete too many hormones is likely to act overly emotionally.

Exocrine

Definition: **adj.** relating to glands that secrete fluids such as hormones

Sentence: The body's sweat glands are <u>exocrine</u> glands as they produce sweat that surfaces on our skin.

Endogenous

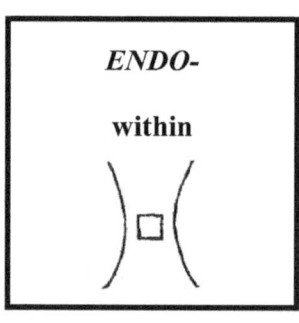

Definition: **adj.** produced or caused from within

Sentence: <u>Endogenous</u> diseases are those with a source inside the organism rather than caused by an outside agent.

Exogenous

Definition: **adj.** produced from outside

Sentence: Viral and bacterial infections are the <u>exogenous</u> result of environmental contact rather than internal dysfunction.

Endoskeleton

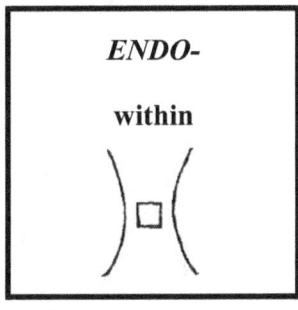

Definition: **n.** a framework within the body of an animal

Sentence: Vertebrates have <u>endoskeletons,</u> an internal framework of bones covered by muscle and skin or exterior tissue.

Exoskeleton

Definition: **n.** a hard external shell or body covering that provides protection or support for an animal

Sentence: Insects and crustaceans such as lobsters have <u>exoskeletons</u> or shell-like bodily coverings that offer housing for internal organs and protect against pests and predators.

Endothermic

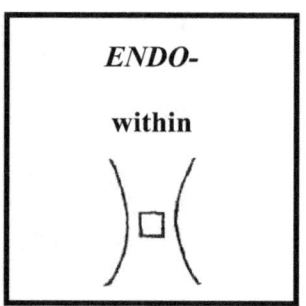
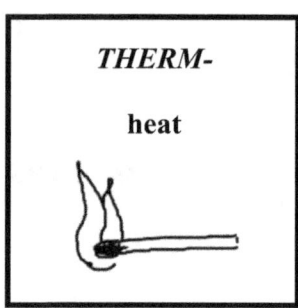

Definition: **adj.** a reaction that absorbs heat; warm-blooded

Sentence: Warm-blooded animals are <u>endothermic</u> in that they maintain a body temperature typically above the temperature of their surroundings.

Exothermic

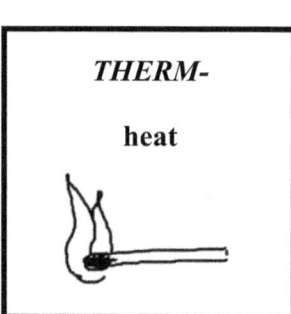

Definition: **adj.** a reaction that releases heat

Sentence: Striking a match generates heat and flame in an energy-producing, <u>exothermic</u> chemical reaction.

Endophyte

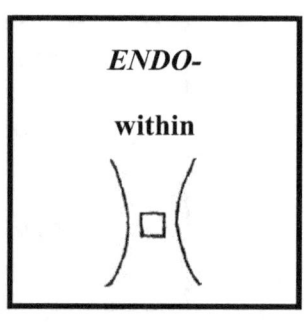
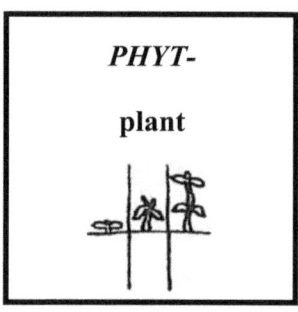

Definition: **n.** a plant growing within another plant

Sentence: A fungus is an <u>endophyte</u> that lives within and gets its nourishment from another plant.

Exoteric

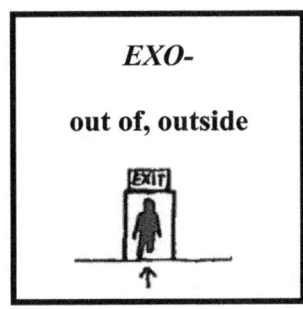

Definition: **adj.** known widely; common knowledge

Sentence: Initially limited to a small group of initiated disciples, Christianity has become a widespread exoteric religion.

Exotic

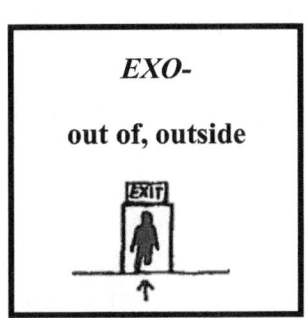

Definition: **adj.** foreign; strikingly unusual

Sentence: That which can be explained simply doesn't require exotic explanations.

Exercise A

1. Ants are known for their strong _____, which can support over 100 times their weight!

2. "2+2=4" is an example of a/an _____ fact. Very few people do not know it.

3. Julianne quickly learned that lighting a sparkler produced an _____ reaction, as she burned her hand on it.

4. There is a theory that grass infused with _____ is healthier because these plants serve to help support the growing grass with nutrients.

5. Salivary glands are _____ glands because they lead to an external secretion.

6. Humans have a/an _____ covered by skin and muscle.

7. Your _____ system contains many glands which internally perspire.

8. From her trip to Africa, my mother brought our family many _____ souvenirs.

9. Humans are _____ as their temperature changes very little with the outside temperature.

10. _____ processes within the earth are responsible for producing mountains and chasms.

11. Any type of therapy or drug administered as a cure is _____ because it was not produced within your body.

Exercise B

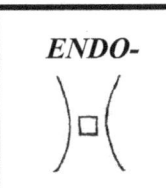 ENDO- _____  EXO- _____

 KRIN- _____  GENUS- _____

 SKELL- _____  THERM- _____

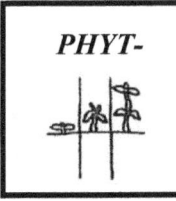 PHYT- _____

EXERCISE C

Complete the following crossword puzzle on Lesson 5:

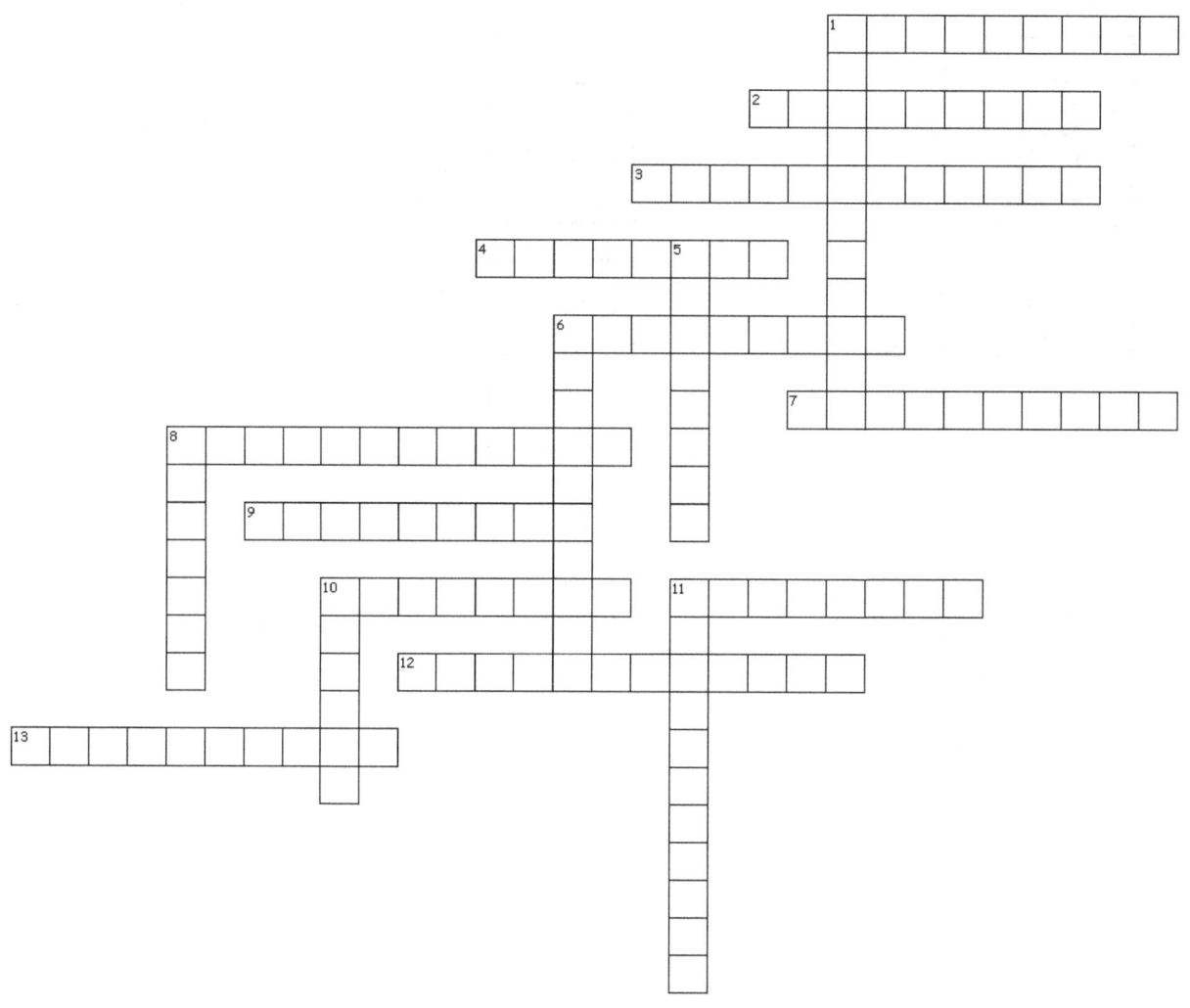

Across:
1. Produced from outside
2. Diffusion outward
3. An internal framework
4. Tissue lining the digestive tract
6. Plant growing within another
7. Produced from inside
8. Internal parasite
9. Secreting internally
10. Marriage within a group
11. Secreting externally
12. Inflammation of the heart lining
13. Diffusion inward

Down:
1. An external framework
5. Widely known
6. Releasing heat
8. Marriage outside of a group
10. Foreign
11. Absorbing heat

EXERCISE D

Match the word with the letter of its definition.

1. ___ endocrine
2. ___ exocrine
3. ___ endogamy
4. ___ exogamy
5. ___ endogenous
6. ___ exogenous
7. ___ endoskeleton
8. ___ exoskeleton
9. ___ endosmosis
10. ___ exosmosis
11. ___ endothermic
12. ___ exothermic
13. ___ endocarditis
14. ___ endoderm
15. ___ endoparasite
16. ___ endophyte
17. ___ exoteric
18. ___ exotic

a) diffusion outward
b) an external framework
c) widely known
d) marriage within a group
e) tissue lining the digestive tract
f) produced from within
g) releasing heat
h) an internal framework
i) secreting externally
j) plant growing within another
k) foreign
l) internal parasite
m) inflammation of the heart lining
n) produced from outside
o) diffusion inward
p) marriage outside of a group
q) absorbing heat
r) secreting internally

Lesson VI

Ephemeral

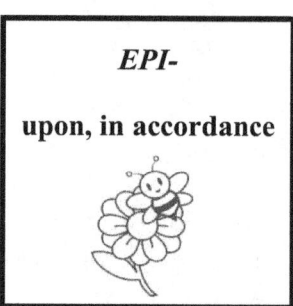

Definition: **adj.** short lived; fleeting

Sentence: Living but a few days, the mayfly is an ephemeral creature.

Epicenter

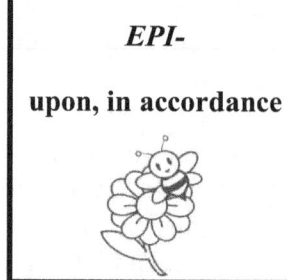
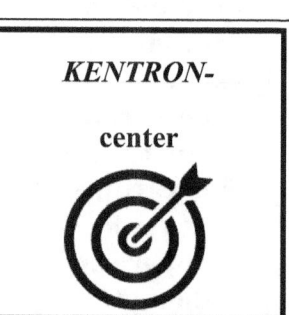

Definition: **n.** the point on the earth's surface directly above an earthquake; a focal point

Sentence: Located over the San Andreas fault line, California is the epicenter of many earthquakes.

Epidemic

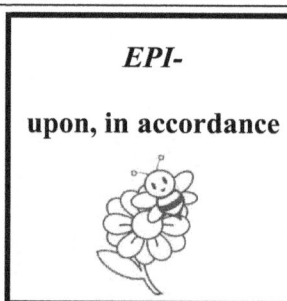

Definition: **adj.** spreading quickly and extensively
n. a rampant and wide-spreading growth or development; an outbreak of a contagious disease

Sentence: In the Great Depression of the 1930's, unemployment reached epidemic proportions.

Epidermis

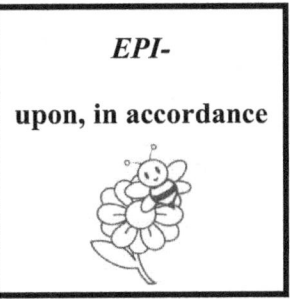
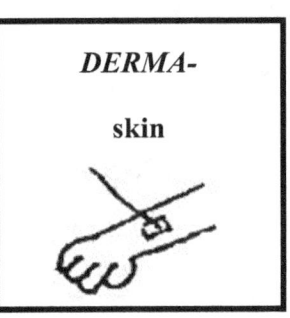

EPI- — upon, in accordance

DERMA- — skin

Definition: **n.** the layer of protective, non-vascular skin covering the dermis or the outer layer of cells covering the leaves of a plant.

Sentence: Athlete's foot is an itchy fungus that infects the <u>epidermis</u> of the foot.

Epilogue

EPI- — upon, in accordance

LOGOS- — word, speech, study

Definition: **n.** an afterword or short addition or concluding portion to a play or literary work after the main story has been finished

Sentence: The <u>epilogue</u> to the championship game was riotous celebration in the hometown streets.

Epitaph

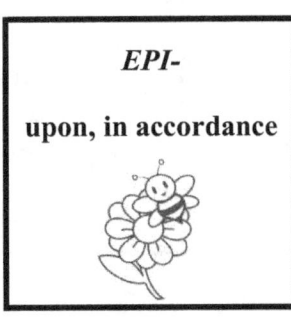
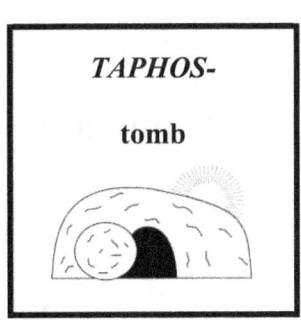

EPI- — upon, in accordance

TAPHOS- — tomb

Definition: **n.** an inscription on a tombstone in memory of the deceased buried there

Sentence: The <u>epitaph</u> on his tombstone makes no mention of Thomas Jefferson's presidency or authorship of the Declaration of Independence.

Eugenics

Definition:	**n.** the study of improving the human race via selective breeding
Sentence:	Hitler initiated special pairings of SS-men and healthy Aryan women aimed at creating a master race through <u>eugenics</u>.

Eulogize

Definition:	**v.** to praise highly in speech or writing (especially of a deceased person)
Sentence:	My uncle was <u>eulogized</u> at his funeral, praised as a fine father, husband, and citizen.

Euphemism

Definition:	**n.** substitute to an otherwise taboo word or offensive subject; auspicious; praise
Sentence:	The term 'pass away' is a <u>euphemism</u> for the blunter, shied away from word 'die'.

Euphonious

Definition:	**adj.** good sounding, pleasing to the ear
Sentence:	The flowing voweled speech of French is generally considered to be more <u>euphonious</u> than the gutteral, consonantal sounds of German.

Euphoria

Definition:	**n.** a feeling of great happiness or being
Sentence:	In the Buddhist tradition, the ultimate goal is to reach a blissful state of <u>euphoria</u> known as nirvana.

Hemisphere

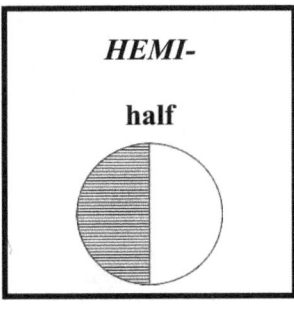 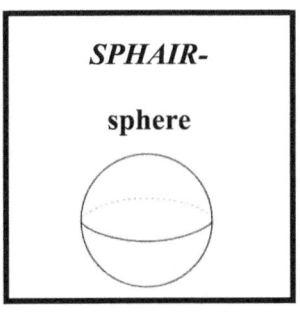

Definition:	**n.** half of a sphere; half of a roughly spherical object
Sentence:	Two copper bowls or <u>hemispheres</u> joined at the rim and held together only by a vacuum could not be separated by horses in the famous Magdeburg experiment.

Hemiplegia

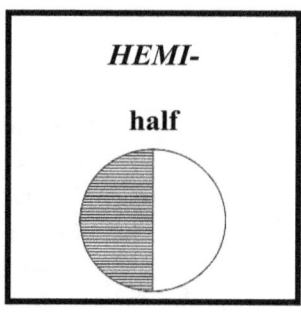

Definition:	**n.** paralysis in half the body
Sentence:	Though it does not necessarily paralyze half the sufferer's body, cerebral palsy is often referred to as <u>hemiplegia.</u>

Exercise A

1. Being the oldest grandson, Mark was asked to _____ his grandmother at her funeral.

2. In 2004, Hong Kong was ridden with a SARS _____ which was spreading rapidly and uncontrollably.

3. Before Columbus sailed across the Atlantic Ocean, people had no concept of the Western _____ – they believed the land was flat and that they had discovered all of the existing land.

4. When Susan's pet dog died, Susan's mother told her that it went to "doggy heaven" in the hopes that this _____ would not upset Susan.

5. In the _____ of the book, the author reveals that the main couple in the book, despite their apparent romance, end up in a messy divorce.

6. Because it is directly above the San Andreas Fault line, California is the _____ for many earthquakes.

7. Suffering from _____ , the man had no use of the left side of his body.

8. Because man is a/an _____ creature, many people do great deeds in attempt to have their memory preserved forever.

9. When Edgar fell off of his bike, he skinned his _____ , leaving an open wound over his thigh.

10. Bach's music is so _____ that my ears perk up whenever I hear it.

11. The _____ on the man's headstone read "Here lies a brave man that believed in his country and died for it."

12. Ice cream is my favorite food. Every time I eat it I feel as though I am entering a state of _____ .

13. Many people disagree with _____ , saying that to choose who is allowed to breed and who is not is not natural.

Exercise B

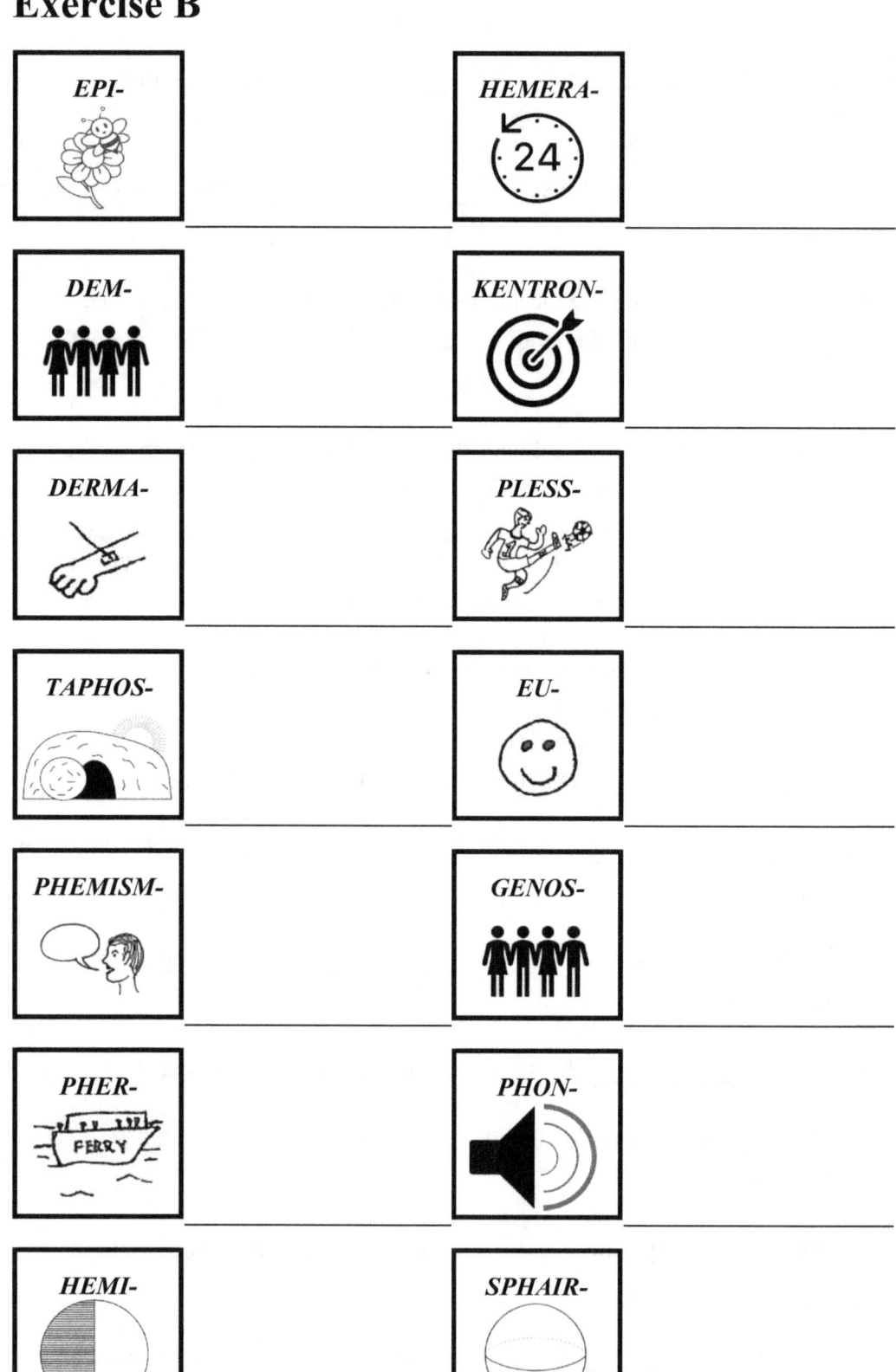

EXERCISE C

Complete the following crossword puzzle on Lesson 6:

Across:
1. Focal point
2. Praise a deceased person
3. Good sounding
5. Addition at the end of a book
7. Paralysis in half of the body
9. Substitute for an offensive word
10. Inscription on a tombstone
11. Short lived
13. Semicircle

Down:
1. Protective layer of skin
4. Pain in half of the body
6. Devoted to gluttony
7. Half of a round object
8. Widespread outbreak
9. Extreme happiness
11. Study of improving humanity by selective breeding
12. Good digestion

13. The _____ on the man's headstone read "Here lies a brave man that believed in his country and died for it."

14. Strokes can produce paralysis on one half of the body or head in a condition known as _____.

15. The boy had particularly good digestion. This _____ helped him to be the hot dog eating champion.

16. Ice cream is my favorite food. Every time I eat it I feel as though I am entering a state of _____.

17. Many people disagree with _____, saying that to choose who is allowed to breed and who is not is not natural.

EXERCISE D

Match the word with the letter of its definition:

1. ___ ephemeral
2. ___ epicenter
3. ___ epicurean
4. ___ epidemic
5. ___ epidermis
6. ___ epilogue
7. ___ epitaph
8. ___ eugenics
9. ___ eulogize
10. ___ eupepsia
11. ___ euphemism
12. ___ euphonious
13. ___ euphoria
14. ___ hemialgia
15. ___ hemicycle
16. ___ hemisphere
17. ___ hemiplegia

a) good sounding
b) protective layer of skin
c) substitute for an offensive word
d) praise a deceased person
e) focal point
f) paralysis in half of the body
g) addition at the end of a book
h) short lived
i) extreme happiness
j) inscription on a tombstone
k) having good digestion
l) devoted to gluttony
m) half of a round object
n) pain in half of the body
o) widespread outbreak
p) semicircle
q) study of improving humanity by selective breeding

Test 1

Choose the correct meaning for the underlined vocabulary word in each sentence.

1. "This was the shocking thing; that the slime of the pit seemed to utter cries and voices; that the amorphous dust gesticulated and sinned; that what was dead, and had no shape, should usurp the offices of life."
   Dr. Jekyll and Mr. Hyde by Robert Louis Stevenson

   (a) waterless (b) lacking a name (c) shapeless (d) without germs
   (e) ailment free

2. "Citizens of feudal states are alarmed at our democratic institutions lapsing into anarchy, and the older and more cautious among ourselves are learning from Europeans to look with some terror at our turbulent freedom."
   Essays, Second Series by Ralph Waldo Emerson

   (a) lawlessness (b) biography (c) iron deficiency (d) authority
   (e) freedom

3. "One day I gave, as a devoir, the trite little anecdote of Alfred tending cakes in the herdsman's hut, to be related with amplifications."
   The Professor by Charlotte Bronte

   (a) chaotic state (b) remedy (c) deficiency (d) brief account
   (e) abnormality

4. "Tulkinghorn being always correct and exact; still that does not," says Sir Leicester, "that does not lessen the anomaly, which is fraught with strange considerations-- startling considerations, as it appears to me."
   Bleak House by Charles Dickens

   (a) authorship (b) deviation (c) place of refuge (d) authority
   (e) short history

TEST 1

5. "You know, one of those uncouth new people one's so often coming across nowadays, one of those free-thinkers you know, who are reared d'emblee in theories of <u>atheism</u>, scepticism, and materialism"

Anna Karenina by Leo Tolstoy

(a) godlessness   (b) deterioration   (c) irregularity   (d) without ailment
(e) deviation

6. "This paralysis lasted, however, but a short time; for Tess's energies returned with the <u>atrophy</u> of his, and she walked as fast as she was able past the barn and onward."

Tess of the d'Urbervilles by Thomas Hardy

(a) without substance   (b) injury   (c) deterioration   (d) account
(e) refuge

7. "But this hard body might be a bony covering, like that of the antediluvian animals; and I should be free to class this monster among <u>amphibious</u> reptiles, such as tortoises or alligators."

20,000 Leagues Under The Sea by Jules Verne

(a) scaly   (b) structural   (c) round theater   (d) aquatic
(e) living in and out of water

8. "Hermann, that Glaucon and Adeimantus are not the brothers but the uncles of Plato, or the fancy of Stallbaum that Plato intentionally left <u>anachronisms</u> indicating the dates at which some of his Dialogues were written."

The Republic by Plato

(a) outdated things   (b) separations   (c) scientific structures   (d) repetitions
(e) exhibitions

9. "Colleville had a passion for reading the horoscopes of famous men in the <u>anagram</u> of their names."

Bureaucracy by Honore de Balzac

(a) out of order in time   (b) rhetorical effect   (c) reordering of letters in a word
(d) person of power   (e) something believable

10. "In their room, however, all is bustle and confusion, for the doctors are about to make an <u>autopsy</u> on the corpse."

Poor Folk by Fyodor Dostoyevsky

(a) structure   (b) examination   (c) surgery   (d) account of one's life
(e) signature

11. "Twice he had exposed himself and been fired at, while he had failed to catch a single glimpse of his antagonist."
Adventure by Jack London

(a) adversary (b) fungus (c) protein (d) remedy (e) hostility

12. "And the invocation was uttered in such a tone as to indicate a rooted antipathy to anything so commonplace, even if she had not added that sequins gave her the sick."
Of Human Bondage by W. Somerset Maugham

(a) likeness (b) adage (c) strong aversion (d) orbit (e) erroneous

13. "Speaking of the moon, she is nearest to the earth in her perigee, and farthest from it in her apogee."
Round The Moon by Jules Verne

(a) regret (b) power (c) opposition (d) apex (e) support

14. "The marriage was to make no change in their place of residence; they had been able to extend it, by taking to themselves the upper rooms formerly belonging to the apocryphal invisible lodger, and they desired nothing more."
A Tale Of Two Cities by Charles Dickens

(a) preventing infection (b) bringing on the end of the world
(c) in opposition to (d) to ward off evil (e) of questionable authenticity

15. "The hour of the intended cataclysm was approaching apace."
The Lair of the White Worm by Bram Stoker

(a) waterfall (b) inflammation (c) catastrophe (d) passageway
(e) biblical teaching

16. "But if this whale be a king, he is a very sulky looking fellow to grace a diadem."
Moby Dick by Herman Melville

(a) electrode (b) royal power (c) chart, graph (d) adornment
(e) banded train

17. "He was to learn a dialect, in which he could be assisted by no affinity with the languages he already knew."
Grandfather's Chair by Nathaniel Hawthorne

(a) form of language (b) geometric relationship (c) half a circle
(d) slant (e) form of writing

TEST 1

18. "The little <u>diatribe</u> with which you have just favored me is exactly the reply we should have expected to receive formally from Downing Street."

    The Illustrious Prince by E. Phillips Oppenheim

    (a) abnormal function   (b) denunciation   (c) reading disorder
    (d) muscular atrophy   (e) unhappiness

19. "We don garment after garment, as if we grew like <u>exogenous</u> plants by addition without."

    Walden & on the Duty of Civil Disobedience by Henry David Thoreau

    (a) internal   (b) marriage outside the group   (c) produced   (d) layered
    (e) framework

20. "It is easy to point out the different modes of government, and we have already settled them in our <u>exoteric</u> discourses."

    A Treatise on Government by Aristotle

    (a) popular, common   (b) plant   (c) foreign, distant   (d) parasitic
    (e) unknowing, strange

21. "The general tuckermanities are arrant Bubbles - <u>ephemeral</u> and so transparent - But this is, now, - you may depend upon it - Stable, opaque, immortal - all by dint Of the dear names that lie concealed within 't."

    Poems by Edgar Allan Poe

    (a) centered   (b) diurnal   (c) fleeting   (d) pleasurable
    (e) spreading

22. "She followed the traditions of the <u>epicurean</u> churchman to whom this valuable garden owed its origin; but Benassis himself regarded it with sufficient indifference."

    The Country Doctor by Honore de Balzac

    (a) devoted to pleasure   (b) tired   (c) heavyset   (d) short-lived
    (e) photographed regularly

23. "And this was the <u>epitaph</u> of a dead dog on the Northland trail--less scant than the <u>epitaph</u> of many another dog, of many a man."

    White Fang by Jack London

    (a) selective breeding   (b) short addition   (c) selective speech
    (d) tombstone inscription   (e) cellular layer

24. "It was something of a <u>euphemism</u> to call him a well-known man about town.
The Man Who Knew Too Much by Gilbert K. Chesterton

(a) good digestion (b) mild expression for a harsh term (c) flattery
(d) happy feeling (e) high praise

25. "I heard of the discovery of the American <u>hemisphere</u> and wept with Safie over the hapless fate of its original inhabitants."
Frankenstein by Mary Shelley

(a) semicircle (b) half the body (c) half the Earth (d) equator
(e) diameter

Lesson VII

Homogeneous

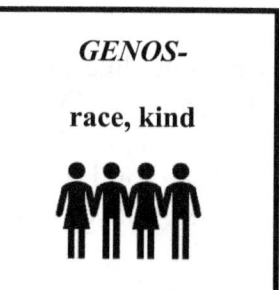

Definition: **adj.** of the same or similar kind or nature

Sentence: To be effective, concrete must be stirred into a <u>homogenous</u> mixture of cement, sand, gravel, and water before application.

Heterogeneous

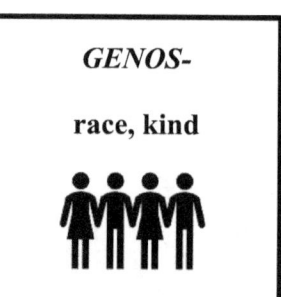

Definition: **n.** a rival

Sentence: The tortoise and the hare were seemingly ill-matched <u>competitors</u>.

Homology

Definition: **n.** being similar or corresponding in position, function, or structure

Sentence: Similar in structure and basic function, the flippers of a seal and human hands exemplify biological <u>homology</u>.

Homonym

 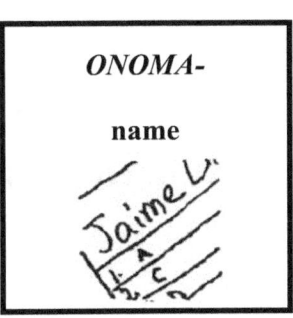

Definition: **n.** word that sounds the same but is spelled differently and has a different meaning from another

Sentence: The words 'their,' 'they're,' and 'there' are <u>homonyms</u> and as a result are commonly confused.

Heteronym

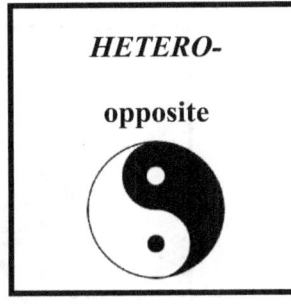 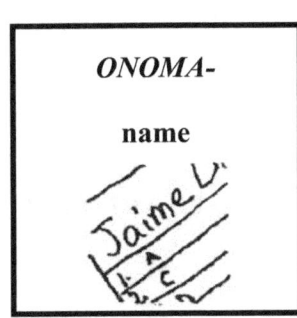

Definition: **n.** word that sounds different but is spelled the same and has a different meaning from another

Sentence: The words 'wind,' as in 'the movement of air,' and 'wind' as in 'to turn' are <u>heteronyms</u>.

Homosexual

Definition: **n.** someone who is attracted to the same gender as himself or herself
adj. sexually oriented towards persons of the same gender

Sentence: Provincetown, MA, located at the tip of Cape Cod, has a large <u>homosexual</u> community of gays and lesbians.

Heterosexual

Definition: **n.** someone who is attracted to the opposite gender as himself or herself.
adj. sexually oriented towards persons of the opposite gender

Sentence: "Women seeking men" is a heading in the Personals section of the newspaper for <u>heterosexual</u> women interested in dating men.

Heterodox

Definition: **adj.** not in agreement with usual beliefs; having unorthodox beliefs

Sentence: Many of the great philosophers of history have had <u>heterodox</u> beliefs that ran counter to accepted popular wisdom.

Homophonic

Definition: **adj.** all instruments play the same melodic line; having the same sound

Sentence: The 'Ode to Joy' in Beethoven's Ninth Symphony examplifies a <u>homophonic</u> composition in which all instruments and choral members perform the same melody in triumphant unison.

Exercise A

1. Many students confuse "principal" and "principle" because with _____ it is hard to remember which one means which thing.

2. The _____ between a human and a chimpanzee is astonishing. We share 99.7% of the same D.N.A. makeup as chimps do.

3. The scholar's views on conventional economics were not mainstream but often rather _____ due to his stance national debt and deficit spending.

4. Even today, there are still places in rural America where racism is prevalent. In many _____ communities, where they have scarcely encountered someone of another race, citizens are frightened of the unusual.

5. The word "bass" as in a fish and the word "bass" as in bass guitar are _____ because they are spelled the same, but they are pronounced differently.

6. Massachusetts is the first state to legalize _____ marriages.

7. The United States has a/an _____ population, accruing immigrants from every nation on the planet.

8. The Catholic church is against gay marriages, saying that _____ relationships are God's natural intention.

9. Beethoven's "Ninth Symphony" is a great example of _____ as all the instruments play the same melodic line.

Exercise B

 HOMO- _____    GENOS- _____

 HETERO- _____    LOGOS- _____

 ONOMA- _____    SEX- _____

 DOXA- _____    PHON- _____

EXERCISE C

Complete the following crossword puzzle on Lesson 7:

Across:
3. Attracted to the same sex
9. Of various kinds or natures
11. Of unorthodox thought
12. Attracted to the opposite sex
13. Difference in structure or form

Down:
1. Of similar kind or nature
2. Words with the same sound but different spellings
4. Anomaly
5. Of varied colors
6. Playing the same melodic line
7. Similarity in structure or form
8. Sharing the same center
9. Words that are spelled the same but mean different things
10. Of one color

EXERCISE D

Match the word with the letter of its definition:

1. ___ homochromatic
2. ___ heterochromatic
3. ___ homogeneous
4. ___ heterogeneous
5. ___ homology
6. ___ heterology
7. ___ homonym
8. ___ heteronym
9. ___ homosexual
10. ___ heterosexual
11. ___ heteroclite
12. ___ heterodox
13. ___ homocentric
14. ___ homophonic

a) attracted to the opposite sex
b) similarity in structure or form
c) of similar kind or nature
d) anomalous
e) of one color
f) of unorthodox thought
g) attracted to the same sex
h) words with the same sound but different spellings
i) of varied colors
j) difference in structure or form
k) of various kinds or natures
l) playing the same melodic line
m) sharing the same center
n) words that are spelled the same but mean different things

Lesson VIII

Hyperglycemia

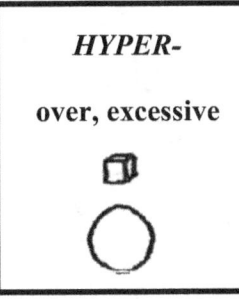  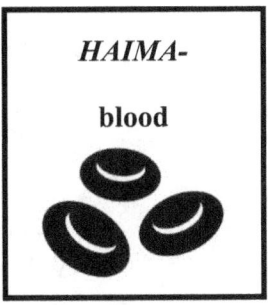

Definition:	**n.** condition of high blood sugar level
Sentence:	<u>Hyperglycemia</u> is the presence of abnormally elevated blood sugar (glucose) levels.

Hypoglycemia

Definition:	**n.** condition of low blood sugar level
Sentence:	<u>Hypoglycemia</u> can result from diabetes treatment but can be treated easily by drinking sugary fluids such as soda or juice.

Hypertension

Definition:	**n.** condition of high blood pressure
Sentence:	Although largely genetic, <u>hypertension</u> is an elevated blood pressure condition that can be induced by not exercising or an unhealthy diet.

Hypotension

Definition:	**n.** condition of low blood pressure
Sentence:	People who have <u>hypotension</u> are at risk for dizziness and hunger as not enough blood reaches their organs.

Hyperthermia

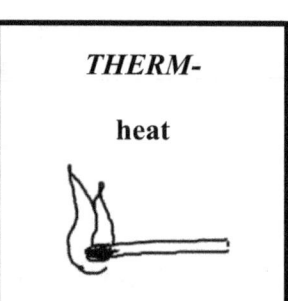

Definition:	**n.** high fever or high body temperature
Sentence:	<u>Hyperthermia</u>, an unusually high body temperature, is a serious medical condition that needs to be treated with cooling.

Hypothermia

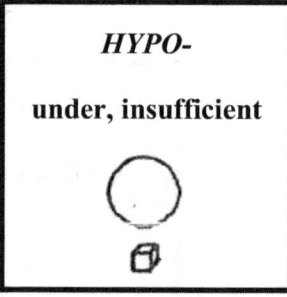
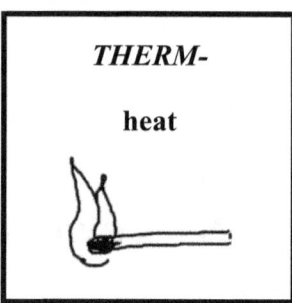

Definition:	**n.** low body temperature
Sentence:	People exposed to the cold for long periods of time with insufficient clothing fall victim to loss of bodily heat and <u>hypothermia</u>.

Hyperbole

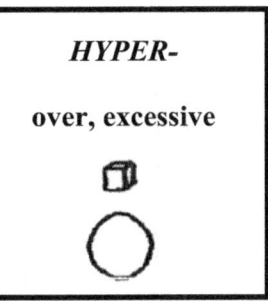

Definition: **n.** exaggeration for rhetorical effect

Sentence: 'I've told you a million times' or 'I nearly died laughing' are examples of <u>hyperbole</u>.

Hyperactive

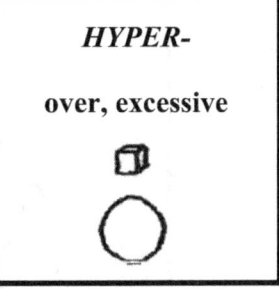

Definition: **adj.** overactive; excessively energized

Sentence: Rambuctious little children may seem <u>hyperactive</u> to older folks who have lost their youthful energy and live at a slower pace.

Hypercritical

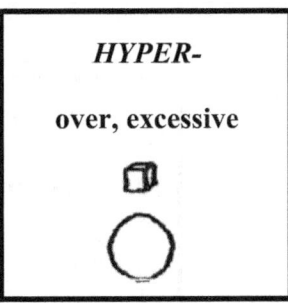

Definition: **adj.** overcritical; captious

Sentence: 'Constant nit-picking and fault-finding make for a <u>hypercritical</u> personality.

Hypocrite

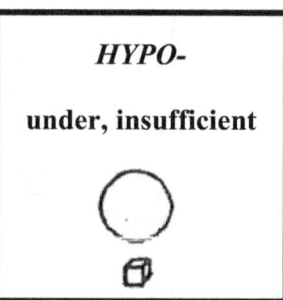
HYPO-
under, insufficient

KRIN-
distinguish, judge

Definition: **adj.** someone who acts in contradiction to his or her stated beliefs

Sentence: The pro-life politician was labeled a hypocrite after it was revealed that he told his mistress to get an abortion.

Hypersensitive

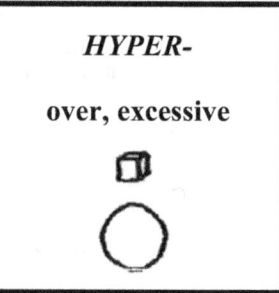
HYPER-
over, excessive

SENT-, SENS-
to think, to feel

Definition: **adj.** abnormally sensitive

Sentence: Having a stutter or lisp may make a person <u>hypersensitive</u> about public speaking.

Hypodermic

HYPO-
under, insufficient

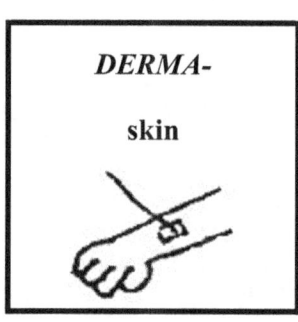
DERMA-
skin

Definition: **adj.** injected beneath the skin
n. a syringe used for such an injection

Sentence: Injected into the skin via the <u>hypodermic</u> needle of a sterile syringe, most vaccine shots cause a patient to wince in brief discomfort.

Hypothesis

Definition:	**n.** proposition asserting an outcome, made prior to experimentation
Sentence:	An early hypothesis that AIDs could be transmitted via kissing was proven wrong by experiment and observation.

Exercise A

1. From eating too much McDonald's and from not exercising enough, I developed _____ and had to find a way to start to lower my blood pressure.

2. The _____ boy was running around for hours, even though his mother was constantly asking him to sit still.

3. When camping in frigid temperatures, I was exposed to too much cold and began to suffer from _____ .

4. In an obvious instance of _____, my brother told me that the boring lecture lasted forever.

5. Using a/an _____ eye, the detective went over the crime scene to find any minuscule clues that he might otherwise have missed.

6. Because the nerves are exposed, cuts are _____ to any touch.

7. Because I suffer from _____, I have to be careful not to eat too many sugary candies.

8. After too much exercise, and not eating enough food, I suffered from _____. My doctor advised me that if my blood pressure dropped any further, I was at a great health risk.

9. When I had the flu, along with my other symptoms, I suffered from _____. My temperature rose to 104.3 degrees.

10. The student made an educated guess about the chemical's behavior, and the experiment proved his _____ correct.

11. When I was diagnosed with _____ , my doctor advised me to always carry around some candy in case my blood sugar level dropped too far.

12. The doctor injected a/an _____ needle deep into my arm in order to numb the area before surgery.

Exercise B

EXERCISE C

Complete the following crossword puzzle on Lesson 8:

Across:
1. High body temperature
3. Overactive
4. Proposition asserting an outcome
9. High blood sugar
10. Overly sensitive
12. Farsightedness

Down:
2. High blood pressure
5. Exaggeration for effect
6. Captious
7. Injected under the skin
8. Low blood pressure
9. Low body temperature
11. Large blood supply

EXERCISE D

Match the word with the letter of its definition:

1. ___ hyperglycemia
2. ___ hypoglycemia
3. ___ hypertension
4. ___ hypotension
5. ___ hyperthermia
6. ___ hypothermia
7. ___ hyperbole
8. ___ hyperactive
9. ___ hypercritical
10. ___ hyperemia
11. ___ hyperopia
12. ___ hypersensitive
13. ___ hypodermic
14. ___ hypothesis

a) low blood sugar
b) low body temperature
c) high body temperature
d) farsightedness
e) overactive
f) high blood pressure
g) low blood pressure
h) proposition asserting an outcome
i) overly sensitive
j) exaggeration for effect
k) high blood sugar
l) captious
m) large blood supply
n) injected under the skin

Lesson IX

Macrocosm

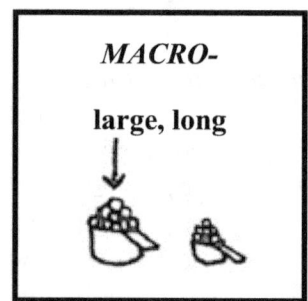
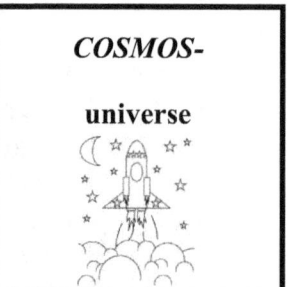

Definition: **n.** the universe; cosmic perspective

Sentence: On the scale of the <u>macrocosm</u> the earth is simply an insignificant speck in an oceanic universe.

Microcosm

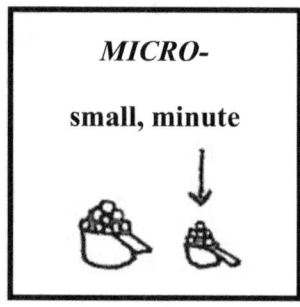

Definition: **n.** smaller group or area representative of a larger group or area

Sentence: Looking through his microscope at the teeming life a drop of pond water, van Leeuwenhoek remarked on the discovery of a biological <u>microcosm</u>.

Macroeconomics

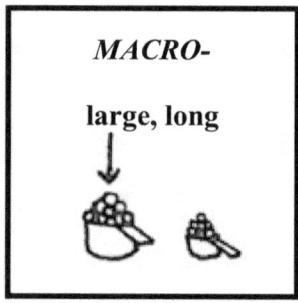

Definition: **n.** the study of overall national economics

Sentence: The U.S. prospers in terms of <u>macroeconomics</u>: the total income, output, and productive relationships in its economic sectors.

Microeconomics

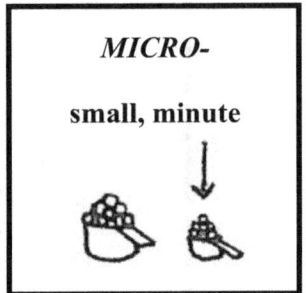

Definition: **n.** the study of individual firms and businesses within a national economy

Sentence: The <u>microeconomics</u> of discrete corporations like Microsoft and IBM have played a major role in boosting the nation's economy as a whole.

Macroscopic

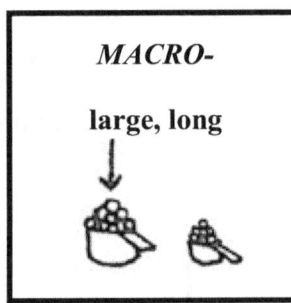

Definition: **adj.** on a great scale; large enough to be perceived by the naked eye

Sentence: The view from 30,000 feet yields a <u>macroscopic</u> scale in which fine details disappear.

Microscopic

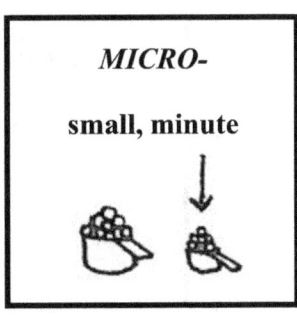
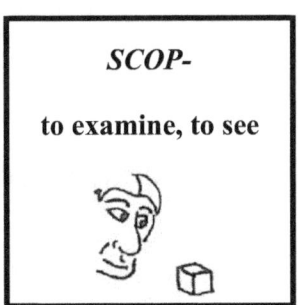

Definition: **adj.** not visible to the naked eye; minute

Sentence: Our bodies are surrounded by and infested with millions of <u>microscopic</u> organisms invisible to the unaided eye.

Microbe

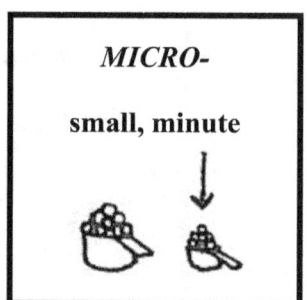
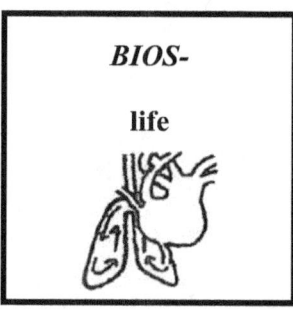

Definition: **n.** a minute life form, especially one that causes disease; a germ or bacterium

Sentence: A given spoonful of dirt contains tens of millions of bacteria or other tiny microbes.

Microfilm

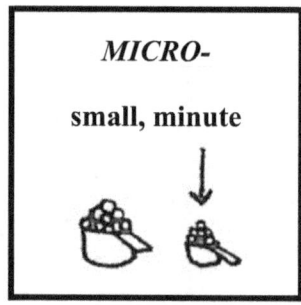

Definition: **n.** a film used to store documents in highly miniaturized form

Sentence: Issues of the *New York Times* from the 1800's to the present are archived in most libraries on microfilm.

Micrometer

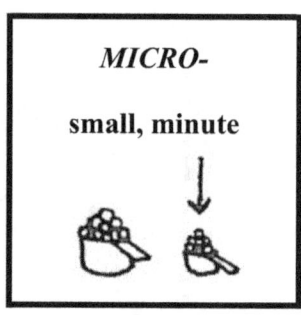
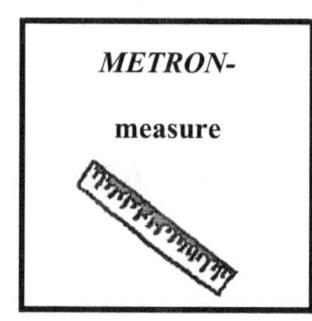

Definition: **n.** device used to measure small distances or intervals; a unit of length equal to one millionth of a meter

Sentence: In Millikan's famous oil-drop experiment, a micrometer is used to measure the diameter of and distance traveled by tiny atomized oil particles.

Microorganism

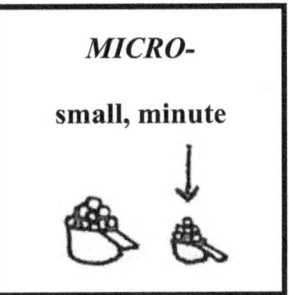 

Definition: **n.** a microscopic animal or plant

Sentence: Huge sea animals such as whales ironically eat millions of tiny microorganisms such as plankton.

Microsecond

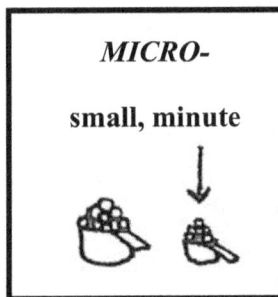 

Definition: **n.** a millionth of a second

Sentence: Some chemical reactions, like the opening of the benzene ring, take place within a span of microseconds, while others, such as the rusting of metal, proceed slowly over a period of years or centuries.

Microwave

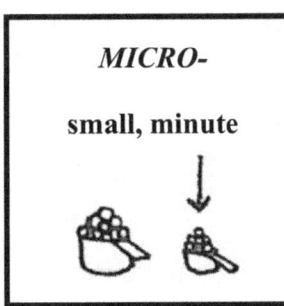 

Definition: **n.** electromagnetic radiation of a low frequency; a device that uses microwaves to warm food

Sentence: The accidental detection of background microwave radiation by a radiotelescope helped confirm the Big Bang theory.

Exercise A

1. While studying _____ , the student focused on Microsoft's influence in the U.S. economy.

2. To measure the width of the fiber, the scientist used a/an _____ because it was so small.

3. After June washes her hands, she is afraid to touch the doorknob because she does not want the _____ she just washed off her hands to immediately return.

4. Though he claimed he would be back in a/an _____ , he was clearly hyperbolizing; He would be at least a minute.

5. I put the frozen burrito in the _____ so that it would be warm enough to eat.

6. Interstellar distances are measured on a _____ macroscopic scale.

7. The village was a _____ of the nation of the nation as a whole.

8. Documents on _____ cannot be read without an optical device.

9. I was unable to see the _____ leak in my boat with my naked eye, but nevertheless my boat still took on water and sank.

10. The _____ is said to have been formed by a Big Bang millions of years ago.

11. During my term studying _____ , I became interested in China's national economy.

12. Though you would never know it, _____ are crawling all over every inch of the ground.

Exercise B

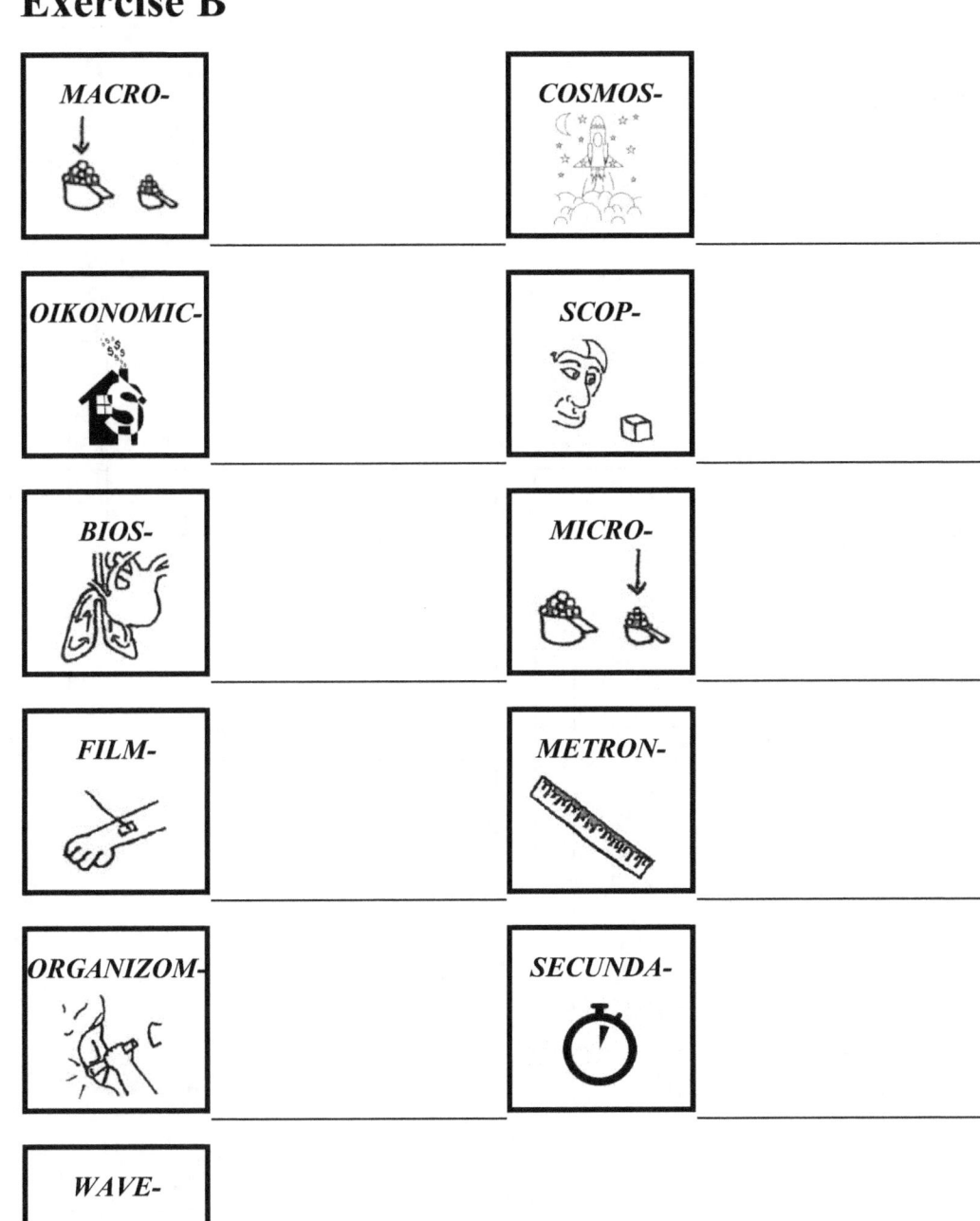

EXERCISE C

Complete the following crossword puzzle on Lesson 9:

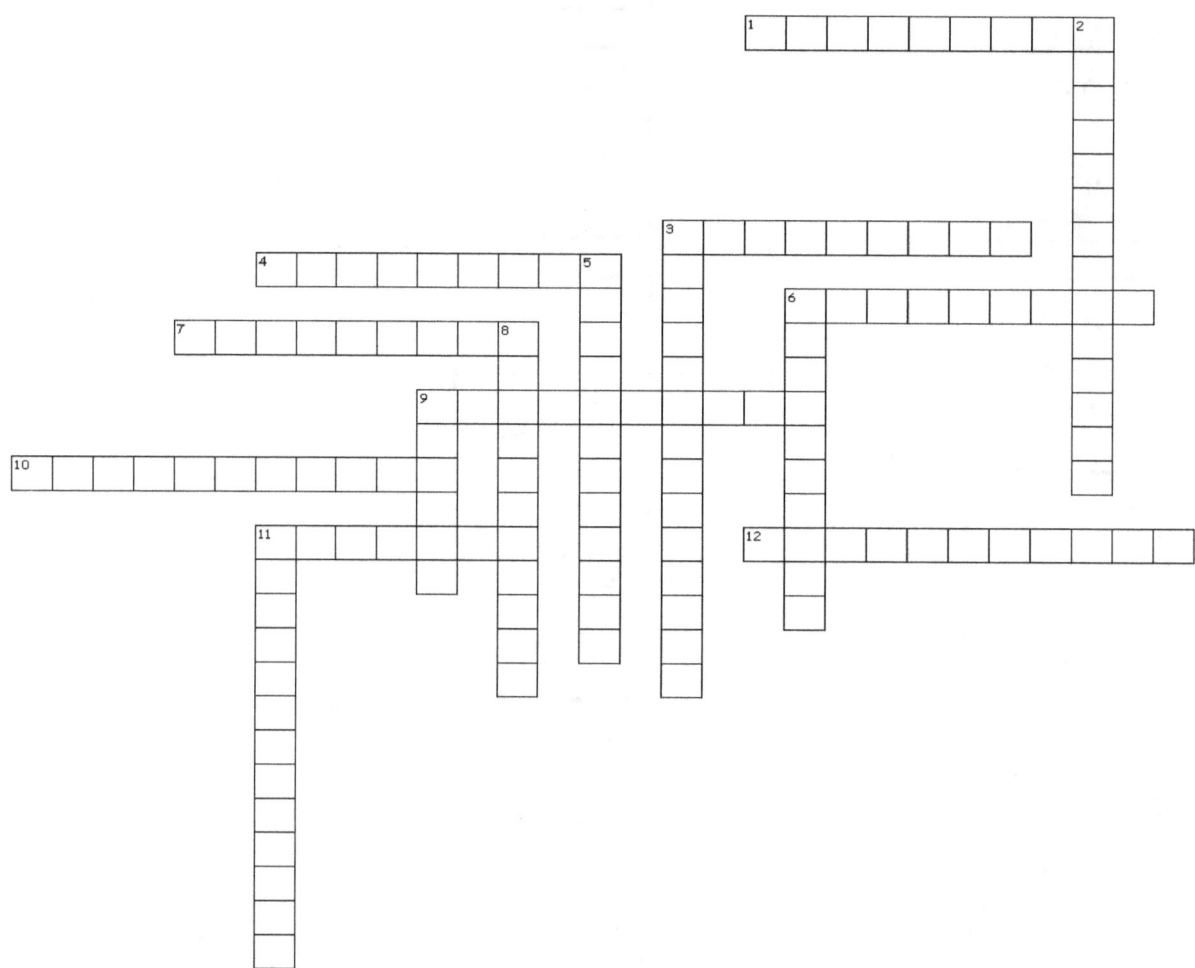

Across:
1. Smaller community analogous to a larger one
3. Low frequency radiation
4. Film that stores documents via images
6. Having small teeth
7. Universe
9. Measures minute distances
10. Not visible to the naked eye
11. Germ
12. Large

Down:
2. Study of firms and businesses
3. Study of a nation's economy
5. Surgery requiring microscopes
6. Representation of equal or greater size
8. Millionth of a second
9. Long mark over a vowel
11. Microscopic plant or animal

EXERCISE D

Match the word with the letter of its definition:

1. ___ macrocosm
2. ___ microcosm
3. ___ macroeconomics
4. ___ microeconomics
5. ___ macroscopic
6. ___ microscopic
7. ___ macrograph
8. ___ macron
9. ___ microbe
10. ___ microdont
11. ___ microfilm
12. ___ micrometer
13. ___ microorganism
14. ___ microsecond
15. ___ microsurgery
16. ___ microwave

a) study of a nation's economy
b) microscopic plant or animal
c) large
d) germ
e) measures minute distances
f) horizontal mark over a vowel
g) film that stores documents via small images
h) low frequency radiation
i) smaller community analogous to a larger one
j) surgery requiring microscopes
k) not visible to the naked eye
l) study of firms and businesses
m) millionth of a second
n) having small teeth
o) representation of equal or greater size
p) universe

Lesson X

Amnesia

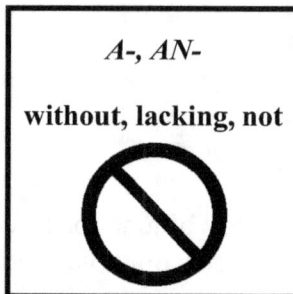

Definition: **n.** the loss of memory

Sentence: Victims of Alzheimer's disease often suffer from <u>amnesia</u>, which makes it difficult for the afflicted to remember loved ones and key events in their own lives.

Metabolism

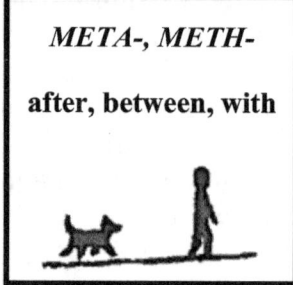
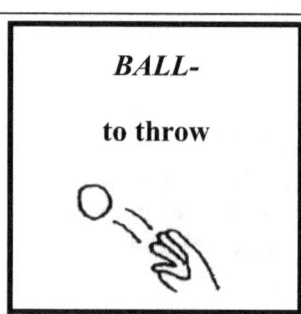

Definition: **n.** the complex of internal physical and internal chemical processes necessary to sustain life

Sentence: A slow <u>metabolism</u> in bodily processing of fat and sugar frequently leads to obesity.

Metamorphosis

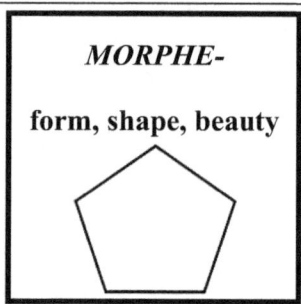

Definition: **n.** a change; transformation

Sentence: "In Kafka's The <u>Metamorphosis</u> poor young Gregor awakens to find himself changed overnight into a repellant cockroach.

Metaphor

Definition: **n.** a literary device used to equate two seemingly dissimilar words, phrases or ideas

Sentence: In *The Red Badge of Courage,* the Civil War hero's wound becomes a metaphor for valorous conduct.

Metaphysics

 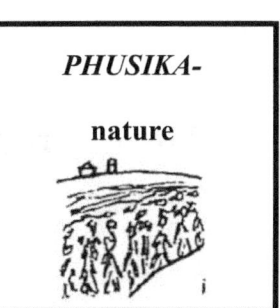

Definition: **n.** the philosophical study of being and knowing

Sentence: Ray Kurzweil, who has written two books about the metaphysics of consciousness, speculates that within 75 years machines will be able to think and act independently on an intellectual and spiritual level.

Method

 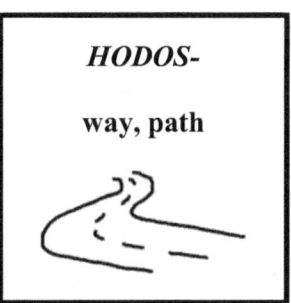

Definition: **n.** means or manner of procedure

Sentence: Carbon paper was a far less efficient method of duplicating a document than the modern photo-copier.

Misandry

 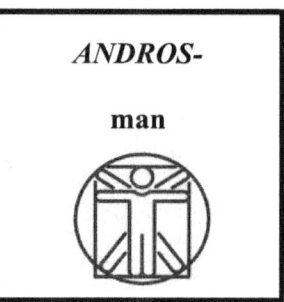

Definition: **n.** hatred of men

Sentence: The Amazons were a mythical race of warrior women that in its <u>misandry</u> disdained men.

Misanthrope

 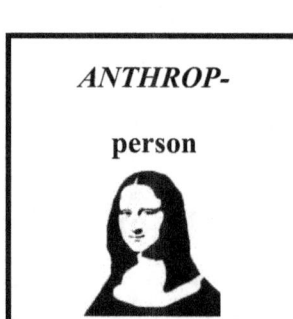

Definition: **n.** one who hates people

Sentence: "I love mankind; it's people I can't stand!" was Charlie Brown's famous formulation of <u>misanthropy</u>.

Misogyny

Definition: **n.** hatred of women

Sentence: The League of Women Voters was appalled when the state elected a known <u>mysogynist</u> as governor.

Mnemonic

Definition: **adj.** intended to aid the memory; **n.** such a retention device

Sentence: The <u>mnemonic</u> name Roy G. Biv (red, orange, yellow, green, blue, indigo, violet) can help one remember the colors of the rainbow.

Neoclassical

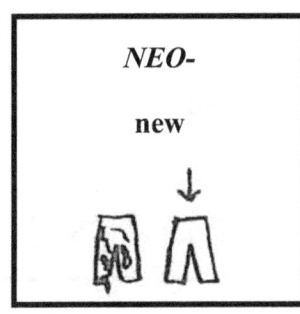 

Definition: **adj.** characteristic of a revival of classical aesthetics

Sentence: Washington D.C. government buildings with their Roman columns and lines represent <u>neoclassical</u> architecture.

Neologism

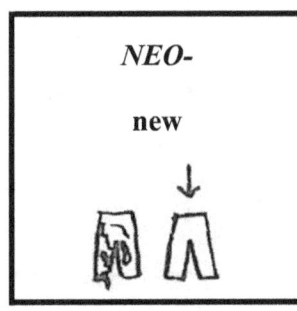 

Definition: **n.** a new word; a made up word; a word coinage

Sentence: "The Jabberwocky" is a poem famous for its use of <u>neologisms</u> like "brillig" and 'slithy toves'.

Neolithic

Definition: **adj.** pertaining to the New Stone Age (10,000 B.C. and later)

Sentence: Agriculture and polished stone tools first appear in the <u>Neolithic</u> period.

Neophyte

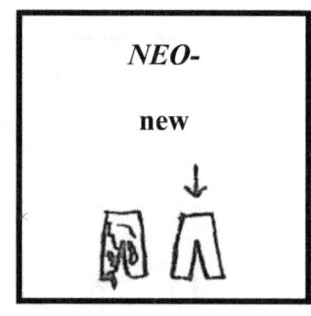 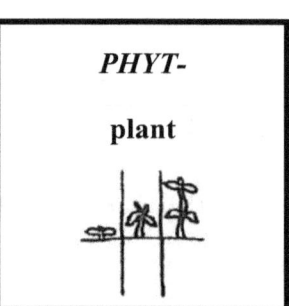

Definition: **n.** recent convert to a belief; a beginner or novice

Sentence: Having previously won an election only to the local school board, the newly appointed representative was a political <u>neophyte</u>.

Neoteric

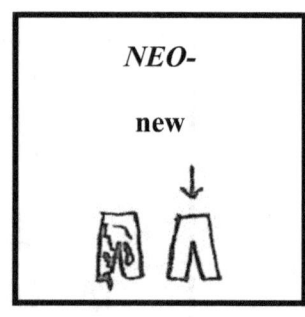

Definition: **adj.** of recent origin; modern

Sentence: Brought to market only recently, plasma TVs are a <u>neoteric</u> home appliance compared black-and-white consoles of the 1950's.

Exercise A

1. The caterpillar went through a/an _____, changing into a butterfly.

2. While digging in Mesopotamia, the archaeologist found fossils from the _____ era.

3. The columns on the White House are a/an _____ style, reminiscent of the ancient columns on Greek and Roman buildings

4. Which _____ did you use to solve the problem – guess and check or algebraic computation?

5. To "google" is a new expression or _____ that has not yet found its way into many dictionaries.

6. The man's wife became fed up with her husband's chauvinism and _____, so she filed for divorce.

7. Many lesbians are criticized for their _____ and so they are stereotyped as "man-haters."

8. An expression referring a crowd as 'a sea of faces' or a phrase like 'fruit of knowledge' a exemplifies a _____.

9. Preferring to live alone rather than to deal with people, the _____ became a hermit.

10. The _____ looked out of place at the church because he was not yet aware of the customs and rituals of the religion.

11. Because of his fast _____, Tom is able to digest and burn calories quicker than many other people of his age.

12. The _____ trend in dieting is a low carbohydrate diet, though historically speaking, trend diets have never worked.

13. I have an affinity for _____, always seeking to learn about knowledge and being.

Exercise B

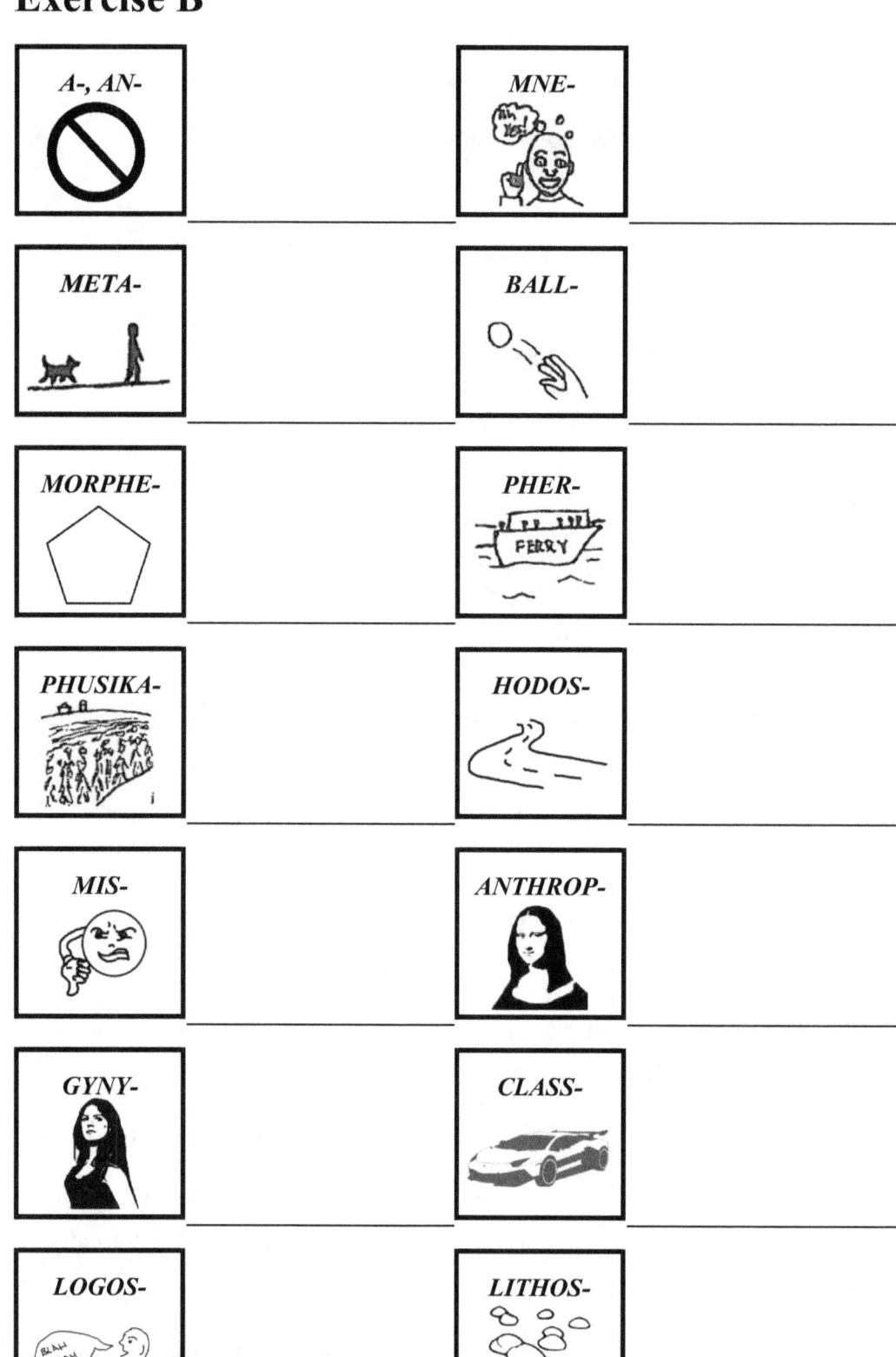

 _____  _____

 _____

EXERCISE C

Complete the following crossword puzzle on Lesson 10:

Across:
6. Stone Age
8. One who hates all people
11. Hatred of new things
12. Hatred of marriage

Down:
1. Change
2. Modern
3. Internal processes necessary to life
4. Means or manner of procedure
5. Characteristic of a revival of classical aesthetics
6. New word
7. Philosophical study of being and knowing
9. Recent convert
10. Hatred of men
11. Comparison between two seemingly unlike things
12. Hatred of women
13. Hatred of logic

EXERCISE D

Match the word with the letter of its definition:

1. ___ metabolism
2. ___ metamorphosis
3. ___ metaphor
4. ___ metaphysics
5. ___ method
6. ___ misandry
7. ___ misanthrope
8. ___ misogamy
9. ___ misogyny
10. ___ misology
11. ___ misoneism
12. ___ neoclassical
13. ___ neologism
14. ___ Neolithic
15. ___ neophyte
16. ___ neoteric

a) hatred of new things
b) new word
c) change
d) hatred of logic
e) comparison between two seemingly unlike things
f) hatred of marriage
g) internal processes necessary to life
h) characteristic of a revival of classical aesthetics
i) means or manner of procedure
j) hatred of women
k) recent convert
l) one who hates people
m) modern
n) Stone Age
o) philosophical study of being and knowing
p) hatred of men

Lesson XI

Litotes

LITOS-
single, simple, meager

Definition: **n.** an expression expressing irony or understatement in which a negative can evoke a positive or a positive invoke a less harsh negative. understatement for rhetorical effect

Sentence: An example of <u>litotes</u> is when people say 'not bad at all' to mean it was good.

Monogamy

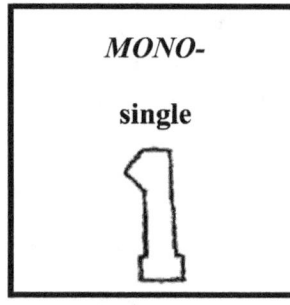 

MONO- single

GAM- marriage

Definition: **n.** practice of having one marriage or marriage partner

Sentence: It is the American tradition to practice <u>monogamy</u>, the condition of having only one spouse in a marriage.

Polygamy

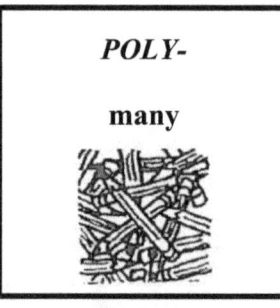 

POLY- many

GAM- marriage

Definition: **n.** practice of having multiple marriages and marriage partners

Sentence: The pre-statehood Mormons of Utah practiced <u>polygamy</u>, in which one man might take several wives.

Monosyllabic

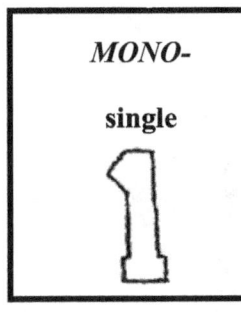  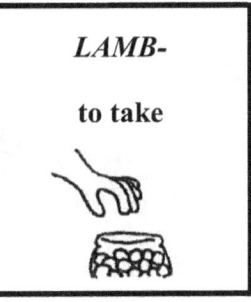

Definition:	**adj.** (of a word) having one syllable or sound
Sentence:	The musical scale is represented by the <u>monosyllabic</u> words: "do, re, mi, fa, sol, la, ti, do!"

Polysyllabic

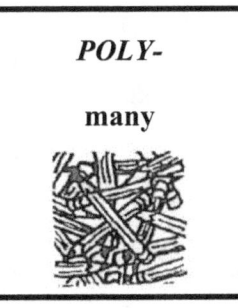  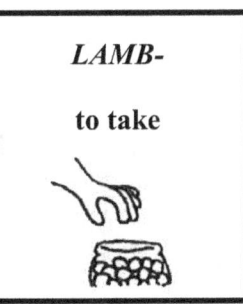

Definition:	**adj.** words having multiple syllables or sounds
Sentence:	Latinate words in English tend more toward the <u>polysyllabic</u> than the typically shorter Anglo-Saxon derived terms.

Monotheism

Definition:	**n.** belief in the existence of one god
Sentence:	Akhenaton established the first <u>monotheism</u> by abolishing the many gods of the prior Egyptian religion in favor of the single deity, the sun god Aton.

Polytheism

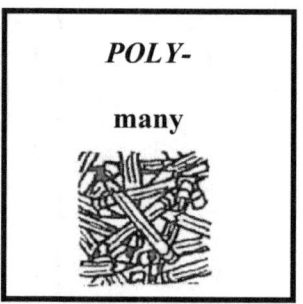 

Definition:	**n.** belief in the existence of multiple gods
Sentence:	Pagan religions practiced <u>polytheism</u>, a belief in multiple gods inhabiting all of nature.

Monarchy

Definition:	**n.** rule by one person (usually used of a system of government involving royalty)
Sentence:	The power of the English <u>monarchy</u> was first weakened when King John was forced to agree to the terms of the nobles' rights outlined in the Magna Charta.

Monocle

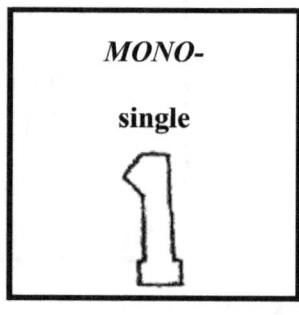 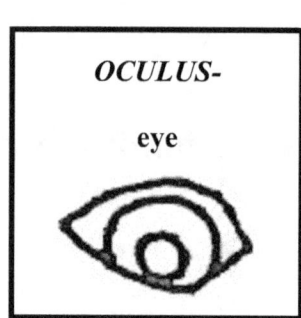

Definition:	**n.** single corrective lens
Sentence:	Mr. Micawber of 'David Copperfeld' used a single lens eyepiece called a <u>monocle</u>.

Monogram

 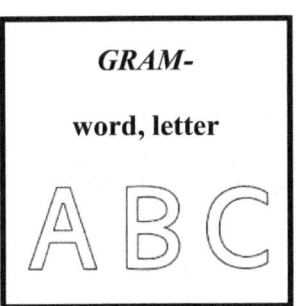

Definition: **n.** design incorporating multiple letters as one picture, often used as a distinguishing mark (often initials)

Sentence: H.M.S is a British government vessel's <u>monogram</u>, standing for "His Majesty's Ship."

Monolithic

 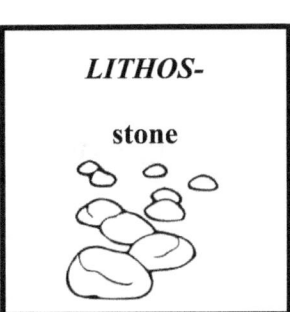

Definition: **adj.** massive, solid, and uniform

Sentence: Stonehenge is an ancient <u>monolithic</u> structure of great stone circles on the Salisbury plain.

Monotonous

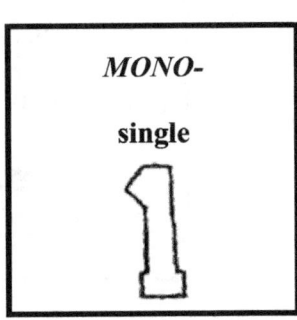 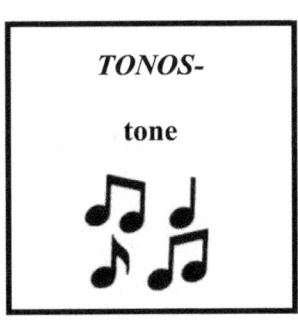

Definition: **adj.** tediously repetitive; spoken in a singular tone of voice

Sentence: Repetitive, boring, unskilled tasks make for <u>monotonous</u> work.

Polemic

Definition:	**n.** a controversial argument or discussion
Sentence:	The <u>polemic</u> between conservatives and liberals on the topic of abortion is not likely to find a conclusion that both sides will agree on.

Polyandrous

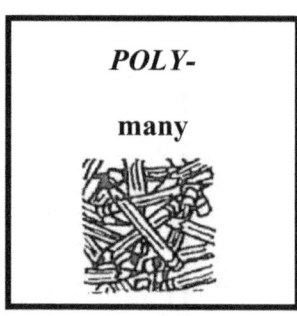 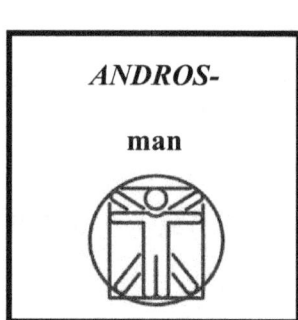

Definition:	**adj.** having multiple husbands at the same time
Sentence:	<u>Polyandrous</u> female insects mate with several males during the breeding season.

Polyglot

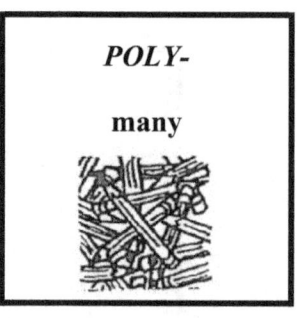 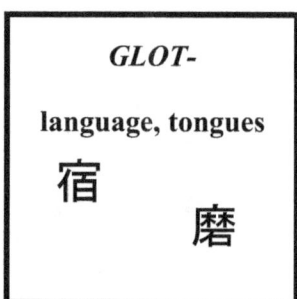

Definition:	**n.** person with the ability to speak many languages; something comprised of many languages
Sentence:	Switzerland is a <u>polyglot</u> nation in which French, Italian, German, and Romish are all official government languages.

Polygon

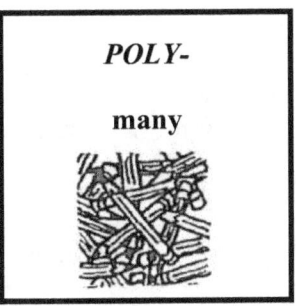
POLY-
many

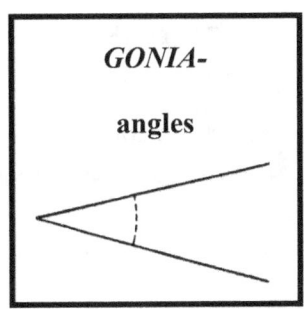
GONIA-
angles

Definition:	**n.** shape consisting of multiple sides
Sentence:	A triangle represents a <u>polygon</u> of three sides, while a pentagle has five.

Polyphonic

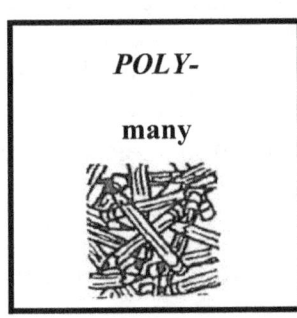
POLY-
many

PHON-
sound, voice

Definition:	**adj.** comprised of multiple melodic lines
Sentence:	Complex symphonies utilize a <u>polyphonic</u> melody, in which different instruments play different melodic lines.

Exercise A

1. The Mormon religion was originally founded with the principle of _____, though U.S. law permits only one spouse.

2. The word "halt" is _____ because it only has one sound.

3. In the British _____, there is no King currently, but instead the rule is by a Queen.

4. The Bible is a/an _____ as it was composed in multiple languages.

5. The eccentric dandy sported a _____ over his left eye.

6. The word "harmony" has three separate sounds; it is _____.

7. The _____ woman managed to keep the secret from both of her husbands that she was not monogamous.

8. It was not right of her to have multiple husbands, and there is no reason why she could not be content with _____.

9. An example of a/an _____ is Islam, which holds that Allah is the one true god.

10. On the girl's bag was a/an _____ of her initials, showing that it belonged to her.

11. A few examples of _____ are squares, triangles, and pentagons.

12. The instruments each had to pay attention to their own line of music, as the piece was incredibly _____ and required many parts playing their own piece at the same time as every other part.

13. Having bologna sandwiches for lunch every day made for a _____ diet.

14. Animism is a/an _____, as it teaches that every animal has its own god and spirit governing that animal.

15. The _____ statue stood over eighty feet tall and weighed fourteen tons.

Exercise B

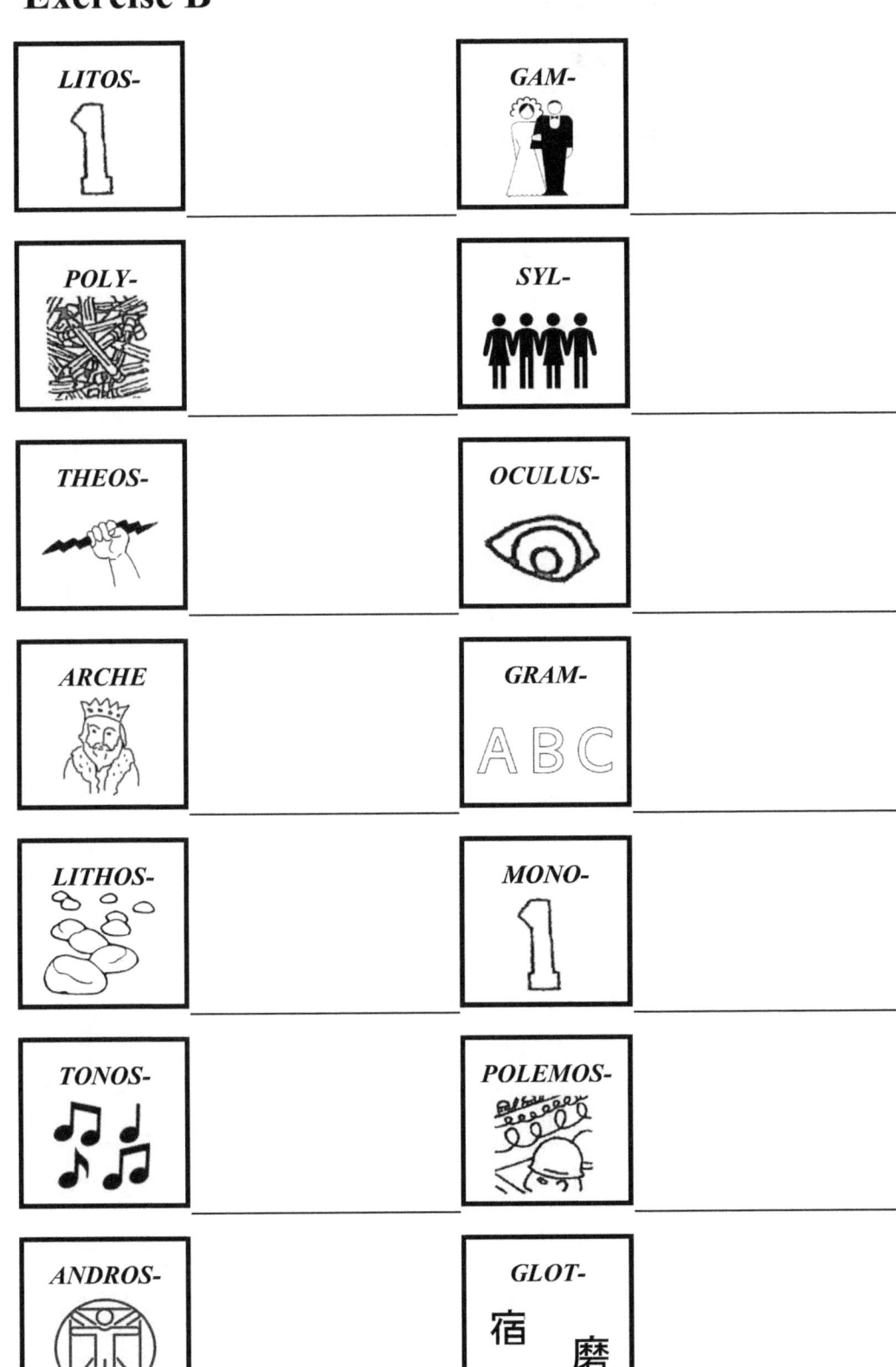

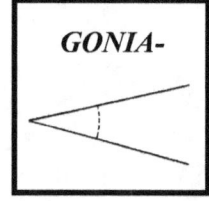 GONIA- _____    PHON- _____

 LAMB- _____

EXERCISE C

Complete the following crossword puzzle on Lesson 11:

Across:
2. Word with multiple sounds
3. Belief in one god
5. Single corrective lens
7. Belief in many gods
9. Many-sided closed shape
10. Having many husbands
14. Single pitched
15. Massive, rigid, and uniform

Down:
1. Word with one sound
4. One marriage
6. Rule by one
7. Composed in many languages
8. Single colored
11. Having multiple melodic lines
12. Letters written as one object
13. Multiple marriages

EXERCISE D

Match the word with the letter of its definition:

1. ___ monogamy
2. ___ polygamy
3. ___ monosyllabic
4. ___ polysyllabic
5. ___ monotheism
6. ___ polytheism
7. ___ monarchy
8. ___ monochrome
9. ___ monocle
10. ___ monogram
11. ___ monolithic
12. ___ monotonous
13. ___ polyandrous
14. ___ polyglot
15. ___ polygon
16. ___ polyphonic

a) belief in many gods
b) word with multiple sounds
c) single pitched
d) rule by one
e) massive, rigid, and uniform
f) multiple marriages
g) single corrective lens
h) single colored
i) composed in many languages
j) word with one sound
k) many-sided closed shape
l) having multiple melodic lines
m) having many husbands
n) letters written as one object
o) belief in one god
p) one marriage

Lesson XII

Pancreas

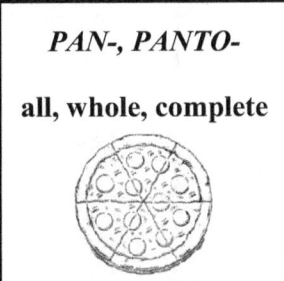
PAN-, PANTO-
all, whole, complete

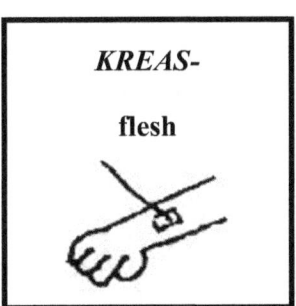
KREAS-
flesh

Definition: **n.** a gland situated behind the stomach that produces insulin

Sentence: A diabetic has problems with the pancreas and its ability to produce sufficient sugar-delivering insulin.

Pandemic

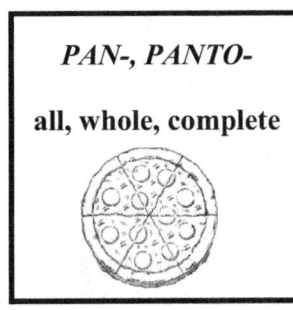
PAN-, PANTO-
all, whole, complete

DEM-
people

Definition: **n.** widespread or worldwide epidemic of infectious disease

Sentence: The influenza outbreak in 1918 quickly became a pandemic that worldwide killed tens of millions of people.

Pandemonium

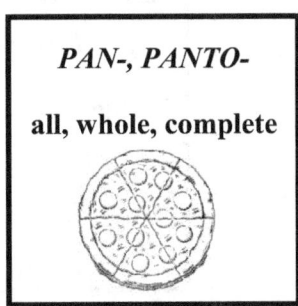
PAN-, PANTO-
all, whole, complete

DAEMON-
spirit, lesser god

Definition: **n.** uproar and noise

Sentence: There was utter chaos and pandemonium beneath the World Trade Towers as they crumbled on the morning of September 11-th.

Pantheon

Definition: **n.** a temple dedicated to all gods

Sentence: The statues of famous U.S. politicians within the rotunda of the Capitol form a <u>pantheon</u> of admired Americans.

Pantomine

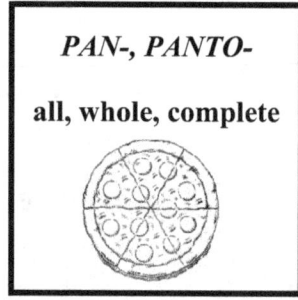 

Definition: **n.** telling of a story without speech through gesture, movement, and facial expression; a performance or performer so characterized
v. to perform such an act

Sentence: As a wordless theatrical performance known as <u>pantomime</u> involves only gesture and movement and may be a challenge to direct.

Parable

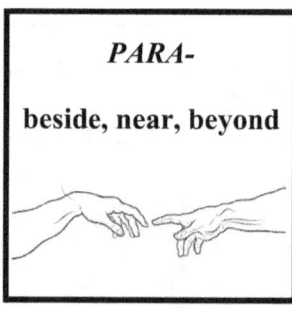 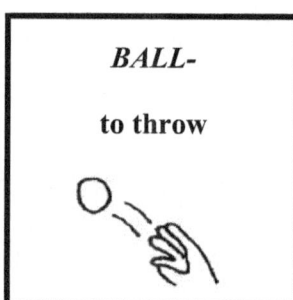

Definition: **n.** a story illustrating a moral or religious lesson

Sentence: The Tortoise and the Hare' is a moralistic <u>parable</u> intended to teach the lesson: "slow and steady wins the race."

Paradigm

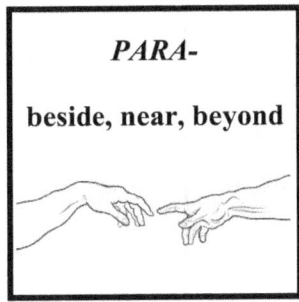 

PARA- — beside, near, beyond

DEIGMA- — pattern, to show

Definition: **n.** framework or model; rubric; theory

Sentence: The Darwinian <u>paradigm</u> of evolution is accepted by most scientists as the explanation for the development of varied life forms.

Paragon

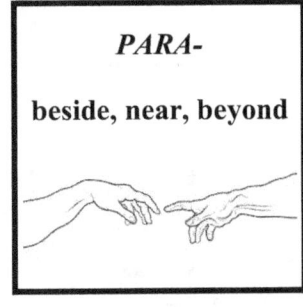 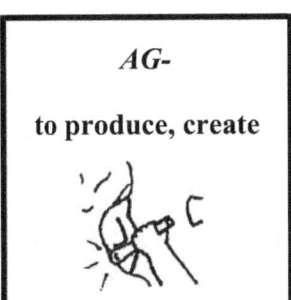

PARA- — beside, near, beyond

AG- — to produce, create

Definition: **n.** a model or pattern of perfection or excellence;

Sentence: Upright, middle-class Malvolio in Shakespeare's *Twelfth Night* thinks of himself as a <u>paragon</u> of virtue compared to the dissolute and drunken nobles he serves.

Parallel

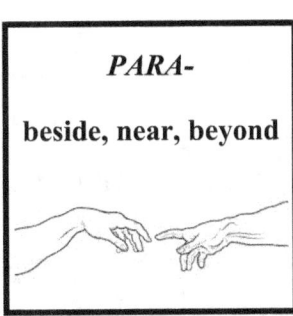 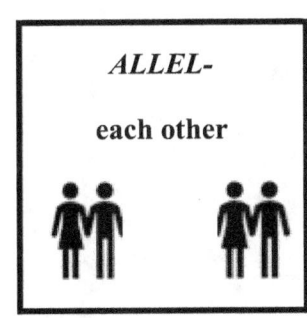

PARA- — beside, near, beyond

ALLEL- — each other

Definition: **adj.** being equidistant at every point; two lines that are coplanar and never intersect
v. to be equidistant to another object at all points

Sentence: The year of Mark Twain's birth and that of his death <u>parallelled</u> the appearances of Halley's comet.

Paranoid

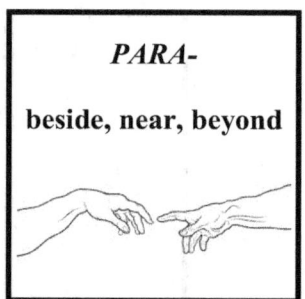
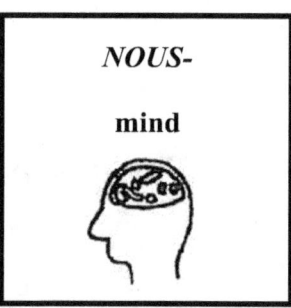

Definition:	**adj.** showing unreasonable distrust or suspicion; worried that someone is unfairly attempting to follow or to persecute them
Sentence:	A <u>paranoid</u> suspect might suffer the delusion or unreasonable belief that everyone is spying on him.

Parasol

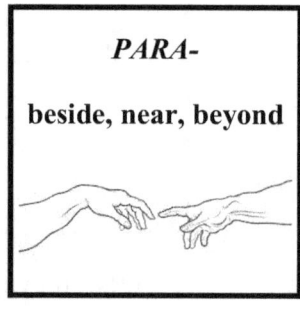
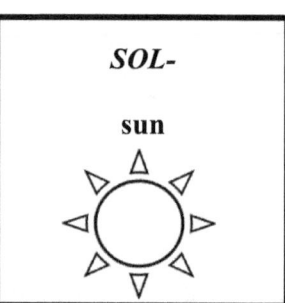

Definition:	**n.** a small, lightweight umbrella carried for shade
Sentence:	Egyptian servants who accompanied royalty carried <u>parasols</u> to shield their masters and mistresses from the African sun.

Perigee

Definition:	**n.** the point nearest the earth in the orbit of the moon
Sentence:	Although indistinguishable by the naked eye, the moon appears largest from the perspective of the earth at the <u>perigee</u> of its orbit.

Perimeter

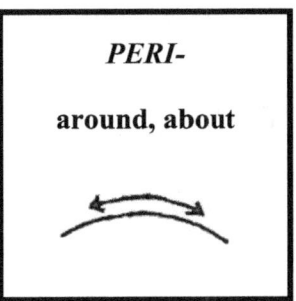 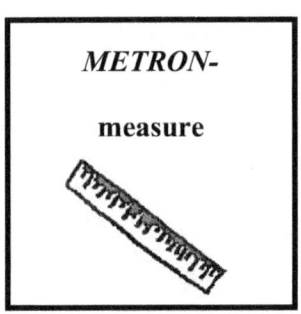

Definition:	**n.** a closed curve bounding an area; the length of such a curve; the distance around an enclosed space
Sentence:	The <u>perimeter</u> of a concentration camp was surrounded by razor wire and armed guard towers to prevent escapees.

Periscope

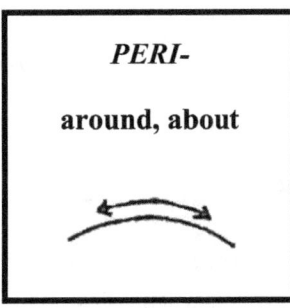 

Definition:	**n.** optical instrument to permit observation of objects not in the line of sight when the direct view line is obscured
Sentence:	Submarines use wave-protruding and turnable <u>periscopes</u> for a 360-degree view of the ocean surface above.

Exercise A

1. Diabetes is the condition in which the _____ does not produce enough insulin.

2. AIDS is currently a/an _____, affecting people all over the world.

3. The SWAT team encircled the _____ of the house, then moved in.

4. The Bible's _____ about the good Samaritan teaches us to be kind to people who need help.

5. A tree's leafy foliage may act like a sunshade on a hot day, serving a weary traveler as a _____.

6. Please reproduce the _____ showing the proper endings of the Latin word "puer."

7. In ancient Greece, there was a/an _____ devoted to worship of all gods.

8. When one of the guests spotted a rat at the upscale party, the party fell into _____ with everyone running and screaming.

9. We traveled on _____ paths for a while, but eventually hers broke off, turning left.

10. In submerged submarines, pilots use _____ to see where they are headed and any obstacles in their path.

11. The street actor performed a _____, acting only in gestures and without any other actors.

12. The traveler's distrust of airplane safety grew to a full-blown _____ about flying.

13. The point closest to earth in the satellite's orbit represented the launched object's _____.

14. The girl's A+ paper was shown to future students as the _____ of excellence.

Exercise B

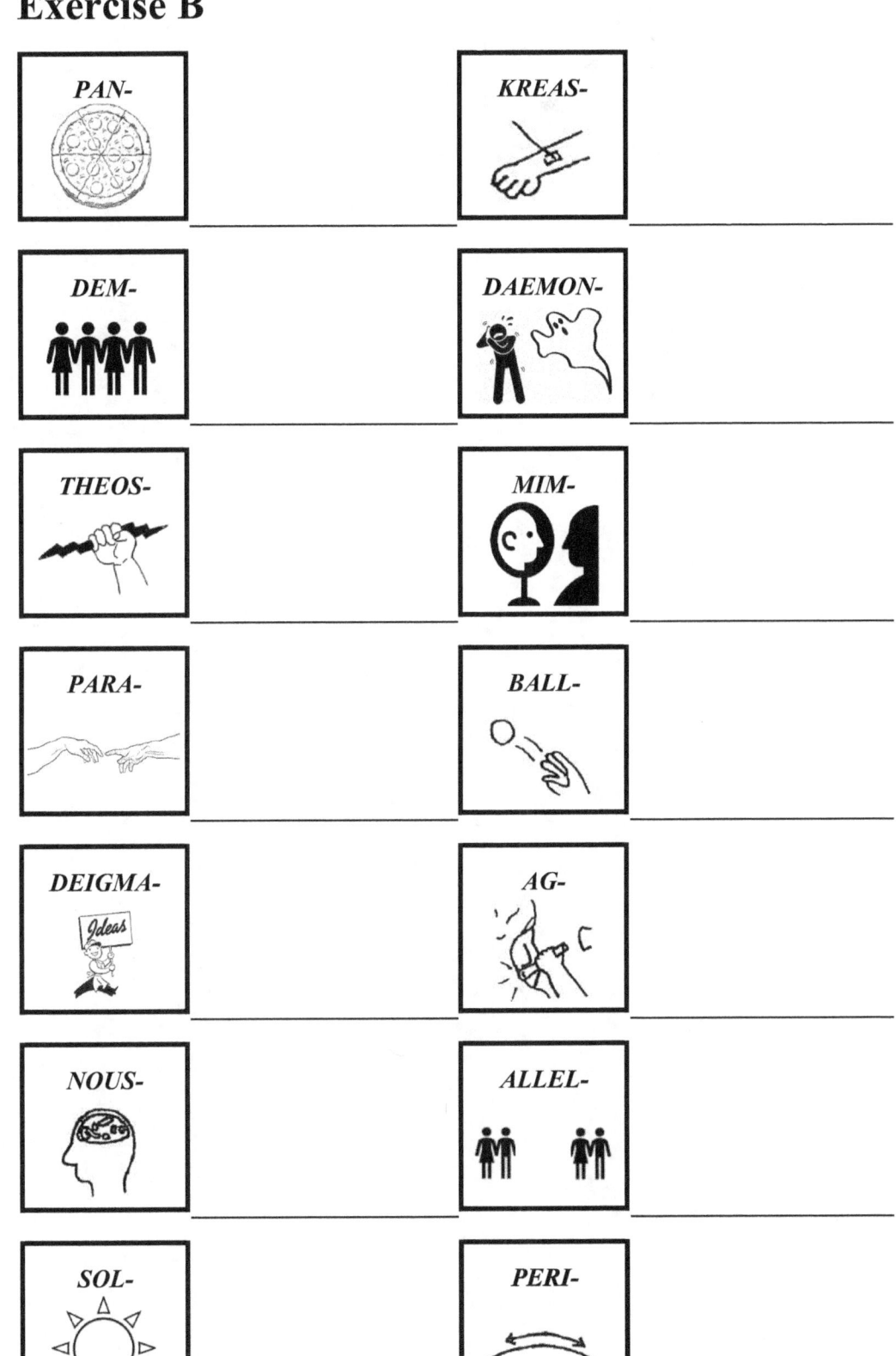

 _____  _____

 _____

EXERCISE C

Complete the following crossword puzzle on Lesson 12:

Across:
4. Optical instrument used by submarines
6. Uproar and noise
7. Temple devoted to all gods
8. Fable with a moral
9. Epitome
10. Boundary line
11. Lightweight sun umbrella
12. Use of circumlocution
13. Closest point to the earth in the moon's orbit

Down:
1. Showing unreasonable suspicion
2. Set of legal codes
3. Traveling by foot
5. Insulin secreting gland
6. Running side by side
8. Single actor play with no words
11. Example or model
12. Worldwide epidemic

EXERCISE D

Match the word with the letter of its definition:

1. ___ pancreas
2. ___ pandect
3. ___ pandemic
4. ___ pandemonium
5. ___ pantheon
6. ___ pantomime
7. ___ parable
8. ___ paradigm
9. ___ paragon
10. ___ parallel
11. ___ paranoid
12. ___ parasol
13. ___ perigee
14. ___ perimeter
15. ___ peripatetic
16. ___ periphrasis
17. ___ periscope

a) worldwide epidemic
b) optical instrument using reflections
c) epitome
d) use of circumlocution
e) uproar and noise
f) traveling by foot
g) running side by side
h) closest point to the earth in the moon's orbit
i) set of legal codes
j) showing unreasonable suspicion
k) fable with a moral
l) temple devoted to all gods
m) insulin secreting gland
n) boundary line
o) lightweight sun umbrella
p) example or model
q) single actor play with no words

Lesson XIII

Protocol

PROTO- first	KOLLEMA- glued together

Definition: **n.** code or set of rules of correct conduct; an agenda

Sentence: American <u>protocol</u> requires that graveside 'Taps' be played to honor fallen soldiers and that a 21-gun salute be fired for officers.

Prototype

PROTO- first	TYPOS- type, form
	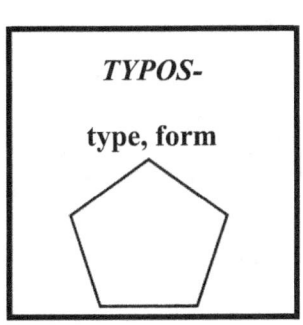

Definition: **n.** an original or experimental type or form used as a model for later stages

Sentence: The Germans' WWII initially developed V-1 rocket was merely a <u>prototype</u> of its deadlier and more accurate V-2 rocket successor weapon.

Protozoan

PROTO- first	ZOA- animal life
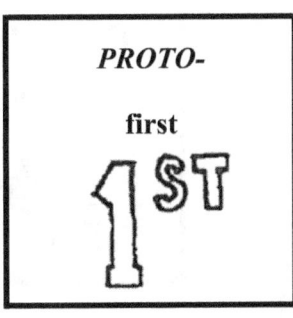	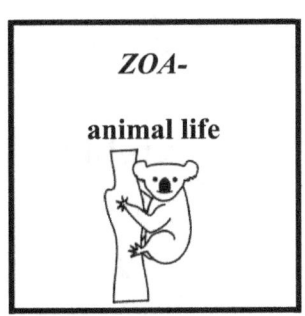

Definition: **n.** a single-celled organism, including the most primitive form of animal life

Sentence: Though life on earth developed from unicellular <u>protozoans</u> to complex multicellular organisms with organ systems and conscious brains, those simple organisms still exist.

Syllabus

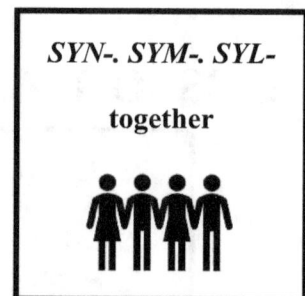

Definition:	**n.** outline of the subjects of a text or course of study
Sentence:	The Roman 'trivia' <u>syllabus</u> or 'three roads' of academic study consisted of grammar, rhetoric, and logic.

Syllogism

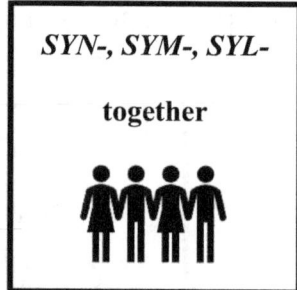 

Definition:	**n.** a form of deductive reasoning containing a major premise, minor premise, and conclusion
Sentence:	"If all men are mortal, and Socrates is a man, then Socrates is a mortal" exemplifies the three-step logical <u>syllogism</u> employed in Aristotelian deductive logic.

Symbiosis

 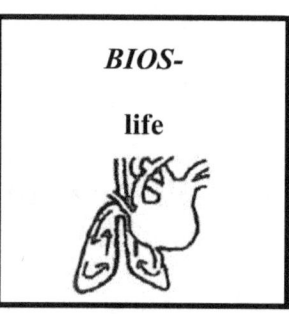

Definition:	**n.** the relationship between two or more different organisms in close association
Sentence:	The <u>symbiosis</u> of fungi and algae – two organisms living in mutual supportive growth - comprise the familiar lichens found on granite rocks and tree bark.

Symmetrical

 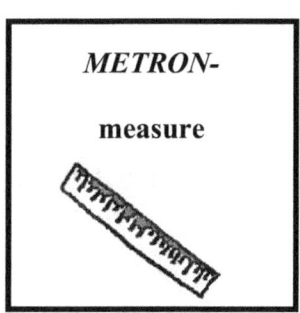

Definition: **adj.** having exact correspondence between opposite sides of a dividing line

Sentence: American nuclear armaments poised against equally threatening Soviet weapons posed a symmetrical opposition of mutually assured destruction.

Sympathetic

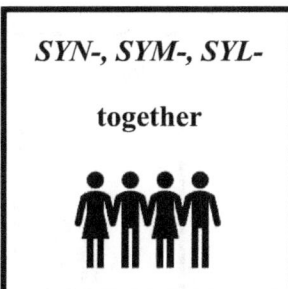 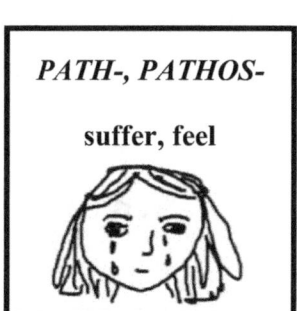

Definition: **adj.** feeling or expressing a mutual knowledge of another's emotions or feelings; of friendly or likable character; having vibrations of the same frequency

Sentence: Soldiers in march tempo across a bamboo suspension bridge may initiate sympathetic vibrations in the platform to cause the bridge's swaying and collapse.

Symposium

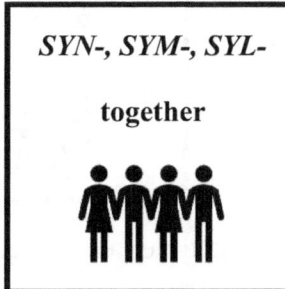 

Definition: **n.** meeting or conference for discussion on a specific topic

Sentence: The conference of professors was a gathering in a symposium to discuss the merits of non-violent protest in modern history.

Synagogue

Definition: **n.** a building for Jewish worship

Sentence: One Gospel account has Jesus overturning the tables of money-lenders in the Jerusalem's Jewish house of worship, the <u>synagogue</u>.

Synapse

Definition: **n.** the point at which a nerve impulse passes between neurons

Sentence: Alcohol widens the <u>synapses</u> or brain-based intracellular, electric connecting arcs in the brain, causing delayed transmission and decreased reaction time.

Synchronize

 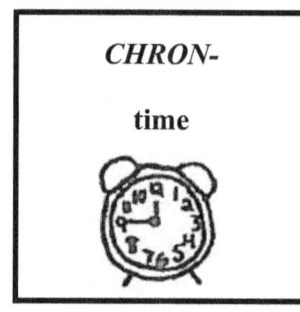

Definition: **v.** to occur at the same time; to operate in unison; to cause to operate simultaneously

Sentence: To attain the exact time, chronometers may be <u>synchronized</u> with the atomic clock in Greenwich, England, which records exact time to the nearest millisecond.

Synergy

 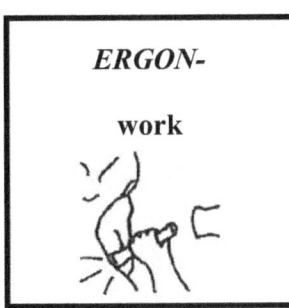

Definition:	**n.** the act of two or more organisms or forces producing a mutually beneficial result that could not be produced by either individually
Sentence:	The <u>synergy</u> of foul weather prohibiting allied air-cover and a German counterattack led to a near-disastrous Battle of the Bulge for Americans in December 1944.

Synonym

 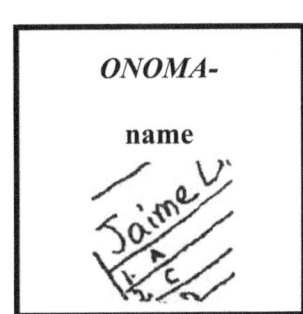

Definition:	**n.** two words that share the same meaning
Sentence:	Words of the same or nearly the same meaning, such as 'gastronome' and 'epicurean' are denoted <u>synonyms</u>.

Syntax

 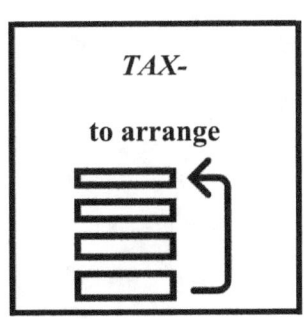

Definition:	**n.** the way in which words are put together to form sentences and clauses
Sentence:	"<u>Syntax</u>" derives from Greek words meaning "together" and "order" and indicates the rules by which parts of speech may be combined.

Synthetic

Definition:	**n.** produced by a non-natural process; man-made
Sentence:	Many fabrics today are <u>synthetic</u> or man-made, like nylon and polyesther, versus natural fibers from flax (linen) or cotton plants.

Exercise A

1. It is important to follow the correct _____ when meeting people of great importance.

2. A mirror exhibits reflectional _____, giving an exact correspondence between an object and its image in the mirror.

3. The sport of _____ swimming is a mix of dance and gymnastics usually performed in a pool by swimmers in unison.

4. Using the _____ between the banking corporation and the doughnut outlet, they were able to offer a drive-through teller and doughnut window.

5. On the first day of the class, the teacher handed out a/an _____ outlining what would be covered this term.

6. In papers that use the same word over and over, it is important to think up a/an _____ to avoid the repetition.

7. Many people prefer _____ motor oil to natural motor oil because it is a more refined product and is of a better quality.

8. The leaders of the G-8 are meeting in a/an _____ on global hunger.

9. Every Friday, the Weinbergs go the local _____ for their Jewish services.

10. I have a blueprint and a working _____ of the product. We should model the rest of our production off of these.

11. I am _____ to the AIDS prevention cause because my uncle died of AIDS.

12. Using the _____ form of logic, one might deduce that all dogs have fur.

13. The excessive use of drugs may impair the _____ in the brain. Drugs damage the neurons so that they can not fire correctly.

14. The _____ relationship between a dog and a person is beneficial to both.

15. Many students have a hard time forming sentences with proper _____ and grammar.

16. It is believed that the earliest forms of life were single-celled _____.

Exercise B

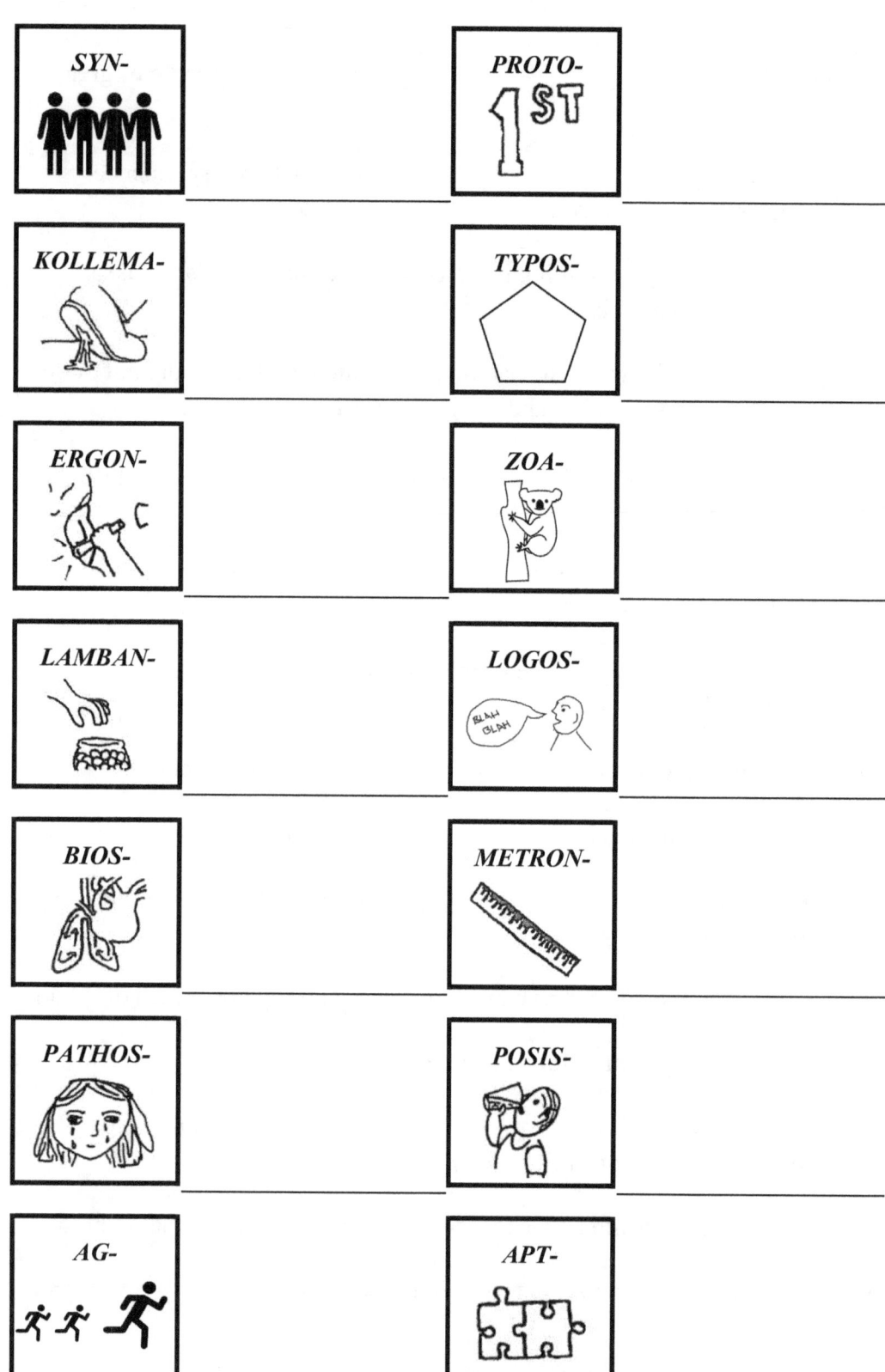

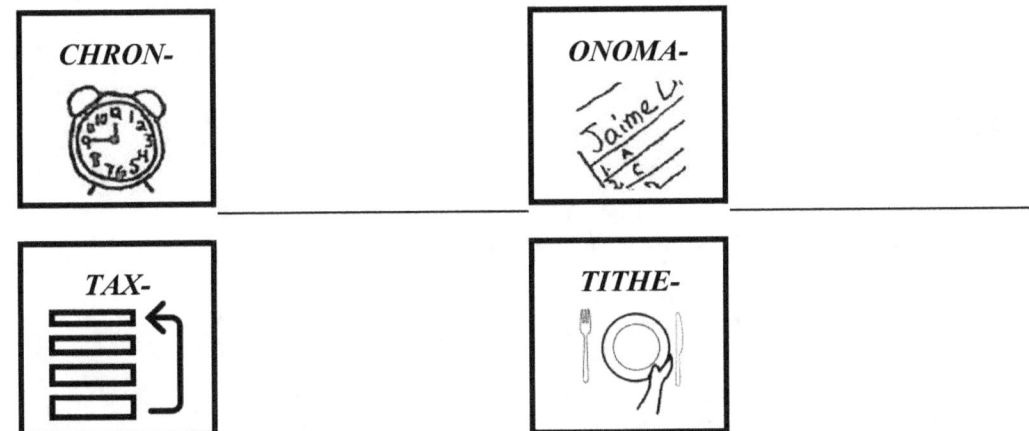

EXERCISE C

Complete the following crossword puzzle on Lesson 13:

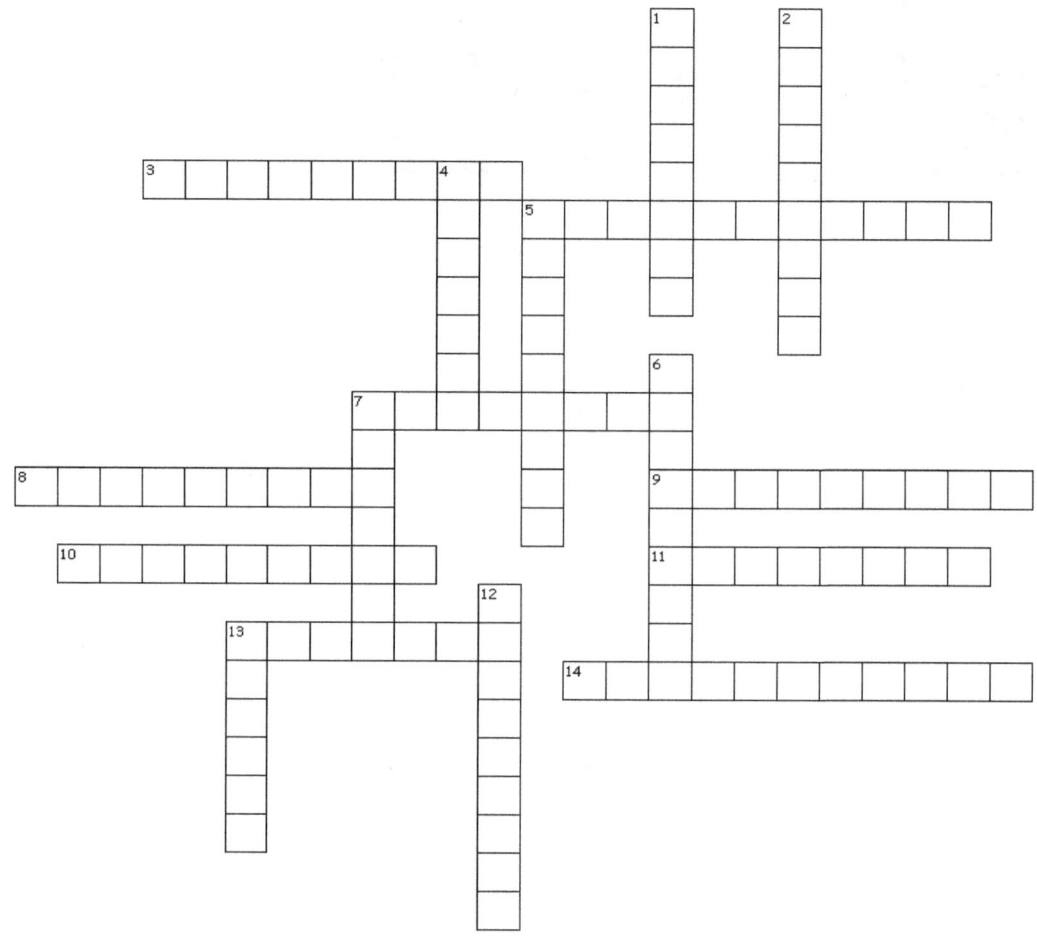

Across:
3. Form of deductive reasoning
5. Causing to occur simultaneously
7. Exact correspondence over a line
8. Type of single celled organism
9. Flexible snout or trunk
10. Model for later versions
11. Outline of main points in a course
13. The result of multiple organisms working together to produce what neither could individually
14. Feeling mutual knowledge of another's emotions

Down:
1. Code of etiquette
2. Relationship between two organisms in close association
4. A word with the same meaning as another
5. Man-made
6. Convention to discuss one topic
7. Point at which impulses pass between neurons
12. Temple for Jewish worship
13. Way in which words are put together to form a sentence

EXERCISE D

Match the word with the letter of its definition:

1. ___ proboscis
2. ___ protocol
3. ___ prototype
4. ___ protozoan
5. ___ syllabus
6. ___ syllogism
7. ___ symbiosis
8. ___ symmetry
9. ___ sympathetic
10. ___ symposium
11. ___ synagogue
12. ___ synapse
13. ___ synchronize
14. ___ synergy
15. ___ synonym
16. ___ syntax
17. ___ synthetic

a) convention to discuss one topic
b) causing to occur simultaneously
c) man-made
d) temple for Jewish worship
e) word with the same meaning as another
f) exact correspondence over a line
g) the result of multiple organisms working together to produce what neither could individually
h) point at which impulses pass between neurons
i) feeling mutual knowledge of another's emotions
j) code of etiquette
k) form of deductive reasoning
l) way in which words are put together to form a sentence
m) type of single celled organism
n) outline of main points in a course
o) model for later versions
p) relationship between two organisms in close association
q) flexible snout or trunk

Test 2

Choose the correct meaning for the underlined vocabulary word in each sentence.

1. "It might be that an Antinomian, a Quaker, or other <u>heterodox</u> religionist, was to be scourged out of the town, or an idle or vagrant Indian, whom the white man's firewater had made riotous about the streets, was to be driven with stripes into the shadow of the forest."
   The Scarlet Letter by Nathaniel Hawthorne

   (a) example is 'wind' (b) different gender (c) unorthodox opinions
   (d) anomalous lifestyle (e) dissimilar structure

2. "Servant, too, of the mightiest <u>homogeneous</u> mass of mankind with a capability for logical, guided development in a brotherly solidarity of force and aim such as the world had never dreamt of."
   Under Western Eyes by Joseph Conrad

   (a) uniform (b) incongruous (c) large (d) colorful (e) same gender

3. "What can be more singular than the relation between blue eyes and deafness in cats, and the tortoise-shell colour with the female sex; the feathered feet and skin between the outer toes in pigeons, and the presence of more or less down on the young birds when first hatched, with the future colour of their plumage; or, again, the relation between the hair and teeth in the naked Turkish dog, though here probably <u>homology</u> comes into play?"
   The Origin of Species by Charles Darwin

   (a) disagreeing (b) being melodic (c) colorfulness
   (d) being similar (e) having a center

4. "We ought not, therefore, to condemn the maid of the inn for her <u>hyperbole</u>, who, when she descended, after having lighted the fire, declared, and ratified it with an oath, that if ever there was an angel upon earth, she was now above-stairs."
   The History of Tom Jones, a Foundling by Henry Fielding

   (a) energy (b) exaggeration (c) farsightedness (d) sensitivity
   (e) injection

TEST 2

5. "You say they are marks of finger-nails, and you set up the <u>hypothesis</u> that she destroyed her child."

   Great Expectations by Charles Dickens

   (a) speech (b) overstatement (c) trap (d) disagreement
   (e) tentative explanation

6. "Beyond us, around us, human nature is at an end, and we are the only population of this <u>microcosm</u> until we become pure Selenites."

   Round The Moon by Jules Verne

   (a) universe (b) miniature model (c) opinion
   (d) national economy (e) cosmic perspective

7. "Physicists distinguish between <u>macroscopic</u> and microscopic equations: the former determine the visible movements of bodies of ordinary size, the latter the minute occurrences in the smallest parts."

   The Analysis of Mind by Bertrand Russell

   (a) millionth of a second (b) minute (c) large, visible to the naked eye
   (d) electromagnetic radiation (e) pictorial representation

8. "So virulent is the <u>microbe</u> of party politics, even in a peaceable old man, that Captain Jim's cheeks were flushed and his eyes were flashing with all his old-time fire."

   Anne's House of Dreams by Lucy Maud Montgomery

   (a) visible to the naked eye (b) measure (c) small plants or animal
   (d) diacritical mark (e) minute life form

9. "It was the shoes that caused the <u>metamorphosis</u> by means of which, unknown to himself, he took upon him the thoughts and feelings of the officer; but, as we have just seen, he felt himself in his new situation much less contented, and now preferred the very thing which but some minutes before he had rejected."

   Andersen's Fairy Tales by Hans Christian Andersen

   (a) life sustaining (b) literary device (c) transformation
   (d) philosophical study (e) state of being

10. "Sometimes too we qualify the <u>metaphor</u> by adding the term to which the proper word is relative."

    The Poetics of Aristotle by Aristotle

    (a) figure of speech (b) study of knowing (c) change
    (d) complex process (e) study of philosophy

11. "Like a plethoric burning martyr, or a self-consuming <u>misanthrope</u>, once ignited, the whale supplies his own fuel and burns by his own body."

Moby Dick by Herman Melville

(a) sinner   (b) story teller   (c) Australian   (d) people hater
(e) optimist

12. "Her whole soul was possessed by the fact that a fuller life was opening before her: she was a <u>neophyte</u> about to enter on a higher grade of initiation."

Middlemarch by George Eliot

(a) modernist   (b) beginner   (c) antecedent   (d) classical revival
(e) doubter

13. "Domestic government is a <u>monarchy</u>, for that is what prevails in every house; but a political state is the government of free men and equals."

A Treatise on Government by Aristotle

(a) marriage with one partner   (b) butterfly   (c) state ruled by one monarch
(d) belief in one god   (e) idea

14. "Brigham Young left Nauvoo for the banks of the Great Salt Lake, where, in the midst of that fertile region, directly on the route of the emigrants who crossed Utah on their way to California, the new colony, thanks to the <u>polygamy</u> practised by the Mormons, had flourished beyond expectations."

Around The World In Eighty Days by Jules Verne

(a) use of multiple syllables   (b) worship of multiple gods
(c) knowledge of multiple languages   (d) practice of having multiple spouses
(e) thinking of multiple ideas

15. "Above this a <u>polyglot</u> babel of signs struggled to indicate the abodes of palmists, dressmakers, musicians and doctors."

The Four Million by O. Henry

(a) linguist, speaking many languages   (b) shaped by many sides   (c) expert
(d) knowing many people   (e) renowned

16. "Sixty feet in the clear, the dim fire occasionally lighted, through shadowy cross-beams, the ridge-pole that was covered with sennit of coconut that was braided in barbaric designs of black and white and that was stained by the smoke of years almost to a <u>monochrome</u> of dirty brown."

Jerry of the Islands by Jack London

(a) rich color   (b) repetition   (c) only one lens   (d) variety of shades   (e) single color

17. "The pandemonium above has ceased almost as suddenly as it arose, passed like a fierce gust of wind; but they know that in the passing it has determined their fate."
    The Adventures of Peter Pan by James Matthew Barrie

    (a) comprehensive treatise (b) extreme confusion and disorder (c) global epidemic
    (d) thunder storm (e) non-speaking actor

18. "The Parable is the designed use of language purposely intended to convey a hidden and secret meaning other than that contained in the words themselves; and which may or may not bear a special reference to the hearer, or reader."
    Fables by Aesop

    (a) example or model (b) two non-intersecting lines
    (c) short moral story (d) lightweight umbrella (e) unreasonable distrust

19. "Janet would make a paragon of a wife -- cheery, economical, tolerant, and a very queen of cooks."
    Anne of The Island by Lucy Maud Montgomery

    (a) unrivaled example (b) story (c) suspicion
    (d) low standard (e) feminist

20. "The perigee distance, therefore, is that which ought to serve as the basis of all calculations."
    From The Earth To The Moon by Jules Verne

    (a) ideal (b) point in an orbit nearest to the body being orbited (c) satellite
    (d) shortest (e) apogee

21. "She had sometimes taken pupils in a peripatetic fashion, making them follow her about in the kitchen with their book or slate."
    Middlemarch by George Eliot

    (a) reflective (b) quick (c) unexpected (d) traveling around
    (e) indirect

22. "The resemblance between the American borderer and his European prototype is singular, though not always uniform."
    The Prairie by James Fenimore Cooper

    (a) typical example (b) code of conduct (c) idea (d) single celled organism
    (e) primitive animal life

23. "Never had he heard such jargon of scholastic philosophy, such fine-drawn distinctions, such cross-fire of major and minor, proposition, syllogism, attack and refutation."

The White Company by Sir Arthur Conan Doyle

(a) course outline (b) close relationship (c) reasoning, deduction
(d) man-made (e) at the same time

24. "I am afraid you find it quite impossible to keep her up at heel, or to mold her personal appearance into harmony with the eternal laws of symmetry and order."

No Name by Wilkie Collins

(a) logic (b) disorder (c) knowledge (d) impulse (e) balance

25. "Orthography, etymology, syntax, and prosody, biography, astronomy, geography, and general cosmography, the sciences of compound proportion, algebra, land-surveying and levelling, vocal music, and drawing from models, were all at the ends of his ten chilled fingers.

Hard Times by Charles Dickens

(a) realism (b) sentence structure (c) operations (d) zoology
(e) two words with the same meaning

Lesson XIV

Archangel

Definition:	**n.** a high-ranking angel
Sentence:	In the Roman Catholic tradition, the three <u>archangels</u> are Michael, Gabriel and Raphael.

Archaeology

Definition:	**n.** the study of prehistoric times centered around artifacts remaining from the time period in examination
Sentence:	Thanks to <u>archaeology,</u> we can almost fully understand the disaster that wiped out most of the city of Pompeii thousands of years ago.

Archenemy

Definition:	**n.** a principal enemy, nemesis, or foe
Sentence:	At the battle in Carthage, Scipio Africanus defeated his Iberian <u>archenemy,</u> Hannibal, razed the city, and plowed salt into the city's fields.

Matriarch

MATER- mother

ARCHE- beginning, rule

Definition: **n.** woman who rules a family, clan, or tribe

Sentence: Queen Victoria was the reigning <u>matriarch</u> of Britain, a woman who ruled for nearly the whole of the nineteenth century.

Oligarch

OLIG- few, little

ARCHE- beginning, rule

Definition: n. a member of a small governing faction

Sentence: The very few, wealthiest families of ancient Rome formed an <u>oligarchy</u> that presided over the empire's early governance.

Patriarch

PATER- father

ARCHE- beginning, rule

Definition: **n.** man who rules a family, clan, or tribe

Sentence: As breadwinners and heads-of-households, the men of the family assumed the role of decision-making <u>patriarchs</u>.

Asterisk

Definition:	**n.** a star-shaped figure (*) used chiefly to indicate an omission, a reference to a footnote, or an unattested word, sound, or affix
Sentence:	Minor historical players are mere <u>asterisks</u> in the grand scheme of events.

Asteroid

Definition:	**n.** any of numerous small celestial bodies that revolve around the sun, with orbits lying chiefly between Mars and Jupiter and characteristic diameters between a few and several hundred kilometers
Sentence:	Extraterrestrial <u>asteroid</u> objects plummet to burn up in earth's atmosphere.

Astrology

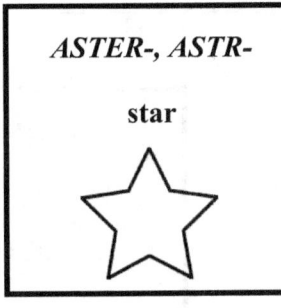 

Definition:	**n.** the study of the positions and aspects of celestial bodies in the belief that they have an influence on the course of natural earthly occurrences and human affairs.
Sentence:	Babylonians trusted in <u>astrology</u>'s notions that future events were readable in the changing star cluster positions in the heavens.

Astronomical

Definition: **adj.** of or relating to astronomy; or, of enormous magnitude; immense

Sentence: The advent of the car had <u>astronomical</u> influence on the infrastructure of modern day society in terms of mobility, highway construction, and everyday routine.

Biography

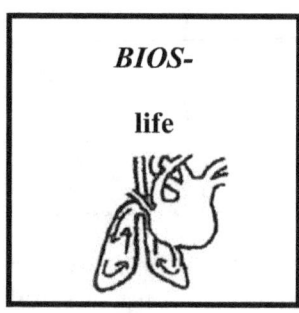

Definition: **n.** an account of a person's life written, composed, or produced by another

Sentence: Many different celebrities have written <u>biographies</u>.

Biological

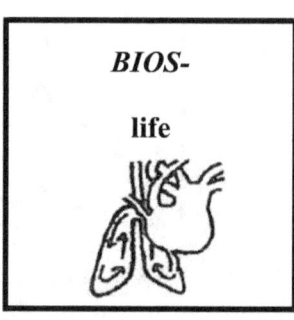

Definition: **adj.** of, relating to, caused by, or affecting life or living organisms; having to do with biology or the science of life

Sentence: <u>Biological</u> differences in the genes constitute 'nature' in human development, whereas environment and upbringing are differences in 'nurture.'

Biology

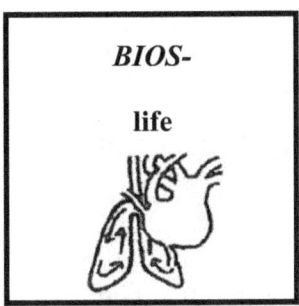

Definition:	**n.** the science of life and of living organisms, including their structure, function, growth, origin, evolution, and distribution
Sentence:	<u>Biology</u> recently has come into its own as the discrete science of life separate from chemistry and physics and with its own irreducible scientific validity.

Bioluminescence

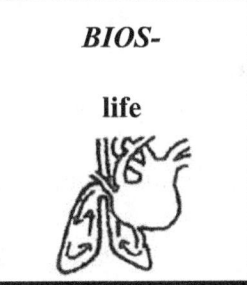

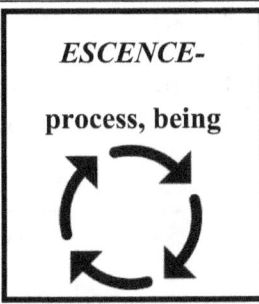

Definition:	**n.** emission of visible light by living organisms such as the firefly and various fish, fungi, and bacteria
Sentence:	Glowworms and deep-dwelling fish contain the glowing enzyme luciferase, whose <u>bioluminescence</u> may scare off predators, lure prey or mates.

Biosphere

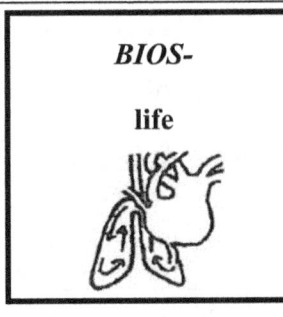
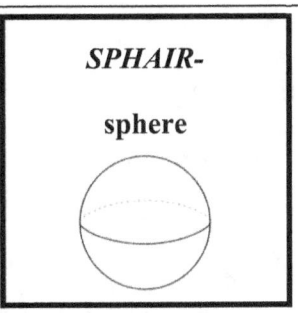

Definition:	**n.** the part of the earth and its atmosphere in which living organisms exist or that is capable of supporting life
Sentence:	The region between deep ocean vents below the earth's crust and earth's highest altitudes constitutes the known realm of all living things - the <u>biosphere</u>.

Exercise A

1. Many African societies, such as the one depicted in Chinua Achebe's *Things Fall Apart*, operate under a/an _____cal philosophy, one in which the men rule and the women are subservient to them.

2. _____, often nicknamed the "life science," is generally taught first in high school curricula before chemistry and physics.

3. *1776*, the newly-released, best-selling _____ of George Washington, outlines his life in great detail, placing special emphasis on his role in the American Revolution.

4. According to Biblical lore, Gabriel, a/an _____, was sent to inform Mary that she was pregnant.

5. The masses of people were disappointed with the few _____s that controlled their society and were interested in instituting a democracy in their place.

6. The _____ belt in our solar system, believed to be a crumbled planet, orbits our sun between Mars and Jupiter.

7. Fireflies, known for their _____, are pretty to watch at night on a dark background.

8. The _____ repercussions of environmental pollution might include respiratory illness and lung damage.

9. In many popular novels, the antagonist must battle his _____ in order to survive.

10. All organisms living on earth subsist within the _____.

11. White dwarf stars and giant red supernovas alike, compared to everyday objects on earth, are of _____ size.

12. Please place a/an _____ next to the terms that are considered to be challenge words so that lower level students will know not to do them.

13. People who study _____ often try to read hands in order to determine events that might transpire later in one's life.

14. The presumptuous housemaid acted as if she were the _____ of the household, constantly directing affairs and acting as if she were the boss.

Exercise B

Exercise C

Fill in the crossword puzzle.

Across:
1. a member of a small governing faction
3. of, relating to, caused by, or affecting life or living organisms
4. a star-shaped figure (*) used chiefly to indicate an omission
5. man who rules a family, clan, or tribe
6. the part of the earth and its atmosphere in which living organisms exist
8. an account of a person's life written, composed, or produced by another
10. a high-ranking angel
12. woman who rules a family, clan, or tribe
13. emission of visible light by living organisms

Down:
2. any of numerous small celestial bodies that revolve around the sun, with orbits lying chiefly between Mars and Jupiter
3. the science of life and of living organisms,
7. a principal enemy, nemesis, or foe
9. the study of prehistoric times centered around artifacts remaining from the time period in examination
10. the study of the positions and aspects of celestial bodies in the belief that they have an influence on the course of natural earthly occurrences and human affairs.
11. of or relating to astronomy

14. The presumptuous housemaid acted as if she were the _____ of the household, constantly directing affairs and acting as if she were the boss.

EXERCISE D

Match the word with the letter of its definition:

1. ___ archangel
2. ___ archenemy
3. ___ matriarch
4. ___ oligarch
5. ___ patriarch
6. ___ asterisk
7. ___ asteroid
8. ___ astrology
9. ___ astronomical
10. ___ biography
11. ___ biological
12. ___ biology
13. ___ bioluminescence
14. ___ biosphere

a) celestial body revolving around the sun
b) principle foe
c) woman who rules a clan
d) part of earth capable of supporting life
e) *
f) affecting life and/or living organisms
g) high ranking angel
h) study of celestial bodies and their effect on human occurrences
i) account of a person's life
j) member of a small governing faction
k) emission of light by living organisms
l) enormous; immense
m) science of life
n) man who rules a tribe

Lesson XV

Cardiac arrest

CARDIO-	AC-, AD-	STARE-
heart	to, toward, very	to stand

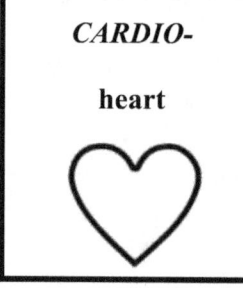 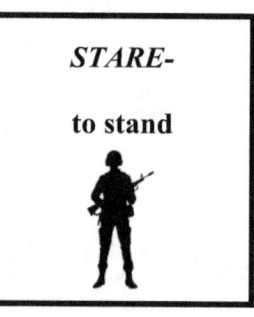

Definition: **n.** sudden cessation of heartbeat and heart function, resulting in the loss of effective circulation

Sentence: Physicians refer to what is commonly called a heart attack – the condition when the heart stops beating – as 'cardiac arrest.'

Cardiologist

CARDIO-	LOGOS-
heart	word, speech, study

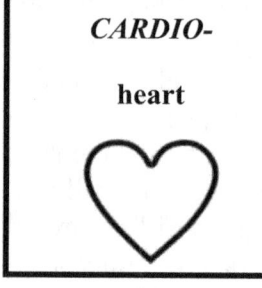 

Definition: **n.** the medical doctor whose specialty is the structure, function, and disorders of the heart

Sentence: A cardiologist may use a stethoscope to detect a heart murmur.

Cardiovascular

CARDIO-	VASCUL-
heart	vessel

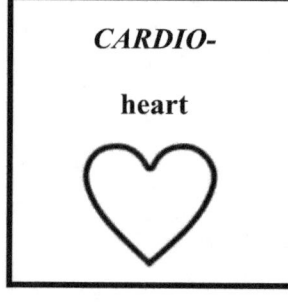 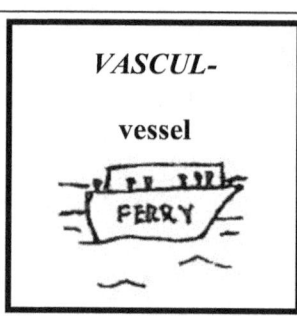

Definition: **adj.** of, relating to, or involving the heart and the blood vessels

Sentence: The cardiovascular system includes the heart and its blood-transporting network of arteries, veins, and capillaries.

Cardiogram

Definition:	**n.** the series of jagged lines traced by a cardiograph, a machine used in the diagnosis of heart disorders
Sentence:	Traced by means of electrodes attached to the skin of the chest, the <u>cardiogram</u> is a graphic recording of the electric currents produced by the heart.

Chronic

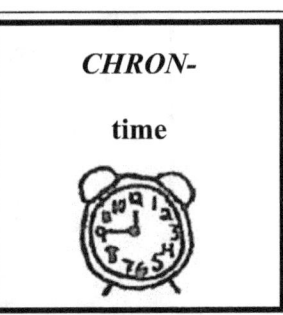

Definition:	**adj.** lasting for a long period of time or marked by frequent recurrence, as certain diseases
Sentence:	A <u>chronic</u> liar is habitually and constitutionally incapable of telling the truth.

Chronicle

Definition:	**n.** an extended account in prose or verse of historical events, sometimes including legendary material, presented in chronological order and without authorial interpretation or comment
Sentence:	Holinshed's *Chronicle of England, Scotland, and Ireland* is a universal history of Britain, which Shakespeare drew on for his many English kings' or History plays, as well as *Macbeth, King Lear,* and *Cymbeline.*

Chronological

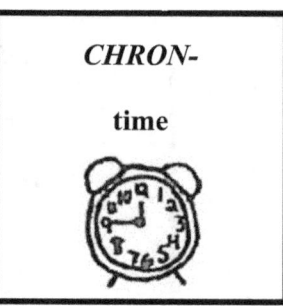

Definition: **adj.** arranged in order of time of occurrence

Sentence: Read from left to right, a timeline graphically represents <u>chronological</u> events.

Cosmic

Definition: **adj.** of or relating to the entire universe, especially as distinct from Earth

Sentence: Millions of extraterrestrial <u>cosmic</u> rays pass unnoticed through our bodies daily.

Cosmology

Definition: **n.** the study or representation of the physical universe considered as a totality of phenomena in time and space

Sentence: Greek <u>cosmology</u> imagined that the stars were fixed on a crystalline celestial sphere rotating about the central earth.

Cosmopolitan

COSM- universe | *POLIS-* city | *POLITES-* citizen

Definition: **adj.** pertinent or common to the whole world; so sophisticated as to be at home in all parts of the world or conversant with many spheres of interest

Sentence: Affecting the entire planet, global warming is an issue of <u>cosmopolitan</u> importance.

Aristocracy

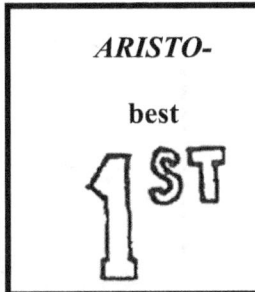 

ARISTO- best | *CRACY-* rule, power

Definition: **n.** a group or class considered superior to others; a hereditary ruling class; nobility.

Sentence: The pecking order characteristic of barnyard fowl exemplifies an avian <u>aristocracy</u>.

Bureaucracy

BUREAU- desk | *CRACY-* rule, power

Definition: **n.** administration of a government chiefly through bureaus or departments staffed with non-elected officials

Sentence: The government of India is infamous for its layered <u>bureaucracy</u> and vast regulations in volumes bound with red tape.

Democracy

Definition: **n.** government by the people, exercised either directly or through elected representatives

Sentence: Whether Athens was a true <u>democracy</u> is debatable, as only men of property were granted voting rights.

Plutocracy

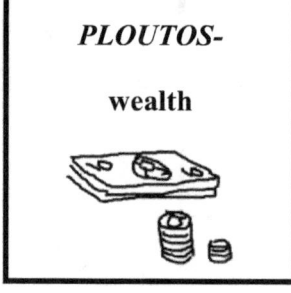 

Definition: **n. a** wealthy class that controls a government

Sentence: Nineteenth century America was in some ways a <u>plutocracy</u> in that wealthy men like Mellon, Carnegie, and Rockefeller controlled the strings of government.

Theocracy

Definition: **n.** a form of government which acknowledges a deity as the supreme ruler and is administered by priests or ministers

Sentence: In a society which did not favor the prospect of becoming a <u>theocracy</u>, the priest's theocentric (centered around God) gubernatorial campaign failed to win him much support.

Exercise A

1. The _____, having completed medical school, was fully trained in the medical study of the structure, function, and disorders of the heart.

2. The sophisticated traveler, at home in many different countries and cultures, was considered a _____ citizen of the world.

3. In the Middle Ages there existed a/an _____ of a few select nobility that was considered superior to the masses.

4. C.S. Lewis's *The _____s of Narnia* is the story of a fantasy world to which several young children find the portal in their attic.

5. When the _____ ceased to register the frequencies of the patient's heart at regular intervals, the doctor assumed that he had lost his patient.

6. To make sure that you get a complete workout, make sure to incorporate both _____ exercises and weight lifting into your routine.

7. Many citizens of the U.S. become frustrated with the tedious _____ involved with government operations.

8. Although it is the aim of the U.S. not to have an effective _____ in control, it is often the case that the few wealthy people in the country have much of the influence and power to effect change.

9. _____ coughing is usually a sign of a sickness.

10. In the U.S. governmental system of _____, every adult has the right to vote.

11. Please describe the events of the evening in _____ order so we can understand exactly how events progressed in time.

12. Many university physics departments offer electives in _____ as a part of their astronomy offerings, since the two topics are closely related.

13. My grandfather, having spontaneously gone into _____, needed to be transported to the hospital immediately to get his blood circulating correctly again through his body.

14. A meteor shower, an exploding star, or the appearance of a comet is considered a _____ event.

Exercise B

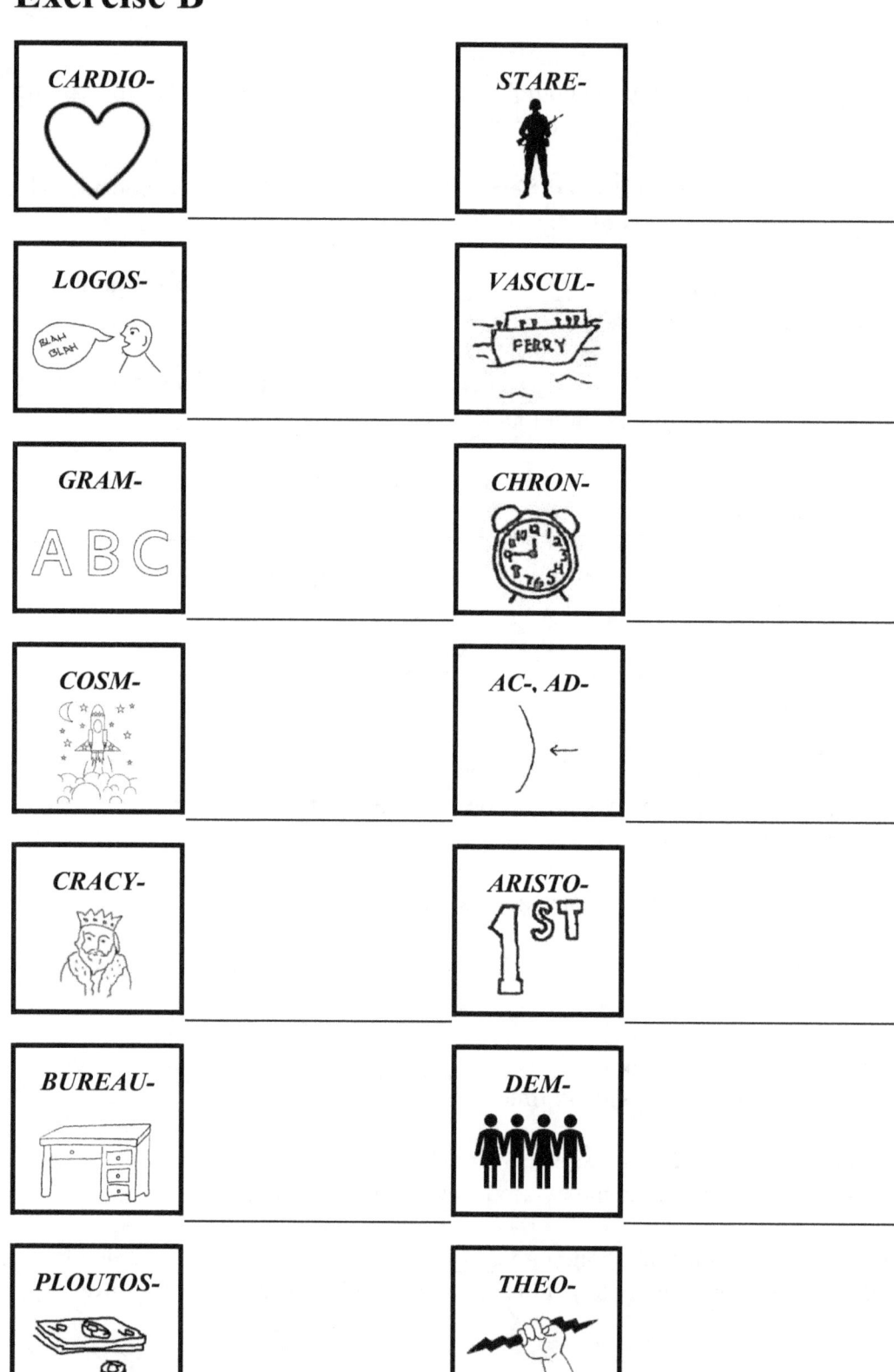

EXERCISE C

Fill in the crossword puzzle.

Across:
4. superior class
7. heart stoppage
9. arranged in order of time
10. involving both the heart and lungs
11. lasting a long time

Down:
1. cause to occur at the same time
2. extended account in prose
3. govt. by the people
5. govt. administration through non-elected officials
6. govt. by the wealthy
7. both the heart and blood vessels
8. study of the physical universe

LESSON 15 CARDIO, CHRON/CHONOS, COSM, CRACY

14. My grandfather, having spontaneously gone into _____, needed to be transported to the hospital immediately to get his blood circulating correctly again through his body.

15. A meteor shower, an exploding star, or the appearance of a comet is considered a _____ event.

EXERCISE D

Match the word with the letter of its definition:

1. ___ cardiac arrest
2. ___ cardiogram
3. ___ cardiologist
4. ___ cardiopulmonary
5. ___ cardiovascular
6. ___ chronic
7. ___ chronicle
8. ___ chronological
9. ___ cosmic
10. ___ cosmology
11. ___ cosmopolitan
12. ___ aristocracy
13. ___ bureaucracy
14. ___ democracy
15. ___ plutocracy

a) curve traced by cardiograph
b) relating to the universe
c) extended account in prose
d) heart doctor
e) government by the wealthy
f) pertinent or common to the whole world
g) govt. by the people
h) govt. administration through non-elected officials
i) involving both the heart and lungs
j) arranged in order of time
k) study of the physical universe
l) heart stoppage
m) involving both the heart and blood vessels
n) superior class
o) lasting a long time

Lesson XVI

Demagogue

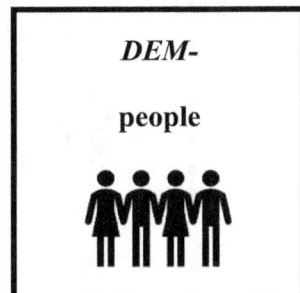 

Definition: **n.** a leader who obtains power by means of impassioned appeals to the emotions and prejudices of the populace

Sentence: In Shakespeare's *Julius Caesar*, Marc Anthony acts the part of demagogue at Caesar's funeral, arousing the mob with his impassioned appeal for revenge against the conspirators.

Endemic

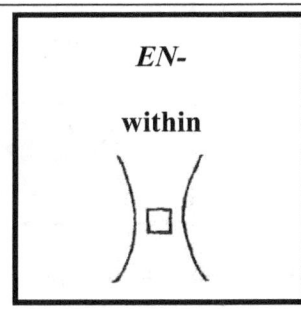 

Definition: **adj.** prevalent in or peculiar to a particular locality, region, or people

Sentence: Not occurring in other racial strains, sickle-cell anemia is a disease endemic to black people.

Demonologist

Definition: **n.** one who studies evil spirits

Sentence: The college's demonologist had an impressive collection of artifacts associated with devil worship.

Democratic

Definition:	**adj.** Of or relating to a government ruled by the will of the people whom it governs
Sentence:	Freedom of speech is an essential part of any true <u>democratic</u> society.

Demographic

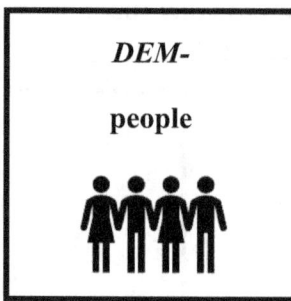

Definition:	**n.** a specific group or section in a population, or a study of such a group
Sentence:	Recent <u>demographics</u> show that African-Americans compromise 13% of the population.

Dermatitis

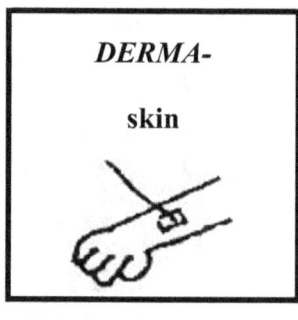
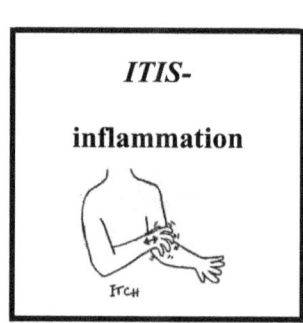

Definition:	**n.** inflammation of the skin
Sentence:	Eczema, rash, and acne are forms of skin irritation collectively known as <u>dermatitis</u>.

Dermatologist

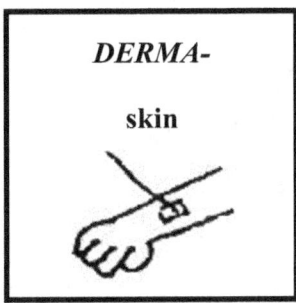 

Definition: **n.** the branch of medicine that is concerned with the physiology and pathology of the skin

Sentence: A <u>dermatologist</u> specialty is the least threatening medical career, since 'the skin patients never get well, and they never die on you.

Dermis

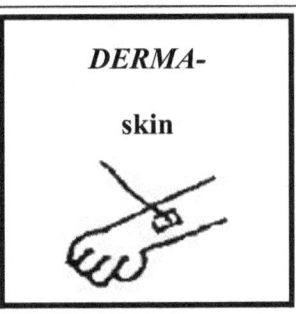

Definition: **n.** the sensitive connective tissue layer of the skin located below the epidermis, containing nerve endings, sweat and sebaceous glands, and blood and lymph vessels

Sentence: The skin or epidermis is a layer protecting the underlying network of glands, nerves, and vessels constituting the <u>dermis</u>.

Taxidermist

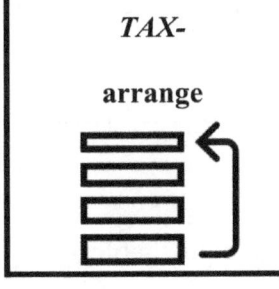 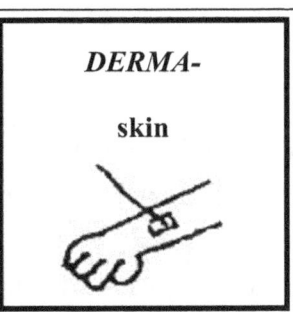

Definition: **n.** a craftsman who stuffs and mounts the skins of animals for display

Sentence: The naturalist Darwin was an accomplished <u>taxidermist</u> who skinned, preserved, and stuffed scores of animal specimens during his three-year voyage on the *HMS Beagle*.

Exercise A

1. The proud hunter had the deer he killed stuffed and mounted for display by a _____.

2. The ambitious politician gained his power as a _____ through his impassioned speeches that appealed to the majority of the voting public.

3. A _____ government depends on a trait called civic virtue by which citizens are willing to give up personal benefit for the greater good of all citizens.

4. An academic who studies the evil spirits worshiped in primitive tribes may be called a _____.

5. For the treatment of a severe skin rash, a patient is advised to consult with a medical specialist known as a _____.

6. Humans have a sensitive inner layer of tissue below the epidermis which is called the _____ and which contains blood vessels, nerves, and oil glands.

7. After the census in the year 2000, _____(s) showed a decrease in the size of the average American family.

8. The Ngowye tribe has certain distinguishable, _____ traits, which ought to give away the tribal affiliation of any of its members.

9. Though he had no clue what kind of rash it was on his arm, Michael recognized it as some form of _____.

Exercise B

Exercise C

Fill in the crossword puzzle.

Across:
2. study of a group in a population
3. leader of the people
6. one who studies evil spirits
9. fear of evil spirits

Down:
1. skin fungi
2. inflammation of the skin
4. common to particular people
5. type of government ruled by the people
6. pertaining to the common people
7. animal skin stuffer
8. skin doctor
9. under epidermis

EXERCISE D

1. ___ demagogue
2. ___ endemic
3. ___ demonologist
4. ___ demonophobia
5. ___ democratic
6. ___ demographic
7. ___ demotic
8. ___ dermatitis
9. ___ dermatophyte
10. ___ dermatologist
11. ___ dermis
12. ___ taxidermist

a) common to particular people
b) speaker using emotional appeal
c) inflammation of the skin
d) skin doctor
e) animal skin stuffer
f) under epidermis
g) fear of evil spirits
h) study of population
i) government by the people for the people
j) skin fungi
k) of the common people
l) one who studies evil spirits

Lesson XVII

Android

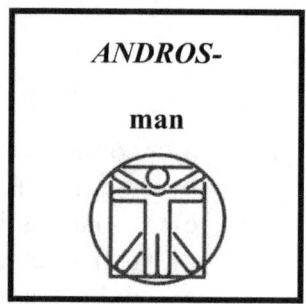

ANDROS- man

EIDOS- form, shape, image

Definition:	**adj.** possessing human features; **n.** a device built to resemble a human
Sentence:	The Stepford Wives' is a movie featuring a suburban community of <u>android</u> women – beautiful, sculpted robots programmed to be perfect housewives.

Idyll

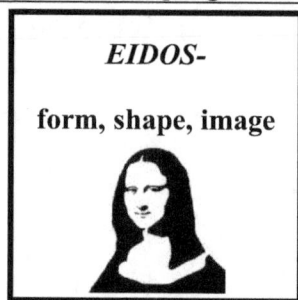

EIDOS- form, shape, image

Definition:	**n.** a short poem or prose piece depicting a rural or pastoral scene, usually in idealized terms; a carefree experience or romantic interlude
Sentence:	Wordsworth's <u>idylls</u> are romantic poems set in an idealized, rustic English countryside.

Tabloid

 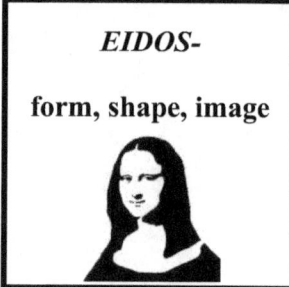

TABLET- tablet

EIDOS- form, shape, image

Definition:	**n.** a small, condensed newspaper; often, a sensational newspaper
Sentence:	Sensationalist <u>tabloid</u> newspapers are usually found at grocery checkout counters.

Kaleidoscope

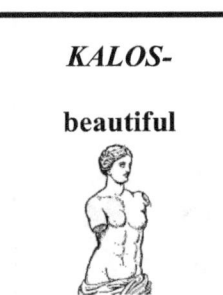 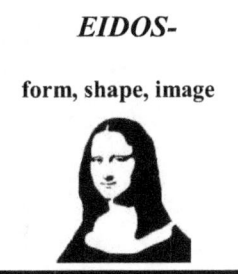 

KALOS- beautiful *EIDOS-* form, shape, image *SCOP-* to examine, see

Definition: **n.** a tube-shaped optical instrument that is rotated to produce a succession of symmetrical designs by means of mirrors reflecting the constantly changing patterns made by bits of colored glass at one end of the tube

Sentence: The laser light show at the concert was a <u>kaleidoscope</u> of visual effect.

Idol

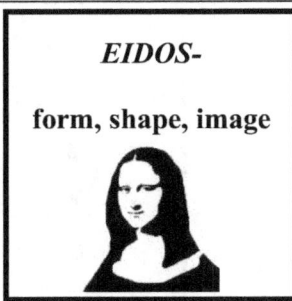

EIDOS- form, shape, image

Definition: **n.** one that is adored, often blindly or excessively; a religious object personifying a deity or spirit

Sentence: While Moses was on the mountain receiving the Ten Commandments, his brother Aaron fashioned a golden calf – an <u>idol</u> for worship in place of the invisible Jehovah.

Geocentric

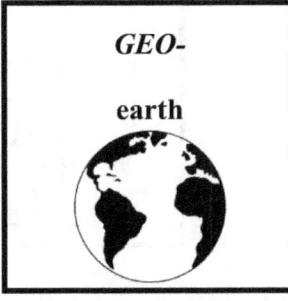 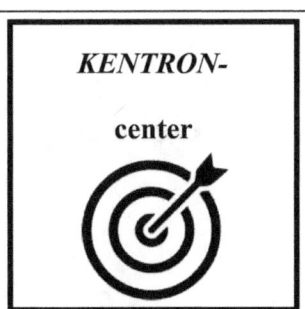

GEO- earth *KENTRON-* center

Definition: **adj.** relating to, measured from, or with respect to the center of the earth

Sentence: Until Polish astronomer Copernicus proposed otherwise, ancient and medieval people believed in a <u>geocentric</u> rather than sun-centered (heliocentric) universe.

Geography

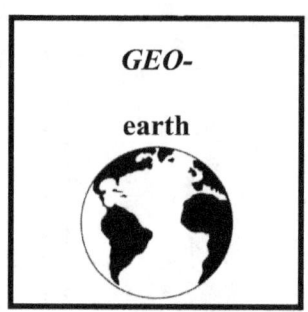
GEO-
earth

GRAPH-
to write, to sign

Definition: **n.** the study of the earth and its features and of the distribution of life on the earth, including human life and the effects of human activity

Sentence: The abandoned urban lot quickly devolves to a <u>geography</u> of weeds, refuse, and cracked pavement.

Geometry

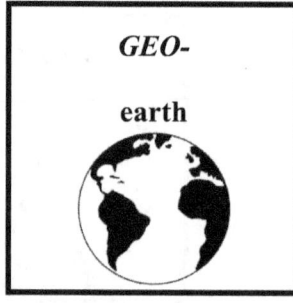
GEO-
earth

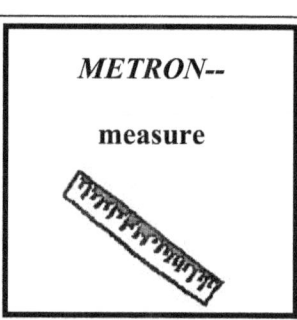
METRON--
measure

Definition: **n.** the mathematics of the properties, measurement, and relationships of points, lines, angles, surfaces, and solids

Sentence: The implicit <u>geometry</u> of the Pyramids shows the Egyptians understood both pi (π) and the Pythagorean theorem long in advance of the Greeks.

Genealogy

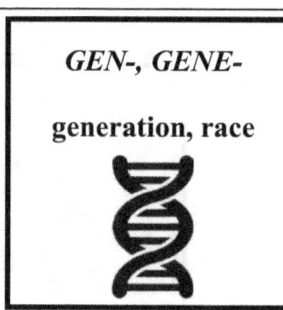
GEN-, GENE-
generation, race

LOGOS-
word, speech, study

Definition: **n.** a record or table of the descent of a person, family, or group from an ancestor or ancestors; a family tree; the study or investigation of ancestry and family histories

Sentence: The <u>genealogy</u> or lineage of ancestors connected most English colonial settlers to America back to the *Domesday Book* compiled after the Norman Conquest of 1066.

Genesis

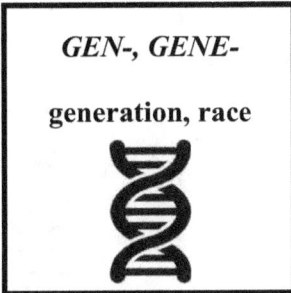

Definition: **n.** the coming into being of something; the origin

Sentence: Otto Hahn's splitting of the atom was the <u>genesis</u> of what eventuated in the A-bomb and the nuclear arms race.

Genius

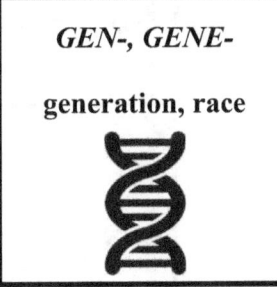 

Definition: **n.** a person of extraordinary intellect and talent
adj. possessing notable intellectual significance or capacity

Sentence: The Romans believed that if someone was a <u>genius</u> it was because he or she had a spirit that guarded and guided him or her from birth.

Genetics

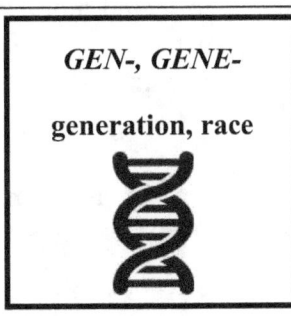

Definition: **n.** the branch of biology that deals with heredity, especially the mechanisms of hereditary transmission and the variation of inherited characteristics among similar or related organisms

Sentence: The Moravian monk Gregor Mendel fathered the science of <u>genetics</u> with his painstaking 'Experiments With Plant Hybrids,' detailing pea plant variations in cross-bred characteristics.

Generation

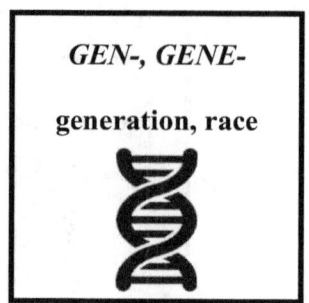

GEN-, GENE-

generation, race

Definition: **n.** all of the offspring that are at the same stage of descent from a common ancestor; the act or process of generating; origination, production, or procreation.
v. the process of creation

Sentence: A human <u>generation</u> or life span from birth to procreation is traditionally reckoned at 25 to 30 years.

Geology

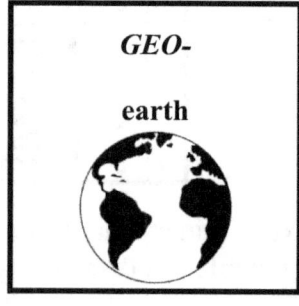 

GEO- earth

LOGOS- word, speech, study

Definition: **n.** the scientific study of the origin, history, and structure of the earth

Sentence: Apollo 11 astronauts collected moon rocks on their mission to explore the <u>geology</u> of the lunar surface.

Genus

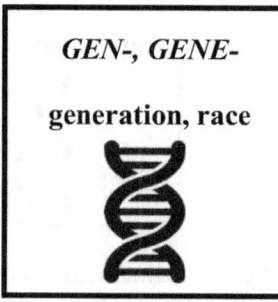

GEN-, GENE-

generation, race

Definition: **n.** a class, group, or kind with common attributes

Sentence: The <u>genus</u> of a biological entity identifies a group of species with similar traits; so, as *homosapiens* we are of the type or <u>genus</u> *homo* (man) and the species *sapiens* (wise).

Exercise A

1. In fourth grade we did a project on ancestry, in which we were asked to determine our _____.

2. Many traits can be attributed to _____, such as hair color, height, and handedness.

3. A popular TV show, "American _____," offers contestants the opportunity to become the next adored singing sensation.

4. Under the influence of hallucinogenic drugs, a user may experience colorful visions that may appear to be made by a _____.

5. Even as a young girl, Sara showed hints of her future career in _____ - she had a rock collection and enjoyed digging in the dirt.

6. In a _____ world, Copernicus was sentenced to jail for his heliocentric ideas.

7. The 6th grader won the _____ competition by correctly naming the capitol of Zimbabwe.

8. Humans can be distinguished from many other species because of their _____: *homo erectus*.

9. Shakespeare, though best known for his plays, also wrote many romantic _____s, only further proving his versatility as a poet.

10. My grandmother insists on reading _____s even though most rational thinkers condemn them as being trashy, gossipy newspapers.

11. Luke Skywalker's _____, C-3PO, possesses an undeniable resemblance to human beings, even though it is clearly a robot.

12. Rick found _____ easier than algebra because he was a visual learner and found shapes easier to work with than formulae.

13. The first book of the Bible is named _____ and tells the story of the beginning of the Earth.

14. Many corporations spend a great deal of money on the _____ of their products, which are often expensive to make.

15. Albert Einstein is the most commonly thought of _____, though there are several other contemporaries that were arguably more intelligent.

Exercise B

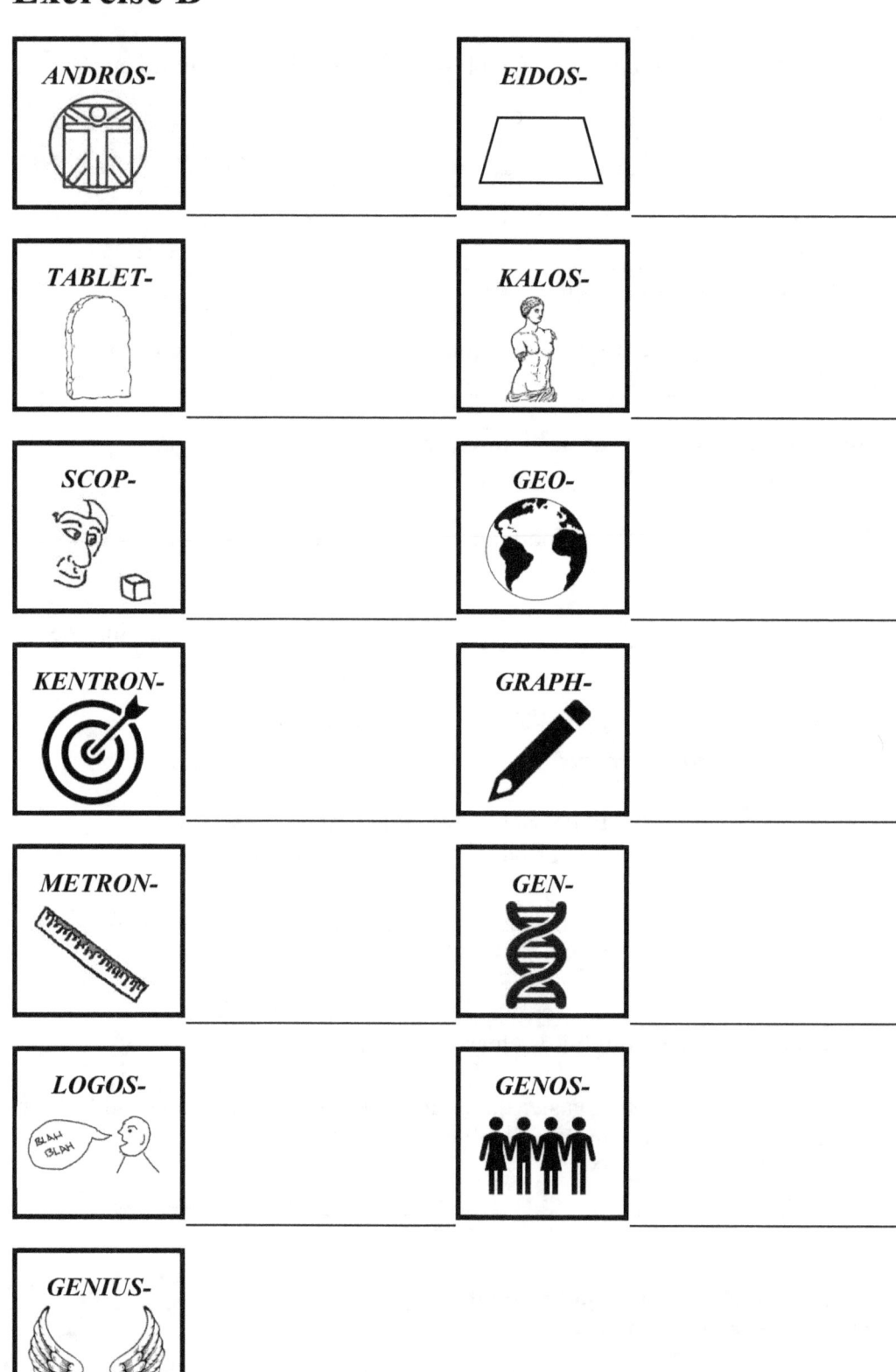

Exercise C

Fill in the crossword puzzle.

Across:
2. one that is adored
4. study of the earth's features
5. short poem or prose piece in ideal terms
6. group with common attributes
8. one's family history
9. process of production
10. mathematical study of points, lines, angles, surfaces and solids
11. condensed newspaper
12. relating to the center of the earth

Down:
1. resembling a human
3. tube shaped optical instrument
4. person of extraordinary intellect
6. origin
7. study of heredity
8. study of the earth's origin

15. Albert Einstein is the most commonly thought of _____, though there are several other contemporaries that were arguably more intelligent.

EXERCISE D

Match the word with the letter of its definition:

1. ___ android
2. ___ idol
3. ___ idyll
4. ___ kaleidoscope
5. ___ tabloid
6. ___ geocentric
7. ___ geography
8. ___ geology
9. ___ geometry
10. ___ genealogy
11. ___ generation
12. ___ genesis
13. ___ genetics
14. ___ genius
15. ___ genus

a) short poem or prose piece in ideal terms
b) study of the earth's features
c) resembling a human
d) one's family history
e) process of production
f) origin
g) study of heredity
h) person of extraordinary intellect
i) relating to the center of the earth
j) tube shaped optical instrument
k) one that is adored
l) condensed newspaper
m) study of the earth's origin
n) mathematical study of points, lines, angles, surfaces and solids
o) group with common attributes

Lesson XVIII

Calligraphy

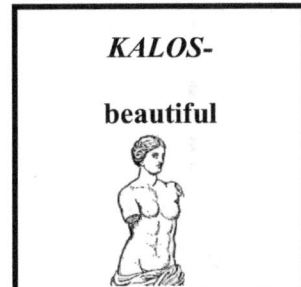
KALOS- beautiful

GRAPH- to write, to sign

Definition: **n.** the art of fine handwriting

Sentence: In Oriental calligraphy, the brush painting of finely wrought linguistic characters is considered an art form.

Cryptogram

KRYPTOS- hidden

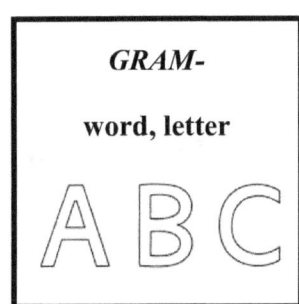
GRAM- word, letter

Definition: **n.** a piece of writing in code or cipher

Sentence: A simple code or cipher known to children is to substitute a number for a letter's alphabetic position; so, the cryptogram 25, 5, 18 would decipher as YES.

Graffiti

GRAPH- to write, to sign

Definition: **n.** writing or drawings defacing a public wall or other surface

Sentence: The graffiti-strewn Berlin Wall was covered by various spray-painted messages and murals before it was ripped down in 1989.

Grammar

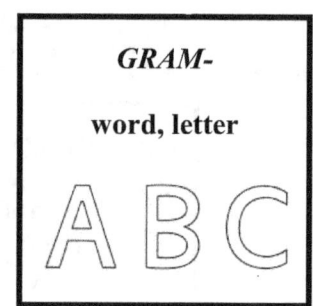

Definition: **n.** the study of how words and their component parts combine to form sentences; the basic rules of an area of knowledge.

Sentence: A gentleman is a person who understands and practices the <u>grammar</u> of mannerly life in polite society.

Hemoglobin

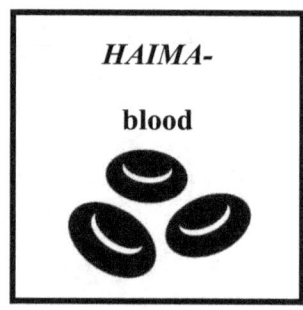 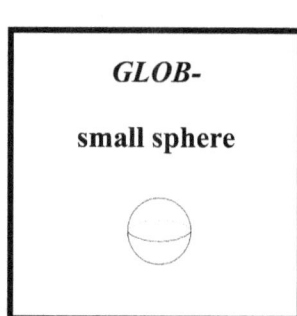

Definition: **n.** the iron-containing oxygen-transporting respiratory pigment in red blood cells of vertebrates

Sentence: Colorless plasma is an emergency substitute for whole blood that lacks red blood cells with their oxygen-transporting chemical <u>hemoglobin</u>.

Hemorrhage

Definition: **n.** excessive discharge of blood from the blood vessels; profuse bleeding

Sentence: Uncontrolled bleeding in the brain caused Franklin Roosevelt to die of cerebral <u>hemorrhage</u>.

Hemorrhoid

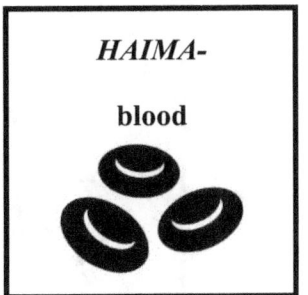
HAIMA- blood

RHEIN- to flow

Definition: **n.** an itching or painful mass of dilated veins in swollen anal tissue

Sentence: Ice packs applied to the rectal area are the preferred home remedy for the swellings known as <u>hemorrhoids</u>.

Ideology

IDEA- idea

LOGOS- word, speech, study

Definition: **n.** the ideas reflecting the social needs and aspirations of an individual, group, class, or culture

Sentence: Terrorists evince an <u>ideology</u> supporting violence and indifference to the taking of innocent life.

Prologue

PRO- before

LOGOS- word, speech, study

Definition: **n.** an introduction or preface, especially a poem recited to introduce a play.

Sentence: Chaucer's twenty-plus *Canterbury Tales* are preceded by a <u>Prologue</u> explaining how the storytellers met at an inn and agreed to narrate tales on their pilgrimage to the cathedral.

Tautology

Definition:	**n.** needless repetition of the same sense in different words; redundancy
Sentence:	A 'true fact' or a trip 'abroad overseas' or 'in my opinion I think' are all common examples of <u>tautologies</u>.

Exercise A

1. It is important to master _____ in order to communicate ideas properly in speaking or writing.

2. _____ is more important to writing in Asian cultures than in our culture because the brush strokes actually affect the meaning of the character in Asian languages whereas in English the brush stroke is irrelevant.

3. Many cities have problems with _____ illicitly written on buildings by gangs and other vandals.

4. It is hard for a rational thinker to agree with Hitler and the Nazi party's racist _____.

5. The _____ to the play informed the audience of the circumstances under which storyline was occurring.

6. After the blood vessels in my uncles head burst, he suffered a _____.

7. Scared that the teacher might intercept his love letter, the young Romeo decided to write it as a _____ that only his sweetheart could decipher.

8. The politician's repeated use of the phrase "in other words" betrayed a tendency toward _____ and rephrasing the same things.

9. A diet low in iron cannot support the manufacturing of sufficient _____.

10. An unfortunate side effect of _____s is pain when sitting.

Exercise B

Exercise C

Fill in the crossword puzzle.

Across:
2. excessive discharge of blood
3. needless repetition
4. blood condition in which blood fails to clot normally
6. rephrasing the same idea
8. elastic cartilage that prevents food from entering the trachea
10. art of fine handwriting
12. drawings made on a public wall
13. introduction or preface to a play

Down:
1. piece of writing in code
2. iron-containing pigment in blood cells
5. ideas reflecting a certain group
7. destruction of red blood cells
9. a study of words and their parts in sentences
11. painful mass of dilated veins

EXERCISE D

Match the word with the letter of its definition:

1. ___ epiglottis
2. ___ calligraphy
3. ___ cryptogram
4. ___ graffiti
5. ___ grammar
6. ___ hemoglobin
7. ___ hemolysis
8. ___ hemophilia
9. ___ hemorrhage
10. ___ hemorrhoid
11. ___ ideology
12. ___ logorrhea
13. ___ prologue
14. ___ tautology

a) excessive use of words
b) excessive discharge of blood
c) destruction of red blood cells
d) needless repetition
e) piece of writing in code
f) elastic cartilage that prevents food from entering the trachea
g) drawings made on a public wall
h) study of words and their parts in sentences
i) blood condition in which blood fails to clot normally
j) painful mass of dilated veins
k) ideas reflecting a certain group
l) introduction or preface to a play
m) iron containing pigment in red blood cells
n) art of fine handwriting

Test 3

Choose the correct meaning for the underlined vocabulary word in each sentence.

1. "He announced himself as the <u>archangel</u> Gabriel, and commanded the captain to jump overboard."

   Moby Dick by Herman Melville

   (a) principal enemy   (b) high ranking foe   (c) head of the church
   (d) high ranking angel   (e) head of a clan or tribe

2. "Manson Mingott, the <u>Matriarch</u> of the line, would dare."

   The Age of Innocence by Edith Wharton

   (a) female leader   (b) female person   (c) a women   (d) a mother   (e) a ruler

3. "These strong <u>oligarchs</u> arose out of the conflict of competition and traveled the inevitable road toward combination."

   The Iron Mask by Jack London

   (a) men who rule   (b) members of a small governing faction
   (c) women who rule   (d) people in a monarchy   (e) priests

4. "He had looked out all the pictures to which an <u>asterisk</u> was affixed in those formidable pages of fine print in his Badeker; his attention had been strained and his eyes dazzled, and he had sat down with an aesthetic headache."

   The American by Henry James

   (a) small celestial orbit   (b) moon shaped body   (c) star shaped character
   (d) a signature   (e) man in the moon

5. "My days I devote to reading and to experiments in chemistry, and I spend many of the clear nights in the study of <u>astronomy</u>."

   The Island of Doctor Moreau by H.G. Wells

   (a) cloud movements   (b) life   (c) the study of anything large
   (d) the moon   (e) the study of outer space

6. "Robert Strickland's innocent biography that it is difficult to avoid feeling a certain sympathy for the unlucky parson."
                                                Moon and Sixpence by W. Somerset Maugham

   (a) habitat for organisms   (b) account of a person's life
   (c) emission of light   (d) study of organisms   (e) the study of ecosystems

7. "Fear and joy may both cause cardiac palpitation, but in one case we find high tonus of the skeletal muscles, in the other case relaxation and the general sense of weakness."
                                                The Analysis of Mind by Bertrand Russell

   (a) study of the liver   (b) used to diagnose kidney disorders
   (c) relating to lungs   (d) relating to the heart   (e) blood vessels

8. "Down the avenue came boastfully sauntering a lad of sixteen years, although the chronic sneer of an ideal manhood already sat upon his lips."
                                                Maggie: A Girl of the Streets by Stephen Crane

   (a) continuing   (b) extended account   (c) at the same time   (d) in order
   (e) occasional

9. "How long ago it is aunt, since we used to repeat the chronological order of the kings of England, with the dates of their accession, and most of the principal events of their reigns."
                                                Mansfield Park by Jane Austen

   (a) simultaneous   (b) arranged in order of time occurring
   (c) lesser known   (d) coincidental   (e) recurring

10. "The gentleman, after looking towards me once or twice, politely accosted me in very good English; I remember I wished to God that I could speak French as well; his fluency and correct pronunciation impressed me for the first time with a due notion of the cosmopolitan character of the capital I was in…"
                                                The Professor by Charlotte Bronte

    (a) spatial   (b) provincial, narrow-minded   (c) worldly, sophisticated
    (d) cosmetic   (e) regional

11. "It is one of her aristocratic tastes, and quite proper, for a real lady is always known by neat boots, gloves, and handkerchief," replied Meg, who had a good many little `aristocratic tastes' of her own."
                                                Little Women by Louisa May Alcott

    (a) characteristic of nobility   (b) government officials   (c) clerical
    (d) representative of the people (e) wealthy officials

12. "There is more liberty of action in England, but for liberty of thought go to <u>bureaucratic</u> Prussia."

    Howards End by E. M. Forster

    (a) relating to nobility   (b) communistic   (c) relating to government officials
    (d) relating to the people   (e) government controlled

13. "In Switzerland they support the Radicals, without losing sight of the fact that this party consists of antagonistic elements, partly of <u>Democratic</u> Socialists, in the French sense, partly of radical bourgeois."

    The Communist Manifesto by Karl Marx & Frederick Engles

    (a) relating to the ruling class   (b) relating to the nobility
    (c) relating to non-elected officials
    (d) relating to government controlled by the majority
    (e) relating to government controlled by the wealthy

14. "His calculation of the membership of these divisions by occupation, from the United States Census of 1900, is as follows: <u>Plutocratic</u> class, 250,251; Middle class, 8,429,845; and Proletariat class, 20,393,137."

    The Iron Heel by Jack London

    (a) relating to the ruling class   (b) relating to the nobility
    (c) relating to non-elected officials   (d) relating to government by the people
    (e) relating to government controlled by the wealthy

15. "The seditious harangues of <u>demagogues</u> in Faneuil Hall have made rebels of a loyal people and deprived me of my country."

    Grandfather's Chair by Nathaniel Hawthorne

    (a) commoners   (b) political agitators   (c) generals   (d) elected officials
    (e) noblemen

16. "Wollaston has discovered the remarkable fact that 200 beetles, out of the 550 species inhabiting Madeira, are so far deficient in wings that they cannot fly; and that of the twenty-nine <u>endemic</u> genera, no less than twenty-three genera have all their species in this condition."

    The Origin of Species by Charles Darwin

    (a) native   (b) impassioned   (c) licensed   (d) diseased   (e) powerful

17. "And by that destiny to perform an act
Whereof what's past is <u>prologue</u>, what to come,
In yours and my discharge."
                                    "The Tempest" by William Shakespeare

    (a) chronicle   (b) introduction   (c) tragedy
    (d) artificial   (e) history

18. "Picture yourself in a boat on a river,/With tangerine trees and marmalade skies/
Somebody calls you, you answer quite slowly,/A girl with <u>kaleidoscope</u> eyes.
                "Lucy in the Sky with Diamonds" by John Lennon and Paul McCartney

    (a) pathological   (b) changing set of colors (c) monochromatic
    (d) parallel   (e) maniacal

19. "Our little <u>idyll</u>," he said, "seems to be the sport and buffet of every one."
                                    The Yellow Crayon by E. Phillips Oppenheim

    (a) one that is adored   (b) optical instrument   (c) carefree interlude
    (d) human looking device (e) small newspaper

20. "So far as the <u>geography</u>, the inhabitants, the animals, and the features of the countries the travelers pass over are described, it is entirely accurate."
                                          Five Weeks in a Balloon by Jules Verne

    (a) study of mathematics   (b) study of ancestors   (c) study of generations
    (d) study of the earth's features (e) study of earth

21. "I was just tracing my mental states for you, in order to show the <u>genesis</u> of the action," he explained."
                                      Moon-Face and Other Stories by Jack London

    (a) beginning   (b) heredity   (c) intellect   (d) talent   (e) scientific class

22. "But the effort that cost her the deepest humiliation was a request to Higgins, whose pet artistic fancy, next to Milton's verse, was <u>calligraphy</u>, and who himself wrote a most beautiful Italian hand, that he would teach her to write."
                                        Pygmalion by George Bernard Shaw

    (a) writing in code   (b) fine handwriting (c) a cartilaginous structure
    (d) public drawing   (e) writing sentences

23. "He tried to reply, but the effort caused him to cough, bringing about a <u>hemorrhage</u> of the lungs and again he fell back exhausted."

The Lost Continent by Edgar Rice Burroughs

(a) release of hemoglobin (b) blood clotting disorder (c) count of red blood cells
(d) profuse bleeding (e) itching dilated veins

24. "I don't differentiate much, except in degree, between people who believe in religion from those who believe in <u>astrology</u>, magic or the supernatural."

Sincerely, Andy Rooney by Andy Rooney

(a) fear of evil spirits (b) beliefs about stars (c) children's stories
(d) mathematical study (e) a story, such as a fable

25. "The declaration itself, though it may be chargeable with <u>tautology</u> or redundancy, is at least perfectly harmless."

Federalist Papers by Alexander Hamilton

(a) individual aspirations (b) knowing several languages
(c) saying the same thing twice (d) poor use of words
(e) clear description

Lesson XIX

Anthropomorphic

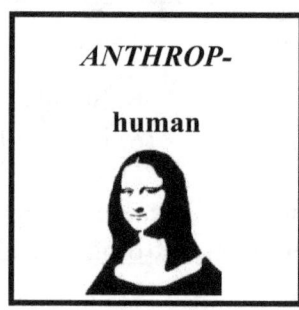
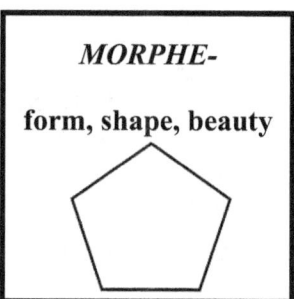

Definition:	**adj.** Having a human form; endowing the non-human with human characteristics
Sentence:	Smiling trees running their arms in the breeze' exemplifies <u>anthropomorphism</u>.

Kleptomania

Definition:	**n.** an obsessive impulse to steal regardless of economic need
Sentence:	A wealthy person repeatedly arrested for shoplifting probably has the psychiatric compulsion known as <u>kleptomania</u>.

Mania

Definition:	**n.** an excessively intense enthusiasm, interest, or desire; a craze
Sentence:	At the height of Holland's 17th century <u>mania</u> for Near Eastern tulip bulbs, a single bulb was valued at as much as $35,000.

Maniacal

Definition: **adj.** suggestive of or afflicted with insanity

Sentence: The extermination of more than 12 million in the concentration camps was Hitler's <u>maniacal</u> solution to the 'racial problems' of gypsies, Jews, and homosexuals.

Megalomania

Definition: **n.** a psychopathological condition characterized by delusional fantasies of wealth, power, or omnipotence

Sentence: King Midas, a <u>megalomaniac</u>, had an unremitting obsession with amassing and hoarding gold.

Pyromania

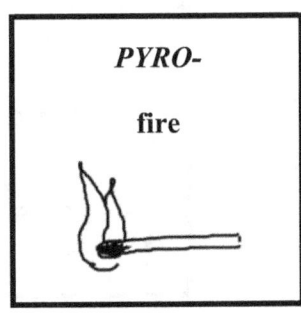 

Definition: **n.** the irresistible urge to start fires

Sentence: *Firestarter* is a Steven King horror novel describing a compulsive <u>pyromaniac</u> fascinated by fire and driven to arson.

Barometer

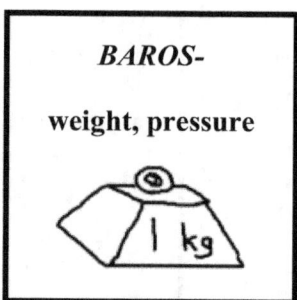

BAROS-

weight, pressure

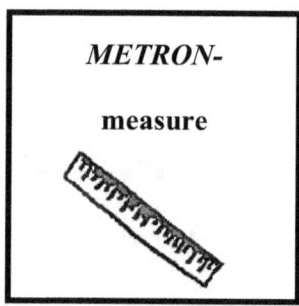

METRON-

measure

Definition:	**n.** an instrument for measuring atmospheric pressure, used especially in weather forecasting; anything that can be used to gauge trends or progress in society
Sentence:	The number of minutes a minimum-wage laborer requires to buy a hamburger at any given time has been used as an economic <u>barometer</u> of the financial health of the US.

Odometer

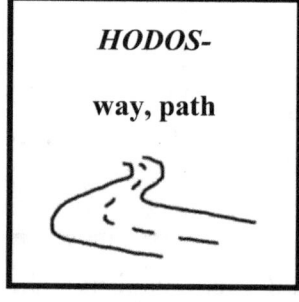

HODOS-

way, path

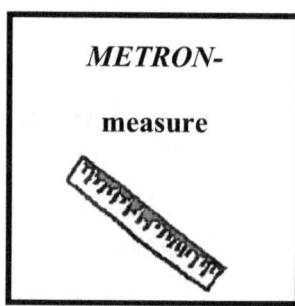

METRON-

measure

Definition:	**n.** an instrument that indicates distance traveled by a vehicle
Sentence:	It is illegal to turn back the <u>odometer</u> in a used automobile for sale to understate the miles the vehicle has traveled.

Speedometer

SPEED-

speed

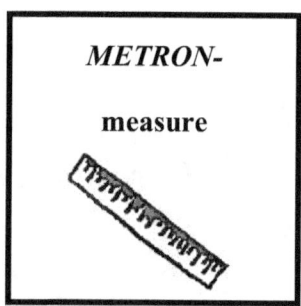

METRON-

measure

Definition:	**n.** an instrument for indicating speed
Sentence:	<u>Speedometers</u> have measured the velocity of major league fastballs at up to 103 mph.

Thermometer

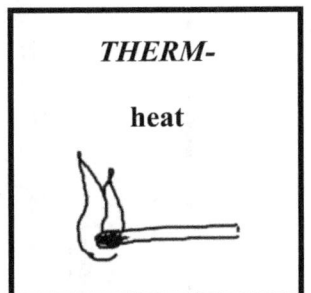
THERM-
heat

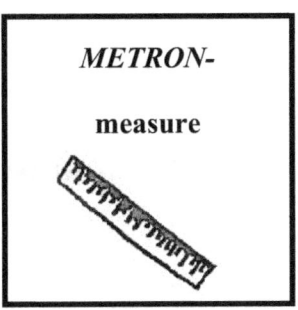
METRON-
measure

Definition: **n.** an instrument for measuring temperature, especially one having a graduated glass tube with a bulb containing a liquid, typically mercury or colored alcohol, that expands and rises in the tube as the temperature increases

Sentence: Before even opening the door, Robert decided it was too hot for him to go outside when he noted that the outdoor <u>thermometer</u> read 98 degrees Fahrenheit.

Isomorphism

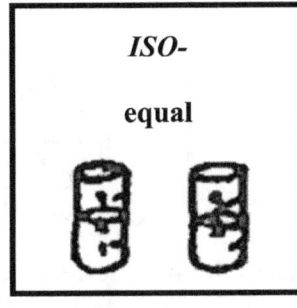
ISO-
equal

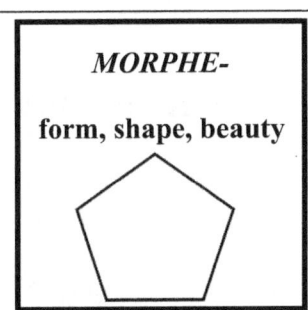
MORPHE-
form, shape, beauty

Definition: **n.** similarity in form, as in organisms of different ancestry.

Sentence: Wings, hands, flippers, and forepaws are evolutionary <u>isomorphisms</u>.

Morphology

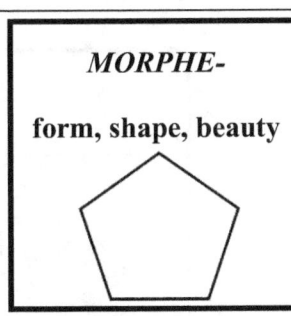
MORPHE-
form, shape, beauty

LOGOS-
word, speech, study

Definition: **n.** the branch of biology that deals with the form and structure of organisms without consideration of function

Sentence: Etymology studies the <u>morphology</u> of words with respect to changes undergone in derivation, compounding, and meaning rather than in inflection or pronunciation.

Agronomy

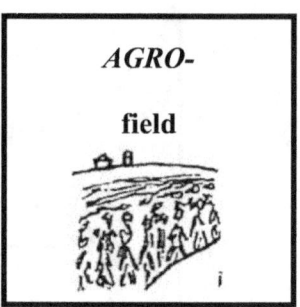

Definition: **n.** application of the various soil and plant sciences to soil management and crop production; scientific agriculture

Sentence: A soil expert or <u>agronomist</u> advises the farmer on nutrient additives, fertilizers, and herbicides.

Economic

Definition: **adj.** of or relating to the production, development, and management of material wealth, as of a country, household, or business enterprise; concise

Sentence: Occam's Razor is the scientific principle of brevity and conciseness: that the most uncomplicated, <u>economic</u> yet valid explanation is the best hypothesis.

Nemesis

Definition: **n.** an opponent that cannot be beaten or overcome; a source of harm or ruin

Sentence: At the Battle of Waterloo in Belgium, the British commander Lord Wellington proved to be Napoleon's <u>nemesis</u> and vanquisher. Nemesis - goddess of vengeance - named after *nomos*.

Meter

METRON-

measure

Definition:	**n.** measuring device; the measured arrangement of words in poetry, as by accentual rhythm, syllabic quantity, or the number of syllables in a line; any of various devices designed to measure time, distance, speed, or intensity or indicate and record or regulate the amount or volume; the international standard unit of length, approximately equivalent to 39.37 inches
Sentence:	The poetic <u>meter</u> in speeches by noble characters in Shakespeare is iambic pentameter – a line of five units, each consisting of an unstressed followed by a stressed syllable: *"The la'dy doth' protest' too much' methinks"*.

Exercise A

1. Realizing that her father's desire for control and power would never be satiated, Alicia saw him for the _____ he really was.
2. The study of the evolution of animals was once entirely based on _____, but now genetic analysis is the most powerful tool in studying the relationship between animals.
3. Cheryl ignored the signs of her son's _____ when she did not question how he had afforded the expensive stereo equipment he had in his room while he did not have a job.
4. The _____ that surrounded Pope's trip to Brazil was unbelievable; citizens lined the streets for hours in hopes of catching the briefest glimpse of him.
5. Most people assume that sea lions and seals are closely related, but in fact their _____ is merely a product of their shared environment.
6. Jack's _____ obsession with acing the SAT was considered unhealthy and perhaps unrealistic by his tutor.
7. Wall Street was unimpressed by George W. Bush's _____ policy and feared that his administration would lead the country into financial ruin.
8. _____ in children is often confused with youthful curiosity about fire, but the condition is far more serious and can lead to dangerous house fires.
9. The _____ on board the skipper's vessel warned that perhaps the planned three hour tour was unwise because the low atmospheric pressure suggested a storm was brewing.
10. Most adults are used to having their temperature taken with an old-fashioned _____ containing mercury, but now most hospitals use a device that is placed in the ear can measure body temperature in a few seconds.
11. Tom's English teacher did not appreciate the genius in his free-form poetry; he insisted that proper poetry followed a consistent _____, such as iambic pentameter.
12. In the original *Batman* movie Jack Nicholson played the part of the Joker, Batman's longtime _____.
13. Although the portion of America's land devoted to agriculture has shrunk as the country has industrialized, modern _____ has allowed farmers to produce more crop from the land they cultivate.
14. According to his mother's directions, the dentist's office was exactly one half mile down the road after exiting the highway, so Jim stared intently at the _____ to make sure he didn't pass it.
15. When he was pulled over for speeding, Mark explained that to the state policeman that his _____ was broken, and he did not realize how fast he was driving.

Exercise B

ANTHROP- 		MORPHE- 	
KLEPTO- 		MANIA- 	
MEGA- 		PYRO- 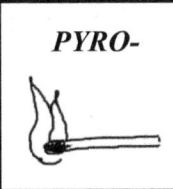	
BAROS- 		METRON- 	
HODOS- 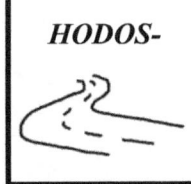		OIKOS- 	
THERM- 		ISO- 	
NOMOS- 		AGRO- 	

Exercise C

Fill in the crossword puzzle.

Across:
4. unbeatable opponent
6. relating to the wealth of a group
9. temperature measurer
10. flow of words in poetry
12. insane
13. sedative drug
14. scientific agriculture
15. mental disease causing desire for power
16. obsessive impulse to steal

Down:
1. indicates speed of a vehicle
2. similarity in form
3. connoisseur of food and drink
5. biology; specifically form studies
7. indicates distance traveled by a vehicle
8. obsessive impulse to light fire
11. an instrument for measuring atmospheric pressure
15. measuring device

EXERCISE D

Match the word with the letter of its definition:

1. ___ kleptomania
2. ___ mania
3. ___ maniacal
4. ___ megalomania
5. ___ pyromania
6. ___ barometer
7. ___ meter
8. ___ thermometer
9. ___ odometer
10. ___ speedometer
11. ___ isomorphism
12. ___ morphine
13. ___ morphology
14. ___ agronomy
15. ___ economic
16. ___ gastronome
17. ___ nemesis

a) atmospheric pressure measurer
b) flow of words in poetry
c) mental disease causing desire for power
d) indicates speed of a vehicle
e) scientific agriculture
f) relating to the wealth of a group
g) connoisseur of food and drink
h) unbeatable opponent
i) biology; specifically form studies
j) obsessive impulse to steal
k) excessive enthusiasm
l) obsessive impulse to light fire
m) temperature measurer
n) indicates distance traveled by a vehicle
o) similarity in form
p) sedative drug
q) having excessive enthusiasm

Lesson XX

Acronym

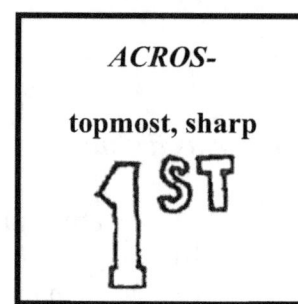
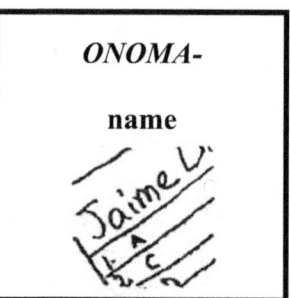

Definition:	**n.** a word formed from the initial letters of a name, such as *WAC* for *W*omen's *A*rmy *C*orps, or by combining initial letters or parts of a series of words, such as *radar* for *ra*dio *d*etecting *a*nd *r*anging.
Sentence:	An S.O.S. is an <u>acronym</u> for the distress signal 'Save our ship!'

Onomatopoeia

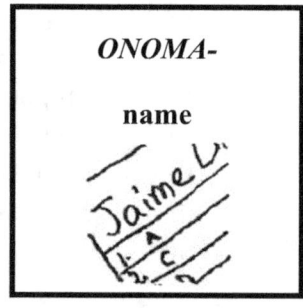
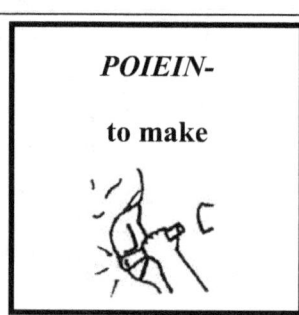

Definition:	**n.** the formation or use of words such as *buzz* or *murmur* that imitate the sounds associated with the objects or actions they refer to
Sentence:	Poe's <u>onomatopoetic</u> use of the word 'tintinnabulation' (of the bells) exemplifies a word coinage that reflects the sound of the thing described.

Pseudonym

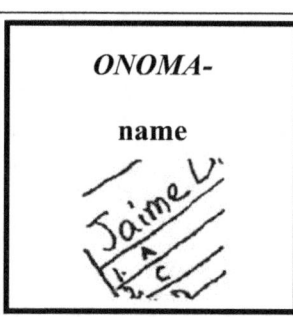

Definition:	**n.** a fictitious name, especially a pen name
Sentence:	Lewis Carroll was the <u>pseudonym</u> Charles Dodgson used as the author of *Alice in Wonderland*.

Orthodontist

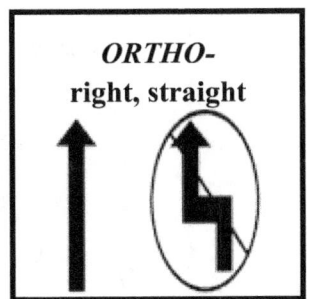 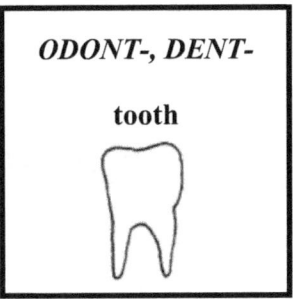

Definition:	**n.** a doctor who specializes in the practice of preventing, straightening and correcting irregularities of the teeth, as by the use of braces
Sentence:	A specialist in dental braces and straightening of teeth, an <u>orthodontist</u> earns considerably more than a run-of-the-mill dentist.

Orthodox

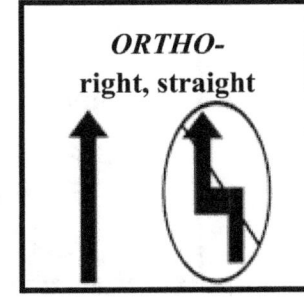 

Definition:	**adj.** adhering to the accepted or traditional and established faith or views, especially in religion
Sentence:	The traditional <u>orthodox</u> cookery dictates a cake prepared from scratch; the modern method is a cake mix or store-bought cake.

Orthography

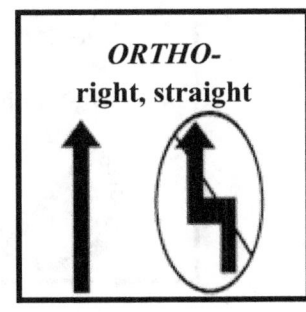 

Definition:	**n.** a method of representing a language or the sounds of language by written symbols; spelling
Sentence:	British and American <u>orthography</u> varies in divergent spelling instances - (begun with Noah Webster) - such as 'honour/honor' and 'theatre/theater.'

Orthopedist

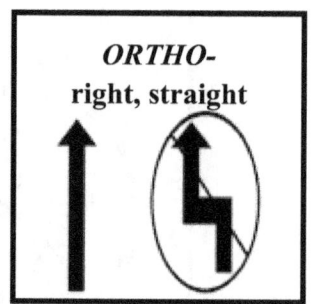 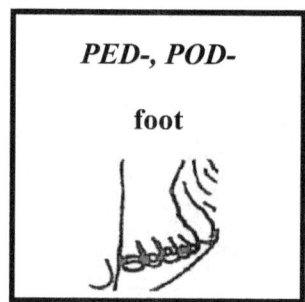

Definition: **n.** a doctor who specializes in the treatment of bones

Sentence: Although originally an <u>orthopedist</u> was a child-bone-straightener, today the profession is concerned with all manner of bone treatments.

Pathos

Definition: **n.** an expression used to evoke sadness, or apprehension of suffering

Sentence: The protagonist's <u>pathos</u> was made evident by his soliloquy during which he described the pains he felt after the death of his father.

Apathy

 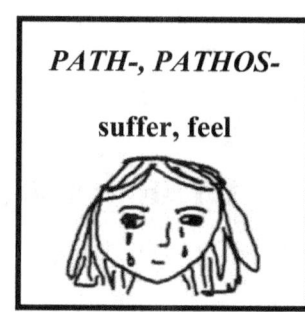

Definition: **n.** lack of interest or concern, especially regarding matters of general importance or appeal; indifference; lack of emotion or feeling

Sentence: That barely 40% of the electorate votes in a presidential election is taken as a sign of voter <u>apathy</u>; the people don't know or care enough to cast a ballot.

Empathy	**EN-** in, into 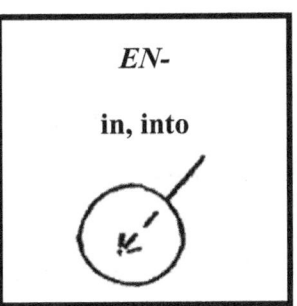	**PATH-, PATHOS-** suffer, feel 

Definition:	**n.** identification with and projection of one's own feelings into another's situation, feelings, and motives
Sentence:	If my dog died and I feel your sorrow at your dog's death, that is <u>empathy</u>; if I've never lost a dog, my sorrow for you is sympathy.

Psychopath	**PSYCH-** soul, mind 	**PATH-, PATHOS-** suffer, feel 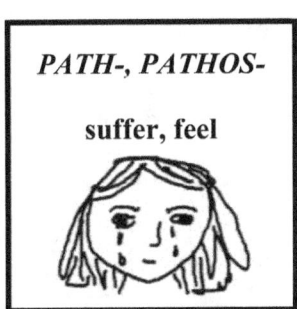

Definition:	**n.** a person with an antisocial personality disorder, manifested in aggressive, perverted, criminal, or amoral behavior without empathy or remorse
Sentence:	Serial killers are <u>psychopaths</u> who can repeatedly kill without shame, guilt, or remorse.

Telepathy	**TELE-** far off 	**PATH-, PATHOS-** suffer, feel 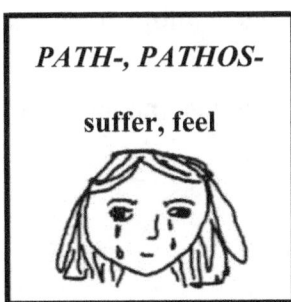

Definition:	**n.** communication through means other than the senses, as by the exercise of an occult power
Sentence:	Using a crystal ball or Ouija board, some mystics claim to be able to communicate with spirits of the dead via <u>telepathy</u>.

Exercise A

1. The army uses _____s composed of the initial letters of words in a phrase such as MIA as an abbreviation for 'missing in action.'

2. Mick Jagger must register at hotels under a _____; otherwise a legion of devoted fans will be waiting at his door every time he returns to his room.

3. Her teeth recently fixed with braces, Rachel now needs to see her _____ once every two weeks to insure that they are adjusted correctly.

4. Informed that "bing" was not a word by his English teacher, Anthony retorted that it was an example of _____, representing the sound of a high-pitched bell.

5. My grandmother's _____ informed her that she might, unfortunately, have osteoporosis, a bone disease characterized by faulty alignment of the spinal chord.

6. The sex scandal in the Catholic Church by no means reflects _____ behavior on the priests' part.

7. The psychiatrist found Jordan's _____ quite disturbing, as he did not seem to care that he had just battered a group of defenseless children.

8. The multiply convicted felon, clearly a _____, was in need of immediate psychological counseling.

9. Only someone who has lost a close family member before it was his time to go can truly feel _____ with a widower whose 30-year-old husband died in action.

10. The _____ of the English language is effective in including a symbol for all the possible sounds we could wish to make.

11. The astrologist claimed that she could use _____ to communicate with otherworldly gods and the deceased.

Exercise B

Exercise C

Fill in the crossword puzzle.

Across:
4. mouth doctor
7. a person with an antisocial disorder
9. word from first letters
10. words spelled like they sound

Down:
1. a fictitious name
2. identify with another's feelings
3. lack of interest or concern
4. spelling
5. communication via mind
6. bone doctor
8. uncontroversial

EXERCISE B

Match the word with the letter of its definition:

1. ___ acronym
2. ___ onomatopoeia
3. ___ pseudonym
4. ___ orthodontist
5. ___ orthodox
6. ___ orthography
7. ___ orthopedist
8. ___ apathy
9. ___ empathy
10. ___ psychopath
11. ___ telepathy

a) word from first letters
b) mouth doctor
c) identify with another's feelings
d) communication via mind
e) a person with an antisocial disorder
f) spelling
g) word imitating a sound
h) a fictitious name
i) lack of interest or concern
j) bone doctor
k) uncontroversial

Lesson XXI

Encyclopedia

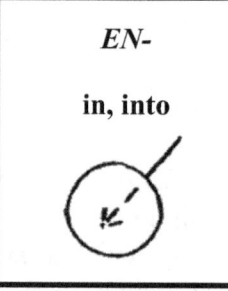
EN-
in, into

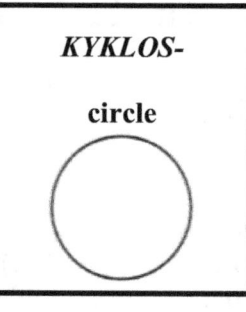
KYKLOS-
circle

PAEDIA-
children, teach

Definition: **n.** a comprehensive reference work containing articles on a wide range of subjects or on numerous aspects of a particular field, usually arranged alphabetically

Sentence: Denis Diderot's 17th century *Encyclopedia* was an attempt to compile all of the world's knowledge in a comprehensive, single set of books.

Pedagogue

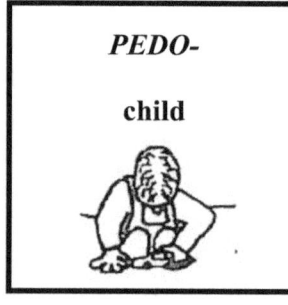
PEDO-
child

AG-, ACT-
to drive, act, urge

Definition: **n.** a schoolteacher; an educator

Sentence: A teacher, a tutor, an instructor or docent is a pedagogue whose job it is to instruct learners.

Pediatrician

PEDO-
child

ICIAN-
one who cures

Definition: **n.** a physician who specializes in pediatrics, or the care of children and babies

Sentence: New or recent mothers are advised to avail themselves of the services of a pediatrician, a doctor specializing in baby and child medical care.

Pedophile

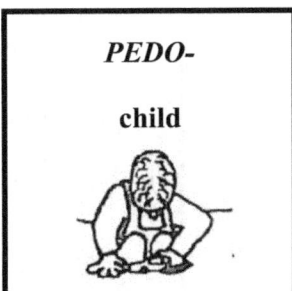 

Definition: **n.** an adult who is sexually attracted to a child or children

Sentence: In the Hellenic age of ancient Greece, carnal or sexual relations between men and boys were deemed natural, whereas today such <u>pedophilic</u> behavior is illegal and severely punished.

Cellophane

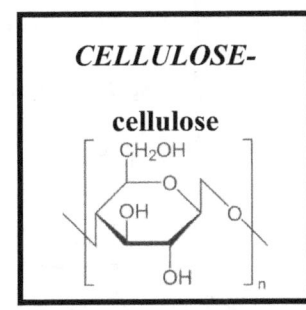 

Definition: **n.** a thin, flexible, transparent cellulose material made from wood pulp and used as a moisture proof wrapping

Sentence: CDs are encased in a transparent <u>cellophane</u> wrapper that is so tightly sealed as to frustrate removal.

Diaphanous

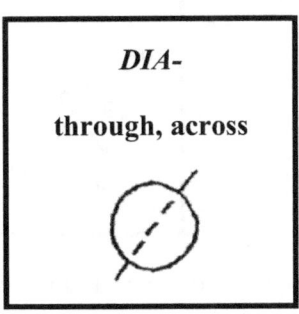 

Definition: **adj.** of such fine texture as to be transparent or translucent

Sentence: The <u>diaphanous</u> gowns of ancient Egyptian royalty permitted close anatomical inspection.

Fantastic

PHANTAS-

imagine, make visible

Definition: **adj.** existing only in the imagination; imaginary; superlative

Sentence: *Peter Pan* is a <u>fantastic</u> story of Lost Boys, pixie-dusted flight, Red Indians, pirates, and a poison potion.

Fantasy

PHANTAS-

imagine, make visible

Definition: **n.** the creative imagination; unrestrained fancy

Sentence: The utterly implausible story of Pocahontas' saving John Smith from the axe was likely a <u>fantasy</u> cooked up by the captain himself years later.

Phantom

PHANTAS-

imagine, make visible

Definition: **n.** something apparently seen, heard, or sensed, but having no physical reality; a ghost or an apparition

Sentence: The '<u>phantom</u> limb' syndrome involves an amputee's sensation of pain in a limb no longer there.

Phenomenal

PHENOMEN-

an appearance

Definition: **adj.** extraordinary; outstanding; of, relating to, or constituting phenomena or a phenomenon

Sentence: After losing the first three games of the 2003 American League Championship Series, the Red Sox made a <u>phenomenal</u> comeback in winning the next four games.

Phenomenon

PHENOMEN-

an appearance

Definition: **n.** an unusual, significant, or unaccountable fact or occurrence; a marvel.

Sentence: A mirage is a <u>phenomenon</u> of an apparent distant pool water caused by heat waves rippling over a hot, distant surface."

Philander

PHIL- love

ANDROS- man

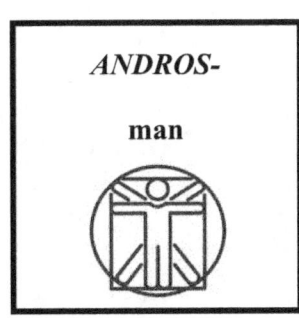

Definition: **v.** to carry on a sexual affair, especially an extramarital affair, with a woman one cannot or does not intend to marry

Sentence: <u>Philanderer</u> Caligula as Roman emperor had numerous affairs with senators' wives and even his own sister.

Philanthropist

Definition:	**n.** someone who makes charitable donations intended to increase human well-being
Sentence:	<u>Philanthropist</u> Andrew Carnegie, after selling his steel company for $20M to Morgan, gave all that largesse to support civic libraries, concert halls, and public institutions.

Philharmonic

Definition:	**adj.** devoted to or appreciative of music; relating to a symphony orchestra
Sentence:	Devotees of symphonic music support their local <u>philharmonic</u> orchestras.

Philosophy

Definition:	**n.** the love or study of knowledge
Sentence:	Speakers Corner in London is an area near Hyde Park where people come together and argue or preach about modern values, current events, and <u>philosophy</u>.

Exercise A

1. The little girl is scheduled for an annual physical and checkup with her _____ on the first of the month.

2. Industrial plants often wrap their products in _____ as to prevent them from becoming scratched or otherwise marred.

3. More and more priests are being found out to be _____s, as many of them have been discovered as having had sexual relations with little boys.

4. Apparitions without substance, such as ghosts and figments of the imagination, often appear in gothic stories such as _____ of the Opera."

5. The _____ performance of the Boston Symphony Orchestra for the Fourth of July fireworks show remains largely unchanged each year, always including classic patriotic songs.

6. As a parent and as a _____, I must insist that you complete all of your homework so that you can pass seventh grade math.

7. Oprah Winfrey is considered to be a great human _____, donating vast sums of money to increase the well-being of humanity and hosting a show that aims to do the same.

8. Classic tales like "Peter Pan" or "Cinderella" are examples of exceptional _____.

9. The window shades were in fact so _____ that they did not work especially well in preventing sunlight from penetrating them.

10. Stephen had a _____ dream, in which he had magical powers and could do almost anything imaginable.

11. It is dishonorable to the person to whom you are married to _____ with another.

12. Having studied with private tutors for two summers, the student accomplished a _____ leap of over 300 points in his SAT score.

13. The Aurora Borealis constitutes one of the greatest observable _____ of the earth's sky.

14. For term paper research, the _____ is a good place to start looking to find an article containing a general overview of a topic.

Exercise B

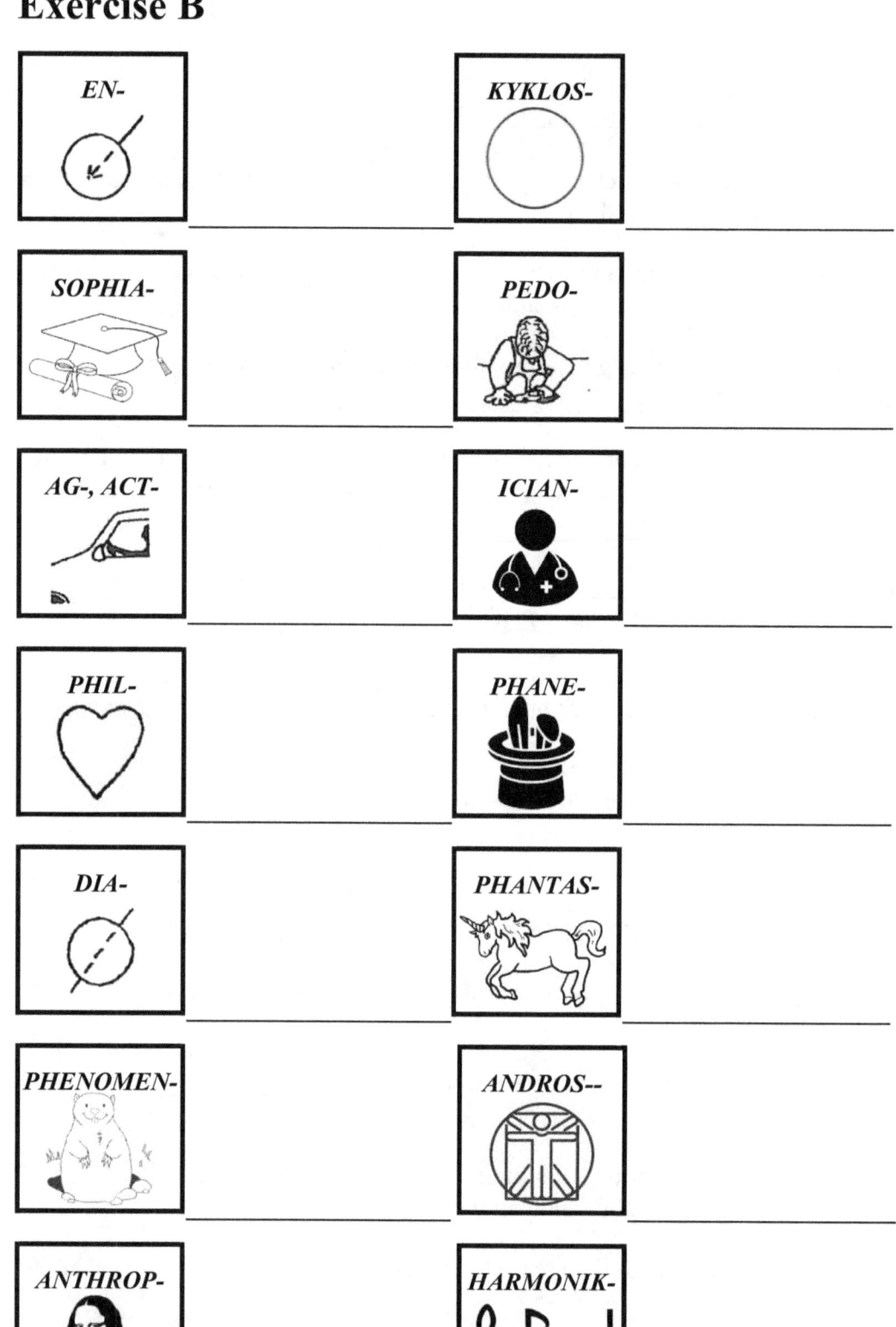

Exercise C

Fill in the crossword puzzle.

Across:
1. a thin, transparent wrapping material
3. adult who is sexually attracted to minors
4. charitable donor
6. carry on a sexual affair
7. wonderful; superb; remarkable
8. one who admires England
10. the creative imagination
11. an unseen ghost
12. baby physician
13. wanting faculty/ highly decorated
14. comprehensive reference work

Down:
2. extraordinary
4. unusual/ spectacular occurrence
5. schoolteacher
6. devoted to music
9. transparent

EXERCISE D

Match the word with the letter of its definition:

1. ___ encyclopedia
2. ___ pedophile
3. ___ pedagogue
4. ___ pediatrician
5. ___ cellophane
6. ___ diaphanous
7. ___ fantastic
8. ___ fantasy
9. ___ phantom
10. ___ phenomenal
11. ___ phenomenon
12. ___ Anglophile
13. ___ philander
14. ___ philanthropist
15. ___ philharmonic

a) unreal
b) carry on a sexual affair
c) unusual/ spectacular occurrence
d) one who admires England
e) a thin, transparent wrapping material
f) physician who treats babies and children
g) the creative imagination
h) a ghost
i) charitable donor
j) devoted to music
k) transparent
l) schoolteacher
m) adult who is sexually attracted to kids
n) wonderful
o) comprehensive research book

Lesson XXII

Agoraphobia

Definition: **n.** an abnormal fear of open or public places

Sentence: A recluse stays secluded from other people, possibly because of <u>agoraphobia</u> – fear of mingling outdoors with others in the marketplace.

Arachnophobia

Definition: **n.** an abnormal fear of spiders

Sentence: The <u>arachnophobic</u> fear of creepy-crawly creatures like spiders is a natural human response based on evolutionary experience.

Phoneme

Definition: **n.** the smallest phonetic unit in a language that is capable of conveying a distinction in meaning

Sentence: The 'b' in 'bat' or the 'p' in 'pat' exemplify English <u>phonemes</u> that create a distinction in meaning.

Phonetic

Definition: **adj.** representing the sounds of speech with a set of distinct symbols, each designating a single sound: *phonetic spelling*

Sentence: The 'ough' sound in English has various pronunciations, so the dictionary gives <u>phonetic</u> spelling or sound indicators to differentiate the 'ough' in 'cough' from the 'ough' in 'dough,' or the 'ough' in 'through.'

Phonics

Definition: **n.** a method of teaching elementary reading and spelling based on the phonetic interpretation of ordinary spelling

Sentence: <u>Phonics</u> is a teaching method for reading that relies on assembling individual sound units of words rather than whole-word recognition.

Phonograph

Definition: **n.** a machine that reproduces sound by means of a stylus in contact with a grooved rotating disk

Sentence: Thomas Edison's first sound recorder was a <u>phonograph</u> consisting of a sound-vibration-inscribed foil wrapped around a turning wax cylinder.

		 *PHON-* sound, voice	 *LOGOS-* word, speech, study

Phonology

Definition: **n.** the study of speech sounds in language or a language with reference to their distribution and patterning and to tacit rules governing pronunciation

Sentence: Because English orthography is only remotely related to <u>phonology</u>, ESL/ELL students have difficulty mastering pronunciation of printed words.

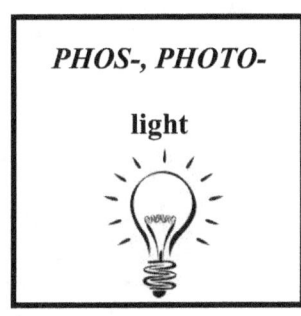 *PHOS-, PHOTO-* light

 *PHER-* to bring

Phosphorous

Definition: **n.** a highly reactive, poisonous, nonmetallic element occurring naturally in phosphate minerals

Sentence: The <u>phosphorous</u> content of certain plankton, deep-dwelling marine creatures, and insects such as fireflies causes them to emit an endothermic glow against a dark background, the glow called phosphorescence.

 *PHOS-, PHOTO-* light

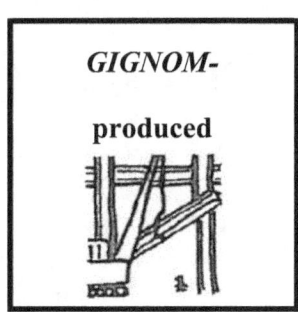 *GIGNOM-* produced

Photogenic

Definition: **adj.** attractive as a subject for photography; caused or produced by light

Sentence: Fashion models are necessarily <u>photogenic</u> in that they must appear naturally beauteous on magazine photo covers.

Photograph

Definition: **n.** an image, especially a positive print, recorded by a camera and reproduced on a photosensitive surface; to take a photograph of

Sentence: The first <u>photograph</u> was produced in 1826 by light rays entering through a pinhole in the blinds of a darkened room ('camera obscura') and striking a light-sensitive varnish to recreate the exterior landscape.

Photon

Definition: **n.** the quantum of electromagnetic energy, regarded as a discrete particle having zero mass, no electric charge, and an indefinitely long lifetime.

Sentence: Einstein proposed that light is emitted in discrete chunks or packets of energy called <u>photons</u> as mathematically described by Max Planck.

Photosynthetic

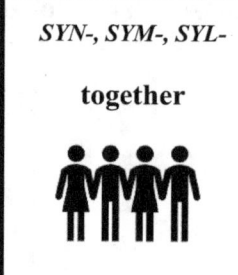

Definition: **n.** the process in green plants and certain other organisms by which carbohydrates are synthesized from carbon dioxide and water using light as an energy source; most forms of photosynthesis release oxygen as a byproduct

Sentence: Plant <u>photosynthesis</u> – the process converting photons, CO2, and water into carbohydrate plant food – has not yet been duplicated in the laboratory.

Pneumatic

PNEUM-

lung, air, gas

Definition:	**adj.** of or relating to air or other gases
Sentence:	Early automobiles used solid rubber tires; in 1888, Dunlop patented the first <u>pneumatic</u> hollow rubber tube filled with air that smoothed the ride.

Pneumonia

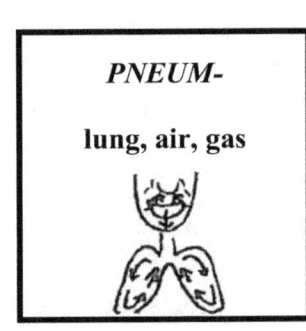

PNEUM-

lung, air, gas

Definition:	**n.** an acute or chronic disease marked by inflammation of the lungs and caused by viruses, bacteria, or other microorganisms and sometimes by physical and chemical irritants.
Sentence:	Thomas Mann's novel *The Magic Mountain* depicts teenaged Hans Castorp's long, maturing stay at a Swiss sanatorium for <u>pneumonia</u> and tuberculosis patients before he is sent to the front in WWI.

Exercise A

1. The letter arrangement "telefone" is clearly a _____ spelling of the word telephone, the "f" representing the sounds in place of the correct spelling.

2. Please do not take any _____s of this old painting as many flashes of cameras over time could cause the paint to fade.

3. My great grandmother refuses to discard her outdated _____ and to replace it with a modern CD player.

4. Though I am not familiar with the _____ of the German language, to my ear the language sounds grating and harsh.

5. If a plant does not receive direct sunlight, its ability to engage in the process of _____ may be hindered, and consequently the plant may not survive.

6. A terrible cough can worsen and turn into a serious condition like _____.

7. Partially provoked because of the public shootings of several presidents and congressional figures, the Senator developed _____ and refused to walk alone down the crowded streets of D.C.

8. The quaint village was so _____ that it attracted many visitors and movie directors.

9. Air conditioners, bicycle pumps, and hair dryers are _____ devices often found in households.

10. Often referred to as tiny "packets" of energy or light, _____s are emitted when an electron jumps down one or more quantized energy levels, thereby releasing energy and producing electromagnetic radiation.

11. _____, the elemental form of the primary ingredient in phosphates, is very reactive and highly poisonous outside of its naturally occurring compounds.

12. Those possessing a severe case of _____ are terrified if they encounter a tarantula or black widow spider.

13. _____ is a subject taught in elementary school that helps pupils to speak and to spell based on words' sounds.

Exercise B

Exercise C

Fill in the crossword puzzle.

Across:
2. the quantum of electromagnetic energy
4. relating to air
6. inflammation of the lungs
7. fear of spiders
8. method of teaching reading and spelling
9. affecting the lungs
10. fear of open spaces
11. a highly reactive element
12. symbols representing sounds of speech

Down:
1. attractive in photographs
2. machine that reproduces sound
3. smallest phonetic unit
5. study of speech sounds in language
6. a positive print of an image
7. fear of water
9. process by which plants synthesize carbohydrates

EXERCISE D

Match the word with the letter of its definition:

1. ___ arachnophobia
2. ___ aquaphobia
3. ___ agoraphobia
4. ___ phoneme
5. ___ phonetics
6. ___ phonics
7. ___ phonograph
8. ___ phonology
9. ___ phosphorous
10. ___ photogenic
11. ___ photograph
12. ___ photon
13. ___ photosynthesis
14. ___ pneumatic
15. ___ pneumonia
16. ___ pneumonic

a) fear of open spaces
b) smallest phonetic unit
c) fear of spiders
d) attractive in photographs
e) study of speech sounds in language
f) machine that reproduces sound
g) a highly reactive element
h) symbols representing sounds of speech
i) method of teaching reading and spelling
j) fear of water
k) relating to air
l) inflammation of the lungs
m) affecting the lungs
n) quantum of electromagnetic energy
o) positive print of an image
p) process by which plants synthesize carbohydrates

Lesson XXIII

Podiatrist

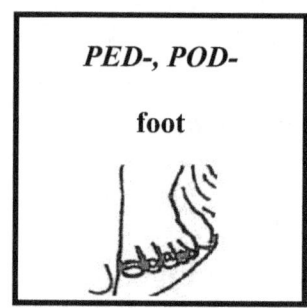

Definition:	**n.** a physician who specializes in the diagnosis, treatment, and prevention of diseases of the human foot
Sentence:	Bunions, corns, ingrown toenails, and related foot ailments are the specialty of doctors called <u>podiatrists</u>.

Podium

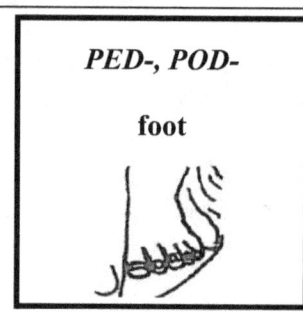

Definition:	**n.** an elevated platform, as for an orchestra conductor or public speaker
Sentence:	The environmentalist used the slagheap of a mine as a <u>podium</u> for his diatribe against corporate polluters.

Psyche

Definition:	**n.** the spirit, mind or soul; the goddess
Sentence:	The goddess <u>Psyche</u> is the maiden representing spirit or soul in psychology, which is the science that investigates behavior and mental processes or disturbances

Arthropod

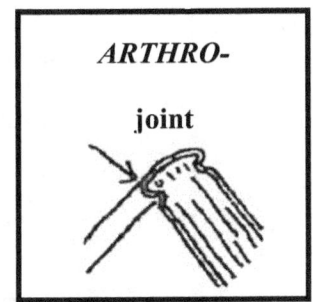
ARTHRO-
joint

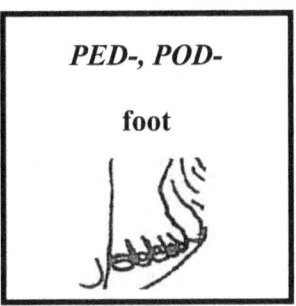
PED-, POD-
foot

Definition: **n.** any of numerous invertebrate animals of the phylum Arthropoda, including the insects, crustaceans, arachnids, and myriapods, that are characterized by a chitinous exoskeleton and a segmented body to which jointed appendages are articulated in pairs

Sentence: The largest group of animals on earth, with their hard exoskeleton shells, arthropods such as cockroaches make a crunching sound when crushed.

Psychedelic

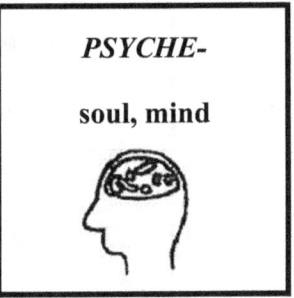
PSYCHE-
soul, mind

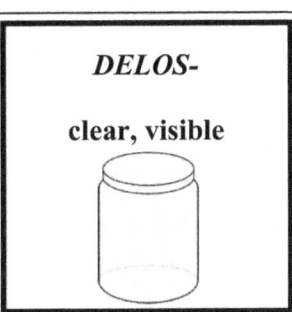
DELOS-
clear, visible

Definition: **adj.** of, characterized by, or generating hallucinations, distortions of perception, altered states of awareness, and occasionally states resembling psychosis

Sentence: A psychedelic drug such as the hallucinogen LSD or peyote can induce kaleidoscopic visions of rainbows.

Psychotic

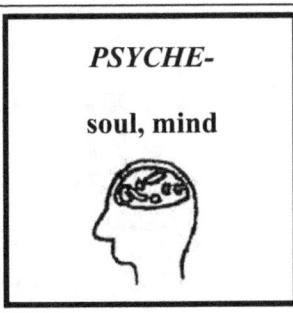
PSYCHE-
soul, mind

Definition: **adj.** of, relating to, or affected by psychosis or a loss of contact with reality

Sentence: Prisoners of war are made irrational, delusional, and psychotic by deprivation of sleep and dream time.

Psychoneurosis

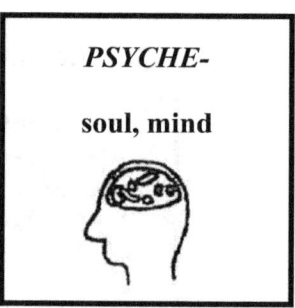
PSYCHE-
soul, mind

NEURON-
string

Definition: **n.** any of various mental or emotional disorders, such as hypochondria or neurasthenia, arising from no apparent organic origin and involving symptoms such as insecurity, anxiety, depression, and irrational fears, but without psychotic symptoms such as delusions or hallucinations

Sentence: The term psychoneurosis has been simplified to 'neurosis' or a malady or affliction with mental or emotional rather than physical causation.

Hydrothermal

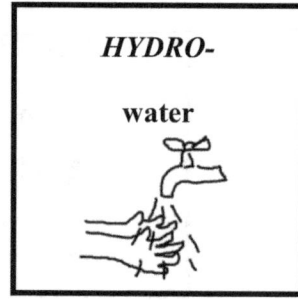
HYDRO-
water

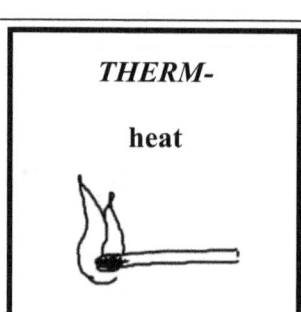
THERM-
heat

Definition: **adj.** of or relating to hot water

Sentence: The entire country of Iceland, situated over hot underground volcanic springs, is heated by hydrothermal energy.

Isotherm

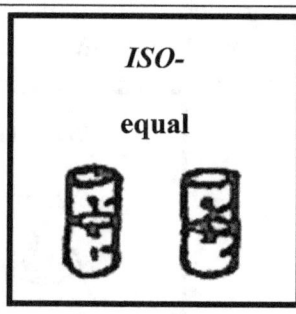
ISO-
equal

THERM-
heat

Definition: **n.** a line drawn on a weather map or chart linking all points of equal or constant temperature

Sentence: The linear connections of regions on a weather map called isotherms indicate regions of equal temperature.

Thermal

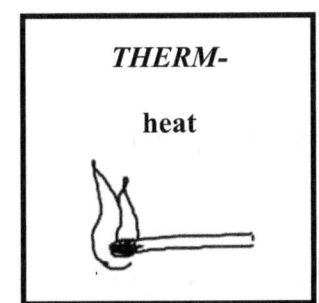

THERM-
heat

Definition: **adj., n.** of, relating to, using, producing, or caused by heat; in meteorology, a rising current of warm air

Sentence: The earth's ozone layer forms a <u>thermal-</u> or heat-trapping blanket that protects creatures below from harmful extraterrestrial ultra-violet radiation.

Dichotomy

DICHO-
two

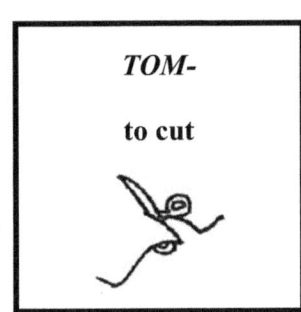

TOM-
to cut

Definition: **n.** division into two usually contradictory parts or opinions

Sentence: The philosopher Descartes insisted on the discrete separation of mind or spirit and body, a <u>dichotomy</u> of human being, which persists as the fundament of religions.

Lobotomy

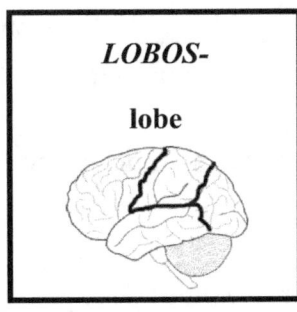

LOBOS-
lobe

TOM-
to cut

Definition: **n.** surgical incision into the frontal lobe of the brain to sever one or more nerve tracts, a technique formerly used to treat certain mental disorders

Sentence: Rarely performed today, a <u>lobotomy</u> or severance (cutting) of the frontal lobes of the brain was once a standard surgical procedure for severely disturbed mental patients.

Exercise A

1. _____ art aims to depict the workings and visions of the psyche that reflect spiritual, and drug experiences.

2. Each of the three presidential candidates will step up to the _____ and deliver a three to five minute persuasive speech.

3. Repeat criminals, particularly murderers, often have deeply-rooted _____ issues that have developed since childhood and have since been untreated.

4. Zoloft is a drug engineered to help to treat many mind disorders and forms of _____, particuarly for the use of making people feel less anxious, depressed, or ostracized.

5. Although there was a time many decades ago when some doctors would have performed a _____ to treat the patient's mental condition, medical experts today realize that it can be cured with simple medications and psychotherapy.

6. The ice hockey player Ray Borque, having contracted another case of athlete's foot, went immediately to see his _____ about treatment.

7. Yoga helps one to achieve equanimity, peacefulness, and balance within the _____.

8. It is strange that the _____ lines on that weather map depict Alaska as having the same temperature as Massachusetts.

9. One way to relieve someone of the chills of full-body frostbite is to use _____ therapy.

10. The deer will not eat insects or any other _____s of the forest; it is strictly a vegetarian.

11. Inflated by _____ expansion, the hot air balloon would shrink immediately if the flames went out, and the balloon would sink and crash.

Exercise B

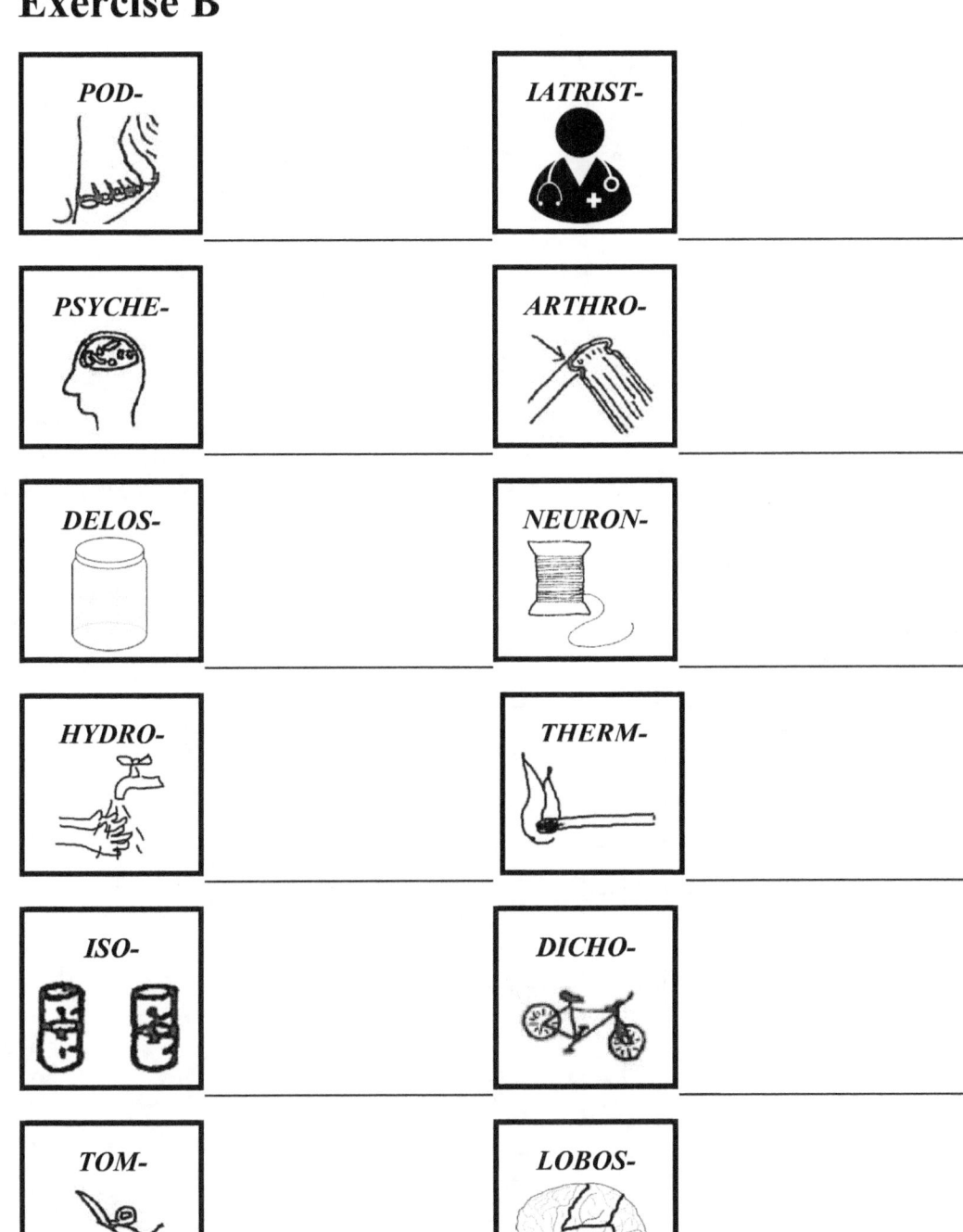

Exercise C

Fill in the crossword puzzle.

Across:
3. a group of mental diseases
6. surgical incision of the trachea to aid breathing
7. a rising current of warm air/ producing heat
9. the spirit or soul
10. elevated platform for victors or conductors
11. division into two contradictory parts

Down:
1. cutting off the frontal lobe of the brain
2. foot doctor
3. affected by psychosis
4. of hot water
5. a line on a weather map
6. a temperature or generating current measurer
8. an invertebrate having jointed appendages

13. Every modern personal computer is equipped with a _____, which engages an automatic shutoff for safety purposes when the internal temperature exceeds a certain limit.

EXERCISE D

Match the word with the letter of its definition:

1. ___ arthropod
2. ___ podiatrist
3. ___ podium
4. ___ psyche
5. ___ psychoneurosis
6. ___ psychotic
7. ___ hydrothermal
8. ___ isotherm
9. ___ thermal
10. ___ thermopile
11. ___ dichotomy
12. ___ lobotomy
13. ___ tracheotomy

a) surgical incision of the trachea to aid breathing
b) cutting off the frontal lobe of the brain
c) affected by psychosis
d) the spirit or soul
e) elevated platform for victors, conductors, or orators
f) division into two contradictory parts
g) a temperature or generating current measurer
h) a line on a weather map
i) a group of mental diseases
j) a rising current of warm air/ producing heat
k) foot doctor
l) an invertebrate having jointed appendages
m) of hot water

Test 4

Choose the correct meaning for the underlined vocabulary word in each sentence.

1. "Featherstone's heir; that old gentleman's pride in him, and apparent fondness for him, serving in the stead of more exemplary conduct--just as when a youthful nobleman steals jewellery we call the act <u>kleptomania</u>, speak of it with a philosophical smile, and never think of his being sent to the house of correction as if he were a ragged boy who had stolen turnips."

    Middlemarch by George Eliot

    (a) intensive enthusiasm   (b) an obsessive impulse to steal   (c) disorderly
    (d) fantasies of power   (e) a pathological impulse to start fires

2. "When they struck up a frantic dance, with <u>maniacal</u> gestures, idiotic stampings, and somersaults like those of the boneless clowns in the circus."

    Round The Moon by Jules Verne

    (a) enthusiastic   (b) obsessive-compulsive   (c) wild, disorderly
    (d) powerful   (e) malodorous

3. "She could only guess at the distance she had been carried for she could not believe in the correctness of the high figures that had been piled upon the record of her <u>odometer</u>."

    The Chessmen of Mars by Edgar Rice Burroughs

    (a) mileage traversed   (b) wind velocity   (c) temperature
    (d) atmosphere   (e) speed

4. "The chief-justice was not above entering the chamber of council where Mariette held court; he cast the eye of a <u>gastronome</u> around it, and offered the advice of a past master in cookery."

    An Old Maid by Honore de Balzac

    (a) wealth manager   (b) opponent   (c) gourmet   (d) land owner
    (e) sea anemone

5. "The Nemesis of the delicate ones was creeping on apace."

The Time Machine by H.G. Wells

(a) type of infection   (b) opponent   (c) growing power   (d) insurrection
(e) source of harm or ruin

6. "If the sound of the words actually imitates the sound of the thing indicated, the effect is called Onomatopoeia."

A History of English Literature by Robert Huntington Fletcher

(a) an allusion   (b) a fictitious name
(c) a word that mimics its sound   (d) pen name   (e) a monogram

7. "But the nervousness that assailed him at the door of that inglorious haunt - a pawnshop - and the effort necessary to invent the pseudonym (which, somehow, seemed to him a necessary part of the procedure), had taken more time than he imagined: and when he returned to the billiard-room with the spoils, the bank had already closed its doors."

Tales and Fantasies by Robert Louis Stevenson

(a) hieroglyph   (b) fictitious name   (c) christening   (d) monogram
(e) letters

8. "Van Helsing had taken the key of the hall door from the bunch, and locked the door in orthodox fashion, putting the key into his pocket when he had done."

Dracula by Bram Stoker

(a) lugubrious   (b) inimical   (c) quick   (d) traditional, established
(e) contemporary

9. "Pierrat turned the handle of the screw-jack, the boot was contracted, and the unhappy girl uttered one of those horrible cries which have no orthography in any human language."

Notre-Dame de Paris by Victor Hugo

(a) writing system   (b) sounds of language   (c) bird study
(d) precedent   (e) contemporary history

10. "She had sunk into a dreary apathy and would not be roused."

Tom Sawyer by Mark Twain

(a) isolationism   (b) indifference   (c) recklessness   (d) defensiveness
(e) irreverence

11. "Thus, by divers little makeshifts, in that ingenious way which is commonly denominated "by hook and by crook," the worthy <u>pedagogue</u> got on tolerably enough, and was thought, by all who understood nothing of the labor of headwork, to have a wonderfully easy life of it."
    The Legend Of Sleepy Hollow by Washington Irving

    (a) child   (b) doctor   (c) educator   (d) student   (e) parent

12. "This phantom wore many faces, but it always had golden hair, was enveloped in a <u>diaphanous</u> cloud, and floated airily before his mind's eye in a pleasing chaos of roses, peacocks, white ponies, and blue ribbons."
    Little Women by Louisa May Alcott

    (a) opaque   (b) remarkable   (c) fanciful   (d) airy, transparent
    (e) troublesome, menacing

13. "Easily, and without correction by reason, her imagination made pictures, superb backgrounds casting a rich though <u>phantom</u> light upon the facts in the foreground."
    Night and Day by Virginia Woolf

    (a) dangerous   (b) indistinguishable   (c) farcical   (d) bright
    (e) illusional

14. "He is a man of good birth and excellent education, endowed by nature with a <u>phenomenal</u> mathematical faculty."
    Memoirs of Sherlock Holmes by Sir Arthur Conan Doyle

    (a) extraordinary   (b) imaginative   (c) ghostly   (d) superb
    (e) paranormal

15. "But she had been kept up late every night, and put upon an unlimited allowance of gin-and-water from infancy, to prevent her growing tall, and perhaps this system of training had produced in the infant phenomenon these additional <u>phenomena</u>."
    The Life and Adventures of Nicholas Nickleby by Charles Dickens

    (a) experiences   (b) imagination   (c) inconveniences   (d) superb
    (e) occurrence perceived by the senses

16. "Do you think I'm going to let you hustle for wages while I <u>philander</u> in the regions of high art?"
    The Four Million by O. Henry

    (a) have a love affair   (b) persevere   (c) become wealthy
    (d) make charitable donations   (e) become a specialist

17. "You remind me of a story Harry told me about a certain philanthropist who spent twenty years of his life in trying to get some grievance redressed, or some unjust law altered--I forget exactly what it was."
    The Picture Of Dorian Gray by Oscar Wilde

    (a) lover (b) Anglophile (c) defendant (d) wealthy benefactor
    (e) musician

18. "It must have been largely in his own despite that he was squeezed into something called a Readership of phonetics there."
    Pygmalion by George Bernard Shaw

    (a) language units (b) system of sounds in speech (c) abnormal fears
    (d) a method of spelling (e) the study of languages

19. "The phial, to which I next turned my attention, might have been about half full of a blood-red liquor, which was highly pungent to the sense of smell and seemed to me to contain phosphorus and some volatile ether."
    Dr. Jekyll and Mr. Hyde by Robert Louis Stevenson

    (a) an attraction to light (b) a positive print (c) a poisonous, non-metallic element
    (d) electromagnetic energy (e) an attractive subject

20. "Over the bookcase hung a photograph of the Tragic Theatre at Pompeii, which he had given me from his collection."
    My Antonia by Willa Cather

    (a) attraction to light (b) printed picture (c) account
    (d) piece of memorabilia (e) video screen

21. "It's the principle of the pneumatic instantaneous shutter for a camera lens."
    The Secret Agent by Joseph Conrad

    (a) relating to the lungs (b) relating to using air (c) pulmonary
    (d) acute repertory disease (e) relating to hearing

22. "Marry them before Lent; I may catch pneumonia any winter now, and I want to give the wedding-breakfast."
    The Age of Innocence by Edith Wharton

    (a) migraine headache (b) aerobic problem (c) physical injury
    (d) acute respiratory disease (e) cardiac palpitations

23. "He asserted that he was going to pick more than anyone that day, but mother; of course no one could pick so much as mother; that reminded him of the trials which Aphrodite put upon the curious Psyche, and he began to tell his children the story of her love for the unseen bridegroom."

Of Human Bondage by W. Somerset Maugham

(a) Greek goddess of love and beauty   (b) Roman goddess of love and beauty
(c) Greek mythological princess   (d) son of Venus   (e) God of warfare

24. "Another thing, Trillium Covert and Madrono Ranch were happily situated in a narrow thermal belt, so that in the frosty mornings of winter the temperature was always several degrees higher than in the rest of the valley."

The Valley of the Moon by Jack London

(a) device to measure temperature
(b) lines on a weather map representing temperature   (c) rising current of warm air
(d) relating to hot water   (e) odometer

25. "His voice had a genuine pathos now, and his large brown hands perceptibly trembled."

Far from the Madding Crowd by Thomas Hardy

(a) tradition   (b) respectability   (c) obsessive impulse
(d) enthusiasm   (e) pity

Answer Key

Lesson I

EXERCISE A

1. asylum
2. anomaly
3. anarchy
4. anesthesia
5. amoral
6. apnea
7. atrophy
8. atheism
9. atypical
10. anonymous
11. amorphous
12. anemia
13. anecdote
14. aseptic
15. atoms
16. asymptomatic

EXERCISE B

1. A-, AN- without, lacking, not
2. MORES- custom
3. MORPHE- from, shape, beauty
4. ARKHE- ruler, rules
5. EKDOTOS- published, given out
6. HAIMA- blood cells
7. AISTHESIS- sensation, feeling
8. ODYNE- pain
9. OMALOS- even, normal
10. ONYMA- name
11. POLITIKOS- political
12. PNEIN- breathing
13. SEPSIS- rotten
14. SYLON- right of seizure
15. SYMPTOMA- indications
16. THEOS- god
17. TOM- to cut
18. TROPHIE- food, nourishment
19. TYPIKOS- impression

Lesson II

EXERCISE A

1. anatomy
2. authentic
3. anachronisms
4. automatic
5. analgesic
6. amphibious
7. anagram
8. automobile
9. anaphora
10. autopsy
11. anabasis
12. autobiography
13. autograph
14. analysis
15. autonomous
16. autocrats
17. automatons
18. amphitheater

EXERCISE B

1. AMPHI- both, about
2. BIOS- life
3. THEATRON- theater
4. ANA- up, against, re-
5. BASIS- go, climb, march
6. CHRONOS- time
7. MATOS- moving
8. GRAM- word, letter
9. ALGEIS- pain
10. LYEIN- to loosen
11. FER- to carry, bring
12. TOM- to cut
13. AUTO- self
14. HENTES- doer
15. GRAPH- to write, to sign
16. OPSIS- sight
17. KRATOS- power, ruling
18. NOMOS- law
19. MOBILE- movable

Lesson III

EXERCISE A

1. antidote
2. antiseptic
3. antibodies
4. apogee
5. aphorism
6. apology
7. antibiotic
8. apostles
9. apocalyptic
10. antagonist
11. apocryphal
12. antipathy
13. antonym
14. apostate
15. antithetical

EXERCISE B

1. ANTI- against
2. AGONIST- contend, compete
3. ONOMA- name
4. BIOS- life
5. BODIG- body
6. DOTOS- to give
7. PATHOS- suffer, feel
8. SEP- rotten
9. THETIKOS- to contend
10. HORIZ- define, limit
11. APO- away, from, out of
12. KALYPT- to cover
13. GEO- earth
14. KRYPT- to hide
15. LOGOS- word, speech, study
16. ISTAMAI- stand, rise, revolt
17. STELL- to send

Lesson IV

EXERCISE A

1. diagram
2. dystopia
3. cataract
4. diameter
5. diagnosed
6. diadem
7. cathode
8. cataclysm
9. cathedral
10. catacombs
11. diagonal
12. dyslexia
13. catalog
14. dialect
15. dysphoria
16. dialogue
17. dysfunction

EXERCISE B

1. CATA- down, wholly, against
2. ARRASS- to strike, to smite
3. KLYZ- to wash away
4. TOMBAS- tomb
5. LOGOS- word, speech, study
6. HEDRA- seat
7. GIGNOSK- to know
8. GRAPH- to write, to sign
9. METRON- measure
10. GONIA- angle
11. LEG- to speak
12. DYS- difficult, faulty
13. HODOS- way, path

14. DIA- through, across
15. DEIN- to bind
16. KATHAIR- to cleanse
17. PHER- to bear
18. TOPOS- place
19. FUNGIO- to perform

Lesson V

EXERCISE A

1. exoskeleton
2. exoteric
3. exothermic
4. endophytes
5. exocrine
6. endoskeleton
7. endocrine
8. exotic
9. endothermic
10. endogenous
11. exogenous

EXERCISE B

1. ENDO- within
2. EXO- out of, outside
3. KRIN- distinguish, judge
4. GENUS- group, progeny
5. SKELL- supporting framework
6. THERM- heat
7. PHYT- plant

Lesson VI

EXERCISE A

1. eulogize
2. epidemic
3. hemisphere
4. euphemism
5. epilogue
6. epicenter
7. hemiplegia
8. ephemeral
9. epidermis
10. euphonious
11. epitaph
12. euphoria
13. eugenics

EXERCISE B

1. EPI- upon, in accordance
2. HEMERA- day
3. DEM- people
4. KENTRON- center
5. DERMA- skin
6. PLESS- to strike, to blow
7. TAPHOS- tomb
8. EU- well, good
9. PHEMISM- speech, fame
10. GENOS- race, people
11. PHER- to bear
12. PHON- sound, voice
13. HEMI- half
14. SPHAIR- sphere

Lesson VII

EXERCISE A

1. heteroclite
2. homonyms
3. homology
4. homocentric
5. heterodox
6. homogeneous
7. homochromatic

8. heteronyms
9. homosexual
10. heterogeneous
11. heterology
12. heterosexual
13. homophony
14. heterochromatic

EXERCISE B

1. HOMO- same, similar
2. GENOS- race, kind
3. HETERO- different
4. LOGOS- word, speech, study
5. ONOMA- name
6. SEX- gender
7. DOXA- opinion, belief
8. PHON- sound, voice

Lesson VIII

EXERCISE A

1. hypertension
2. hyperactive
3. hypothermia
4. hyperbole
5. hypercritical
6. hypersensitive
7. hyperglycemia
8. hypotention
9. hyperthermia
10. hypothesis
11. hypoglycemia
12. hypodermic

EXERCISE B

1. GLYKYS- sweet
2. HAIMA- blood
3. HYPO- under, insufficient
4. TEIN- to stretch
5. THERM- heat
6. BALL- to throw
7. AG-, ACT- to drive, urge, act

8. HYPER- over, excessive
9. KRIN- distinguish, judge
10. SENS- to think, to feel
11. DERMA- skin
12. TITHEM- to place, assume

Lesson IX

EXERCISE A

1. microeconomics
2. micrometer
3. microbes
4. microsecond
5. microwave
6. macroscopic
7. microcosm
8. microfilm
9. microscopic
10. macrocosm
11. macroeconomics
12. microorganisms

EXERCISE B

1. MACRO- large, long
2. COSMOS- universe
3. OIKONOMIC- manage a household
4. SCOP- to examine, to see
5. BIOS- life
6. MICRO- small, minute
7. FILM- skin, membrane
8. METRON- measure

9. ORGANIZOM- assemble complex thing
10. SECUNDA- second
11. WAVE- wave

Lesson X

EXERCISE A

1. metamorphosis
2. Neolithic
3. neoclassical
4. method
5. metaphor
6. misogyny
7. misandry
8. neologism
9. misanthrope
10. neophyte
11. metabolism
12. neoteric
13. metaphysics

EXERCISE B

1. A-, AN- without, lacking, not
2. MNE- memory
3. META- after, between, with
4. BALL- to throw
5. MORPHE- form, shape, beauty
6. PHER- to bear
7. PHUSIKA- nature
8. HODOS- way, path
9. MIS- hate
10. ANTHROP- person
11. GYNY- woman
12. CLASS- first class
13. LOGOS- word, speech, study
14. LITHOS- stone
15. ANDROS- man
16. PHYT- plant
17. NEO- new

Lesson XI

EXERCISE A

1. polygamy
2. monosyllabic
3. monarchy
4. polyglot
5. monocles
6. polysyllabic
7. polyandrous
8. monogamy
9. monotheism
10. monogram
11. polygons
12. polyphonic
13. monotonous
14. polytheism
15. monolithic

EXERCISE B

1. LITOS- single, simple, meager
2. GAM- marriage
3. POLY- many
4. SYL- together
5. THEOS- god
6. OCULUS- eye
7. ARCHE- beginning, rule
8. GRAM- word, letter
9. LITHOS- stone
10. MONO- single
11. TONOS- tone
12. POLEMOS- war
13. ANDROS- man
14. GLOT- language, tongues
15. GONIA- angles
16. PHON- sound, voice
17. LAMB- to take

Lesson XII

EXERCISE A

1. pancreas
2. pandemic
3. perimeter
4. parable
5. parasol
6. paradigm
7. pantheon
8. pandemonium
9. parallel
10. parascopes
11. pantomimed
12. paranoid
13. perigee
14. paragon

EXERCISE B

1. PAN- all, whole, complete
2. KREAS- flesh
3. DEM- people
4. DAEMON- spirit, lesser god
5. THEOS- god
6. MIM- imitator
7. PARA- beside, near, beyond
8. BALL- to throw
9. DEIGMA- pattern, to show
10. AG- to produce, create
11. NOUS- mind
12. ALLEL- each other
13. SOL- sun
14. PERI- around, about
15. GEO- earth
16. METRON- measure
17. SCOP- to examine, to see

Lesson XIII

EXERCISE A

1. protocol
2. symmetry
3. synchronize
4. synergy
5. syllabus
6. synonym
7. synthetic
8. symposium
9. synagogue
10. prototype
11. sympathetic
12. syllogism
13. synapses
14. symbiosis
15. syntax
16. protozoans

EXERCISE B

1. SYN- together
2. PROTO- first
3. KOLLEMA- glued together
4. TYPOS- type, form
5. ERGON- work
6. ZOA- animal life
7. LAMBAN- to take
8. LOGOS- word, speech, study
9. BIOS- life
10. METRON- measure
11. PATHOS- suffer, feel
12. POSIS- drinking
13. AG- to lead, to compel
14. APT- to connect
15. CHRON- time
16. ONOMA- name
17. TAX- to arrange
18. TITHE- to put, to place

Lesson XIV

EXERCISE A

1. patriarch
2. biology
3. biography
4. archangel

5. oligarch
6. asteroid
7. bioluminescence
8. biological
9. archenemy
10. biosphere
11. astronomical
12. asterisk
13. astrology
14. matriarch

EXERCISE B

1. ARCHE- beginning, rule
2. GRAPH- to write, to sign
3. ANGEL- messenger
4. LOGOS- word, speech, study
5. AMIC- friend
6. MATER- mother
7. OLIG- few, little
8. PATER- father
9. IN- not
10. ASTER- star
11. EIDOS- form, shape, image
12. NOMOS- law
13. BIOS- life
14. LUMIN- to light up

Lesson XV

EXERCISE A

1. cardiologist
2. cosmopolitan
3. aristocracy
4. chronicle
5. cardiogram
6. cardiovascular
7. bureaucracy
8. plutocracy
9. chronic
10. democracy
11. chronological
12. cosmology
13. cardiac arrest
14. cosmic

EXERCISE B

1. CARDIO- heart
2. STARE- to stand
3. LOGOS- word, speech, study
4. VASCUL- vessel
5. GRAM- word, letter
6. CHRON- time
7. COSM- universe
8. AC-, AD- to, toward, very
9. CRACY- rule, power
10. ARISTO- best
11. BUREAU- desk
12. DEM- people
13. PLOUTOS- wealth
14. THEO- god

Lesson XVI

EXERCISE A

1. taxidermist
2. demagogue
3. democratic
4. demonologist
5. dermatologist
6. dermis
7. demographic
8. endemic
9. dermatitis

EXERCISE B

1. DEM- people
2. AG-, ACT- drive, urge, act
3. EN- within
4. LOGOS- word, speech, study
5. DAEMON- spirit, lesser god
6. CRAT- rule, power
7. GRAPH- write, to sign
8. DERMA- skin
9. ITIS- inflammation
10. TAX- arrange

Lesson XVII

EXERCISE A

1. genealogy
2. genetics
3. Idol
4. kaleidoscopes
5. geology
6. geocentric
7. geography
8. genus
9. idyll
10. tabloid
11. android
12. geometry
13. Genesis
14. Generation
15. genius

EXERCISE B

1. ANDROS- man
2. EIDOS- form, shape, image
3. TABLET- tablet
4. KALOS- beautiful
5. SCOP- to examine, to see
6. GEO- earth
7. KENTRON- center
8. GRAPH- to write, to sign
9. METRON- measure
10. GEN- generation, race
11. LOGOS- word, speech, study
12. GENOS- race, kind
13. GENIUS- guardian spirit

Lesson XVIII

EXERCISE A

1. grammar
2. calligraphy
3. graffiti
4. ideology
5. prologue
6. hemorrhage
7. cryptogram
8. tautologies
9. hemoglobin
10. hemorrhoids

EXERCISE B

1. KALOS- beautiful
2. GRAPH- to write, to sign
3. KRYPTOS- hidden
4. GRAM- word, letter
5. HAIMA- blood
6. GLOB- small sphere
7. RHAGE- breaking
8. RHEIN- to flow
9. IDEA- idea
10. LOGOS- word, speech, study
11. PRO- before
12. TAUTO- same

Lesson XIX

EXERCISE A

1. megalomaniac
2. morphology
3. kleptomania
4. mania
5. isomorphism
6. maniacal
7. economic
8. pyromania
9. barometer
10. thermometer
11. meter
12. nemesis
13. agronomy
14. odometer
15. speedometer

EXERCISE B

1. ANTHROP- person
2. MORPHE- form, shape, beauty
3. KLEPTO- thief
4. MANIA- madness, enthusiasm
5. MEGA- great
6. PYRO- fire
7. BAROS- weight, pressure
8. METRON- measure
9. HODOS- way, path
10. OIKOS- house
11. THERM- heat
12. ISO- equal
13. NOMOS- law
14. AGRO- field

Lesson XX

EXERCISE A

1. acronym
2. pseudonym
3. orthodontist
4. onomatopoeia
5. orthopedist
6. orthodox
7. apathy
8. psychopath
9. empathy
10. orthography
11. telepathy

EXERCISE B

1. ACROS- topmost, sharp
2. ONOMA- name
3. POIEIN- to make
4. PSEUDO- false
5. ORTHO- right, straight
6. DENT- tooth
7. DOXA- opinion, belief
8. GRAPH- to write, to sign
9. PED- foot
10. PATHOS- suffer, feel
11. A-, AN- without, lacking, not
12. EN- in, into
13. TELE- far off
14. PSYCH- soul, mind

Lesson XXI

EXERCISE A

1. pediatrician
2. cellophane
3. pedophile

4. phantom
5. philharmonic
6. pedagogue
7. philanthropist
8. fantasy
9. diaphanous
10. fantastic
11. philander
12. phenomenal
13. phenomenon
14. encyclopedia

EXERCISE B

1. EN- in, into
2. KYKLOS- circle
3. SOPHIA- knowledge, wisdom
4. PEDO- child
5. AG-, ACT- to drive, act, urge
6. ICIAN- one who cures
7. PHIL- love
8. PHANE- appear, show
9. DIA- through, across
10. PHANTAS- imagine, make visible
11. PHENOMEN- an appearance
12. ANDROS- man
13. ANTHROP- human
14. HARMONIK- musical

Lesson XXII

EXERCISE A

1. phonetic
2. photograph
3. phonograph
4. phonology
5. photosynthesis
6. pneumonia
7. agoraphobia
8. photogenic
9. pneumatic
10. photon
11. phosphorous
12. arachnophobia
13. phonics

EXERCISE B

1. AGORA- open space city market
2. PHOBIA- fear, terror
3. ARACHNE- spider
4. PHON- sound, voice
5. GRAPH- to write, to sign
6. LOGOS- word, speech, study
7. PHOTO- light
8. PHER- to bring
9. GIGNOM- produced
10. SYN- together
11. TITHE- to put, to place
12. PNEUM- lung, air, gas

Lesson XXIII

EXERCISE A

1. psychedelic
2. podium
3. psychotic
4. psychoneurosis
5. lobotomy
6. podiatrist
7. psyche
8. isotherm
9. hydrothermal
10. arthropod
11. thermal

EXERCISE B

1. POD- foot
2. IATRIST- one who cures
3. PSYCHE- soul, mind
4. ANTHRO- joint
5. DELOS- clear, see through
6. NEURON- string
7. HYDRO- water
8. THERM- heat
9. ISO- equal
10. DICHO- two
11. TOM- to cut
12. LOBOS- lobe

Exercise C Answers

Lesson I

Across:
1. atom
2. apnea
5. anomaly
8. anesthesia
9. anemia
10. anarchy
12. anosmia
13. anecdote
14. amoral

Down:
1. anhydrous
2. anonymous
3. asymptomatic
4. atrophy
5. anoxia
6. aseptic
7. asylum
8. atheism
11. amorphous
12. asyndeton
15. atypical

Lesson II

Across:
2. analysis
4. autocrat
6. amphibious
8. anagram
9. anatomy
10. autopsy
11. amphitheater
13. analgesic
14. anachronism
15. authentic

Down:
1. autograph
2. automobile
3. automatic
5. autonomous
6. anaphora
7. autobiography
8. anabasis
12. amphibolous
13. automaton

Lesson III

Across:
1. antibiotic
2. aphorism
3. apostate
6. apocalyptic
8. antagonist
9. apoplectic
10. antibody
11. apogee
12. apology
13. antidote
14. apocryphal

Down:
1. apotropaic
2. antonym
4. apostle
5. antipathy
6. antiseptic
7. aphelion
13. antithetical

Lesson IV

Across:
3. dystrophy
5. dysfunction
6. cathode
8. diacritical
10. dysphoria
11. dialect
12. cataclysm
13. diadem
15. cathedral

Down:
1. cataract
2. diagonal
3. dyslexia
4. diagnose
7. dialogue
8. diagram
9. catarrh
10. dystopia
13. diatribe
14. catacomb
15. catalog
16. diameter

Lesson V

Across:
1. exogenous
2. exosomosis
3. endoskeleton
4. endoderm
6. endophyte
7. endogenous
8. endoparasite
9. endocrine
10. endogamy
11. exocrine
12. endocarditis
13. endosmosis

Down:
1. exoskeleton
5. exoteric
6. exothermic
8. exogamy
10. exotic
11. endothermic

Lesson VI

Across:
1. epicenter
2. eulogize
3. euphonious
5. epilogue
7. hemiplegia
9. euphemism
10. epitaph
11. ephemeral
13. hemicycle

Down:
1. epidermis
4. hemialgia
6. epicurean
7. hemisphere
8. epidemic
9. euphoria
11. eugenics
12. eupepsia

Lesson VII

Across:
3. homosexual
9. heterogeneous
11. heterodox
12. heterosexual
13. heterology

Down:
1. homology
2. homonym
4. heteroclite
5. heterochromatic
6. homophonic
7. homology
8. homocentric
9. heteronym
10. homochromatic

Lesson VIII

Across:
1. hyperthermia
3. hyperactive
4. hypothesis
9. hyperglycemia
10. hypersensitive
12. hyperopia

Down:
2. hypertension
5. hyperbole
6. hypercritical
7. hypodermic
8. hypotension
9. hypothermia
11. hyperemia

Lesson IX

Across:
1. microcosm
3. microwave
4. microfilm
6. microdont
7. macrocosm
9. micrometer
10. microscopic
11. microbe
12. macroscopic

Down:
2. microeconomics
3. macroeconomics
5. microsurgery
6. macrograph
8. microsecond
9. macron
11. microorganism

Lesson X

Across:
6. neolithic
8. misanthrope
11. misoneism
12. misogamy

Down:
1. metamorphosis
2. neoteric
3. metamorphosis
4. method
5. neoclassical
6. neologism
7. metaphysics
9. neophyte
10. misandry
11. metaphor
12. misogyny
13. misology

Lesson XI

Across:
2. polysyllabic
3. monotheism
5. monocle
7. polytheism
9. polygon
10. polyandrous
14. monotonous
15. monolithic

Down:
1. monosyllabic
4. monogamy
6. monarchy
7. polyglot
8. monochrome
11. polyphonic
12. monogram
13. polygamy

Lesson XII

Across:
4. periscope
6. pandemonium
7. pantheon
8. parable
9. paragon
10. perimeter
11. parasol
12. periphrasis
13. perigee

Down:
1. paranoid
2. pandect
3. peripatetic
5. pancreas
6. parallel
8. pantomime
11. paradigm
12. pandemic

Lesson XIII

Across:
3. syllogism
5. synchronize
7. symmetry
8. protozoan
9. proboscis
10. prototype
11. syllabus
13. synergy
14. sympathy

Down:
1. protocol
2. symbiosis
4. synonym
5. synthetic
6. symposium
7. synapse
12. synagogue
13. syntax

Lesson XIV

Across:
1. oligarch
3. biological
4. asterisk
5. patriarch
6. biosphere
8. biography
10. archangel
12. matriarch
13. bioluminescence

Down:
2. asteroid
3. biology
7. archenemy
9. archaeology
10. astrology
11. astronomical

Exercise D Answers

Lesson I

1. e   11. l
2. h   12. i
3. r   13. c
4. n   14. f
5. o   15. d
6. s   16. j
7. q   17. a
8. t   18. g
9. m   19. k
10. p   20. b

Lesson II

1. f
2. o
3. k
4. c
5. i
6. h
7. d
8. a
9. m
10. s
11. n
12. p
13. e
14. j
15. b
16. l
17. r
18. q
19. g

Lesson III

1. d
2. i
3. h
4. e
5. a
6. l
7. j
8. c
9. k
10. m
11. r
12. n
13. q
14. b
15. p
16. g
17. f
18. o

Lesson IV

1. i
2. m
3. d
4. p
5. a
6. g
7. k
8. s
9. f
10. o
11. c
12. r
13. u
14. h
15. b
16. n
17. j
18. e
19. t
20. l
21. q

Lesson V

1. r
2. i
3. d
4. p
5. f
6. n
7. h
8. b
9. o
10. a
11. q
12. g
13. m
14. e
15. l
16. j
17. c
18. k

Lesson VI

1. h
2. e
3. l
4. o
5. b
6. g
7. j
8. q
9. d
10. k
11. c
12. a
13. i
14. n
15. p
16. m
17. f

Lesson VII

1. e
2. i
3. c
4. k
5. b
6. j
7. h
8. n
9. g
10. a
11. d
12. f
13. m
14. l

Lesson VIII

1. k
2. a
3. f
4. g
5. c
6. b
7. j
8. e
9. l
10. m
11. d
12. i
13. n
14. h

Lesson IX

1. p
2. i
3. a
4. l
5. c
6. k
7. o
8. f
9. d
10. n
11. g
12. e
13. b
14. m
15. j
16. h

Lesson X

1. g
2. c
3. e
4. o
5. i
6. p
7. l
8. f
9. j
10. d
11. a
12. h
13. b
14. n
15. k
16. m

Lesson XI

1. p
2. f
3. j
4. b
5. o
6. a
7. d
8. h
9. g
10. n
11. e
12. c
13. m
14. i
15. k
16. l

Lesson XII

14. m
15. i
16. a
17. e
18. l
19. q
20. k
21. p
22. c
23. g
24. j
25. o
26. h
27. n
28. f
29. d
30. b

Lesson XIII

1. q
2. j
3. o
4. m
5. n
6. k
7. p
8. f
9. i
10. a
11. d
12. h
13. b
14. g
15. e
16. l
17. c

Lesson XIV

1. g
2. b
3. c
4. j
5. n
6. e
7. a
8. h
9. l
10. i
11. f
12. m
13. k
14. d

Lesson XV

1. l
2. a
3. d
4. i
5. m
6. o
7. c
8. j
9. b
10. k
11. f
12. n
13. h
14. g
15. e

Lesson XVI

1. b
2. a
3. l
4. g
5. i
6. h
7. k
8. c
9. j
10. d
11. f
12. e

Lesson XVII

1. c
2. k
3. a
4. j
5. l
6. i
7. b
8. m
9. n
10. d
11. e
12. f
13. g
14. h
15. o

Lesson XVIII

1. f
2. n
3. e
4. g
5. h
6. m
7. c
8. i
9. b
10. j
11. k
12. a
13. l
14. d
15. d

Lesson XIX

1. j
2. k
3. q
4. c
5. l
6. a
7. b
8. m
9. d
10. o
11. p
12. i
13. e
14. f
15. g
16. h

Lesson XX

1. a
2. g
3. h
4. b
5. k
6. f
7. j
8. i
9. c
10. e
11. d

Lesson XXI

1. o
2. m
3. l
4. f
5. e
6. k
7. a
8. g
9. h
10.
11. c
12. d
13. b
14. i
15. j

Lesson XXII

1. c
2. j
3. a
4. b
5. h
6. i
7. f
8. e
9. g
10. d
11. o
12. n
13. p
14. k
15. l
16. m

Lesson XXIII

1. l
2. k
3. e
4. d
5. i
6. c
7. m
8. h
9. j
10. g
11. f
12. b
13. a

Test 1

1. amorphous — c. shapeless
2. anarchy — a. lawlessness
3. anecdote — d. brief account
4. anomaly — b. deviation
5. atheism — a. godlessness
6. atrophy — c. deterioration
7. amphibious — e. living in and out of water
8. anachronisms — a. outdated things
9. anagram — c. reordering of letters in a word
10. autopsy — b. examination
11. antagonist — a. adversary
12. antipathy — c. strong aversion
13. apogee — d. apex
14. apocryphal — e. of questionable authenticity
15. cataclysm — c. catastrophe
16. diadem — b. royal power
17. dialect — a. form of language
18. diatribe — b. denunciation
19. exogenous — d. layered
20. exoteric — a. popular, common
21. ephemeral — c. fleeting
22. epicurean — a. devoted to pleasure
23. epitaph — d. tombstone inscription
24. euphemism — b. substitute for an offensive term
25. hemisphere — c. half the Earth

Test 3

1. archangel — d. high ranking angel
2. Matriarch — a. female leader
3. oligarchs — b. member of a small governing faction
4. asterisk — c. star shaped printing character
5. astronomy — e. the science of outer space
6. biography — b. account of a person's life
7. cardiac — d. relating to the heart
8. chronic — a. continuing
9. chronological — b. arranged in order of time occurring
10. cosmopolitan — c. worldly, sophisticated
11. aristocratic — a. characteristic of nobility
12. bureaucratic — c. relating to government officials
13. Democratic — d. relating to government by the people
14. Plutocratic — e. relating to wealthy government control
15. demagogues — b. political agitators
16. endemic — a. native
17. kaleidoscope — c. changing set of colors
18. prologue — b. introduction
19. idyll — c. pastoral poem
20. geography — d. study of earth
21. genesis — a. beginning
22. calligraphy — b. fine handwriting
23. hemorrhage — d. profuse bleeding
24. astrology — b. interpretation of stars
25. tautology — c. duplication

Test 2

1. heterodox — c. unorthodox opinions
2. homogeneous — a. uniform
3. homology — d. being similar
4. hyperbole — b. exaggeration
5. hypothesis — e. tentative explanation
6. microcosm — b. miniature model
7. macroscopic — c. large, seen with the naked eye
8. microbe — e. minute life form
9. metamorphosis — c. transformation
10. metaphor — a. figure of speech
11. misanthrope — d. people hater
12. neophyte — b. beginner
13. monarchy — c. state ruled by one monarch
14. polygamy — d. multiple spouses
15. polyglot — a. linguist, speaking many languages
16. monochrome — d. shades of a single color
17. pandemonium — b. extreme confusion and disorder
18. Parable — c. short moral story
19. paragon — a. unrivaled example
20. perigee — b. the point in an orbit nearest to the body being orbited
21. peripatetic — d. traveling around
22. prototype — a. typical example
23. syllogism — c. reasoning, deduction
24. symmetry — e. balance
25. syntax — b. sentence structure

Test 4

1. kleptomania — b. an obsessive impulse to steal
2. maniacal — c. wild, disorderly
3. odometer — a. mileage traversed
4. gastronome — c. gourmet
5. Nemesis — e. source of harm or ruin
6. Onomatopoeia — c. rhetorical device
7. pseudonym — b. fictitious name
8. orthodox — d. traditional, established
9. orthography — a. writing system
10. apathy — b. indifference
11. pedagogue — c. educator
12. diaphanous — d. airy, transparent
13. phantom — e. unreal, illusional
14. phenomenal — a. extraordinary, outstanding
15. phenomenon — e. occurrence perceived by the senses
16. philander — a. to talk or behave amorously
17. philanthropist — d. benefactor
18. phonetics — b. system of sounds in speech
19. phosphorus — c. poisonous, non-metallic element
20. photograph — b. positive print
21. pneumatic — b. relating to using air
22. pneumonia — d. acute respiratory disease
23. Psyche — c. Greek mythological princess
24. thermal — c. rising current of warm air
25. pathos — e. pity

www.ingramcontent.com/pod-product-compliance
Lightning Source LLC
Chambersburg PA
CBHW082044250426
43661CB00080B/2736